# To Where You Are

## Love, Loss, and Finding the Path Home

**JASON FISHER**

ISBN: 978-1-954614-95-6 (hard cover)
       978-1-954614-96-3 (soft cover)

Edited by: Erika Nein

Published by Warren Publishing
Charlotte, NC
www.warrenpublishing.net
Printed in the United States

*For Mandi:*
*My Wife and Forever Love*


*For Mackenzie:*
*Home and Love Will Never Leave You*

# CHAPTER 1
# Losing Home

JUNE 1, 2012

"Babe!"

Mandi's scream echoed through the house, piercing through the quiet June morning. Rushing downstairs from my office, my feet barely even touched the steps. With the haunting experiences of our NICU journey never far from my mind, I was expecting to find Kenzie in some type of medical turmoil. Going through the trauma of having a child in the neonatal intensive care unit, we had come to expect the unexpected with Kenzie, so my mind immediately went to thoughts of my baby girl in distress.

Rounding the corner into the kitchen, I was stunned to see my young wife half-seated at the kitchen countertop, hunched over, with our daughter's breakfast in front of her. Kenzie, at two and a half years old, was still in her high chair, quietly watching a cartoon video on the DVD player.

"My back. It hurts so bad!" Mandi said in a pained voice. Immediately thinking she strained a muscle, I helped her off the barstool and walked her over to the recliner a few feet away in the living room. "It feels like I'm being stabbed. I can barely breathe."

I quickly got Kenzie out of her high chair and put her on the living room floor to play with her toys. Mandi was squinting in agony.

"Point to where it hurts the worst," I said. She directed my hand to a spot on her back, just above her kidney on her right side. I rubbed the area for a couple of minutes, keeping an eye on both Kenzie and the clock.

It was 8:45 a.m. My conference call with my boss started in fifteen minutes, and I was thinking about what we had on the agenda. Working from home had its privileges, especially for the parents of a special needs child, but I only had a few more minutes to help Mandi before calling my boss.

"My lips are tingling," Mandi said curiously. She asked for my help in gathering a heating pad, grabbing her laptop, and getting her into bed so she could work while she rested her back. Stiff and in pain, Mandi slowly moved to our bedroom, situated just off the living room in our open floor plan. She carefully crawled into bed and got as comfortable as she could.

"Once my call is finished, I will take you to the doctor to get your back X-rayed," I said. Mandi just nodded, her face tight with pain.

I scooped up Kenzie, headed for the playroom, and grabbed my work phone to quickly call Mandi's mom.

"What's wrong with the baby?" Miss Sheri immediately asked.

"Nothing," I replied. "It's Mandi. She hurt her back."

"Is she okay?"

"She wrenched it pretty good," I said. "She's in bed with a heating pad. I'm going to take her to the doctor as soon as I'm finished with my nine o'clock meeting. The call won't take long."

"Are you sure you want to wait, Jason?" she asked. "I don't like the sound of this."

I didn't dismiss the serious nature of what was happening to Mandi. She was in a great deal of pain, but I knew Miss Sheri was always very sensitive to the well-being of her children and grandchild. I attempted to reassure her the best I could.

"I promise, as soon as I'm done, and depending on how she is feeling, we'll either go to the urgent care up the street for an X-ray or perhaps to the hospital. And as soon as we know something, we'll call you."

As I hung up the phone, I turned my attention back to Kenzie. She was playing quietly in the background as I dialed in to my call with Maureen.

Maureen and I had been working on a marketing piece for a potential client, and we needed to review the information I had input into a large spreadsheet. I gave her my thoughts on the best way to lay out the data and show the results of my analysis. Being a bit of a numbers geek, I'm always excited to dive into the information and see what it offers. But my mind wasn't entirely on my work or the call.

"I may be out later, taking Mandi to the doctor for X-rays," I told Maureen after five to ten minutes of discussion. "She hurt her back this morning. I'm multitasking and watching Kenzie now."

"Go tend to Mandi," Maureen quickly said. "That takes priority. I think we have what we need to move forward. We'll discuss it again Monday and finish it up."

I pocketed my phone and proceeded to walk back fifteen feet from the front room where Kenzie was playing to the bedroom to see how Mandi was feeling.

I opened the door to the bedroom to find Mandi on the floor, gasping for breath.

"Call an ambulance," she managed to say in a barely audible voice. A pink plastic bedpan we had used for Kenzie's reflux when she was an infant was lying a few feet away on the floor. The distinct odor of vomit overwhelmed me almost immediately upon entering the room.

Stunned and suddenly confused, my mind immediately tried to understand what I was seeing.

"You want me to call an ambulance?" I said in a slightly panicked tone as I moved toward her.

"Yes," she said as she lay flat on her back. She was staring at the ceiling but looking at nothing in particular. Her eyes looked glazed over, and her skin was a pale, pasty white. She was writhing in obvious discomfort and trying to catch her breath.

Hurriedly, I picked up the phone and dialed 9-1-1. Moments later, the dispatcher confirmed our address and gave me instructions to unlock the front door and stay with my wife.

We lived in a relatively new home in a neighborhood of Semmes, a fast-growing suburb of Mobile, Alabama. Since we lived on the outskirts of town, we did not have city services—including fire and rescue. Instead, the Mobile County EMS covered our neighborhood. Fortunately, they were just down the street, about two miles away.

The audible sound of sirens pierced the quiet morning air of our neighborhood. It had taken just a few minutes for the first responders to arrive, and I let myself breathe a slight sigh of relief. *Paramedics are here ... everything's going to be fine*, I said to myself.

But I knew that something was very wrong. By then, Mandi's look changed to one of desperation. She was struggling mightily. I tried to keep her calm, but it was evident the situation was anything but stable.

Two paramedics rolled a gurney through the front door and down the hallway to our master bedroom, where Mandi was on the floor near my dresser. One paramedic began to immediately monitor her vital signs while the other assessed her condition.

Mandi was obviously in great distress and doing anything she could to relay the desperation she was feeling. She reached out and grabbed the leg of the paramedic who was standing closest to her. In a raspy, barely audible voice, she uttered, "Help me."

Shane, as his name tag displayed, responded harshly. "Take your hands off me!"

Shocked, I looked at Shane, puzzled at first. Mandi was desperate; did Shane understand the seriousness of the situation? My anger built quickly, and I thought for a split second about throwing a punch at his head for his sheer insensitivity, but instead turned my attention back to Mandi.

My mind was racing, my adrenaline pumping. I had told the paramedics that she hurt her back, but it was apparent to even the untrained eye there was more to this than just a strained back muscle. Mandi was deteriorating rapidly, and the circumstances were growing more dire by the second.

Reviewing her symptoms in my head and knowing what I knew about varying medical conditions, I came to a conclusion. "Could she have a blood clot?" I blurted out.

"No," Shane responded somewhat tersely. "If it were a blood clot, she would be much paler. She's hyperventilating because of her back."

Mandi continued to worsen with each tick of the clock. Her skin tone had changed drastically, and she started drifting toward an unconscious state. My heart was pounding and threatening to jump out of my body.

"Are you sure?" I asked sharply, my aggression ticking up.

Before Shane had the chance to answer, the other paramedic interjected. "I'm not getting a blood pressure reading," he said in a surprised tone.

Mandi was fading in and out of consciousness and was nearly motionless. I had seen enough. We were wasting precious time. My stomach in my throat, I shouted at both the paramedics, "We have to get her to the hospital! We're not doing anything for her here!"

At a loss to provide any other reasonable diagnosis, the two paramedics looked at each other, as if they realized I was right. They quickly lifted Mandi onto the gurney and began rolling her toward the front door and the ambulance in the driveway.

The entire time we were in the bedroom with the paramedics, Kenzie was playing quietly in her playroom just down the hall near the front door, unattended and unaware of the chaos unfolding. The morning babysitter we hired to help while we both worked from home was running late. There was nobody there at the moment to watch her. I had one eye on Kenzie and the other on Mandi being hoisted into the ambulance.

Fortunately, Mandi's good friend from high school lived a few houses down. Chelsea had just rushed over after seeing the commotion. She glanced at me and then Kenzie. "What's going on with Mandi?"

"I don't know," I replied frantically. "If you can give me one minute and keep an eye on Kenzie ... I'll be right back."

I walked out of the house and watched the paramedics secure Mandi's gurney to the inside rails of the ambulance. I was torn with indecision. Bringing Kenzie to the hospital was not an option. Do I stay with her or go with Mandi and trust Kenzie would be okay with Chelsea, who had never watched her before?

*What would Mandi want me to do?* I asked myself. Torn between my two loves, I had to choose to either stay by my wife's side as her condition potentially worsened or ensure the well-being of our nonverbal daughter with special needs until I could make sure she would be cared for appropriately.

And then I knew, without a doubt, Mandi would have told me to stay with our daughter. She was extremely protective of Kenzie. When Kenzie was in the NICU, we made a pact that we would always put Kenzie's needs first—it was imperative with Kenzie's medical history.

After I told the paramedics I'd meet them at the hospital, I quickly dialed Miss Sheri. She barely said "hello" before I bit out, "I don't know anything yet, but Mandi's heading to Providence Hospital in an ambulance. This is not just back pain. As soon as I get Kenzie squared away, I'll meet you up there."

Miss Sheri probably said something to the effect of, "I'll call the family and see you soon," but I do not remember the details of that part of the conversation. I remember walking back toward the front door as Ms. Jean—Kenzie's caregiver—parked her car. She hopped out, staring at the ambulance racing away.

"Is everything all right with Kenzie?" she asked.

"Yes, Kenzie's fine," I replied, ushering her inside. "It's Mandi. I don't know what's wrong."

I was so relieved Ms. Jean was finally there, I decided to head to the hospital to be with Mandi. "I can't stay here while she's going through this," I told her and Chelsea, and then gave them a quick rundown. "Kenzie just had breakfast, so don't worry about feeding her. You can let her play with toys in her playroom, and there are cartoon DVDs in the living room if she gets fussy."

I jumped into my car and headed up the cul-de-sac. The ambulance had left just a few minutes ahead of me, so I was sure I would encounter them on the way. I drove at high speeds down Snow Road into West Mobile, watching for traffic to ensure my safety but essentially disregarding the posted speed limit.

A few minutes into the drive, it occurred to me I should call my boss and fill her in. "I don't know what is going on with Mandi," I told Maureen in a mild panic, "but I won't be in the rest of the day—"

She stopped me. "Do whatever you need to do, Jason. Please don't worry about work. It will be there when you get back."

I kept expecting to catch the ambulance, but it never happened. Every minute of that drive was filled with anxiety and bad thoughts. I was hoping and praying for the best while silently fearing the worst. I was kicking myself for taking the call and leaving Mandi in the bedroom with what I had thought was a back injury. I kept thinking about her suffering when I was on the phone, telling myself those ten minutes or so may have made a difference.

When we had chosen to buy our house, we never thought about the distance to the hospital or first responder station. The subject never came up in discussion. I suppose we naïvely assumed we would have normal pregnancies, raise three healthy kids in the growing Mobile suburbs, and enjoy the quiet life until the encroaching city overtook our neighborhood years down the road. I'm confident we were more worried about how close the grocery stores and the local mall were versus the nearest hospital. Our lives to that point had been a fairy tale. But the fairy tale started unraveling with Kenzie's early arrival and diagnosis of a chromosomal disorder. Now, that fairy tale was about to become a nightmare.

\*\*\*

I got to the hospital in fifteen minutes, shaving about five minutes off the normal pace. I made the hard right turn into the entrance and looked for the signs pointing to the emergency room. I pulled into the first open space I could find and jumped out of the car. Sprinting across the parking lot with my feet barely hitting the ground, I triggered the automatic doors at the entrance and immediately entered the waiting room. I was greeted by Mandi's family, huddled in a corner off to the left-hand side.

Somehow, her parents and both sisters beat me to the hospital. Her uncle was there and possibly a few other folks, but I don't recollect exactly whom. At the time, though, it felt good to be surrounded by familiar faces. The drive to the hospital by myself was suffocating, my mind racing to every possible outcome and praying the paramedics were able to help Mandi with the equipment available in the ambulance.

Now, I was face-to-face with the people who loved her the most. I could see the concern and worry on their faces as they grasped at what could be happening. I gave them as much information as I could.

"She did not look good," I admitted nervously. Mandi's mom made eye contact with me long enough, as if to say, "Don't tell me that." My anxiety ran high as I attempted, out loud, to make sense of what I saw. My words were staggered, and I backtracked in my description a time or two, trying to remember the events.

Stunned by how a back strain landed us in the emergency room via ambulance, most everyone was quiet. The family knew something was missing from this equation. Back issues don't present with all the symptoms I described. An eerie silence emanated from a group of typically very animated people. It was serious, and we all knew it.

A few minutes after I had arrived, an emergency room staff member approached the family and asked if we would like to go to a private waiting area. The family was so anxious for news that we jumped at the chance to go back behind the doors and get an update.

The staff member guided us to a medium-sized waiting room directly adjacent to the triage area. The room was large enough to hold seven or eight people comfortably, with an oversized couch along the back wall and several chairs positioned around the room. There was soft lighting, paintings on the wall, and magazines on the side tables. A large cross hung on the far wall as you entered through the door.

As we sat and waited as patiently as possible for any updates, we could hear new patients arrive. There was a doctor or nurse giving instructions somewhat loudly, followed by the unmistakable noise of castor wheels rolling on a ceramic tile floor as a gurney was pushed down the corridor to the patient's assigned area. I envisioned Mandi on her gurney and wondered what was now happening in her triage area.

After waiting for what seemed like twenty to thirty minutes, an ER physician entered the room with a clipboard and an accompanying nurse.

"Mister Fisher?" he said as he scanned the room.

"I'm Jason Fisher ... Mandi's husband," I confirmed.

"Mandi is in a very serious state right now," the doctor said in a purposefully calm voice. "Tell me what you know about what happened. Any information is helpful. Did she complain about breathing difficulty or anything else outstanding that you could pick up on?"

"Yes. She was having issues catching her breath, and her back was hurting." I relayed to him the events of the morning and the symptoms as they presented themselves. I showed the doctor approximately where on her back the pain had been and gave him as much information as possible, including the paramedic's initial diagnosis that she was hyperventilating.

The doctor thanked me, said he would be back as soon as they had additional updates, and left the room. I was extremely anxious; my heart was pounding so hard that the sound echoed through my ears.

In hindsight, I didn't need his actual words to decipher the gravity of the situation. The doctor's demeanor—his hushed tone of voice and his body language—told me he wasn't just fishing for new information but was preparing me for bad news.

Everyone gathered in the room was extremely quiet as we waited for the next update. Minutes felt like hours as the adrenaline flowed nonstop. I sat nervously in the middle of the room, carefully scanning the family's reaction to the doctor. Most of the faces stared blankly straight ahead, unsure of how to feel or what to think. The silence was more prominent than any discussion happening between the family members. Occasionally, the anxiety would overflow, and somebody would wonder out loud why it was taking so long.

Suddenly, there was a knock at the door. Opening cautiously and peeking in, the hospital chaplain walked in. He said nothing about Mandi's condition, but at that moment, I began to understand why our family was moved to a private room. They were preparing us for the strong possibility of bad news.

A new doctor entered the room a minute or two behind the chaplain. He looked around the room at the concerned faces before speaking.

"Who is the spouse?" the doctor asked.

A lump erupted in my throat, and I felt my ability to speak suddenly leave me. I could not respond to his simple question. It was as if my soul was hiding, hoping not to be seen for what was about to come next. I hesitantly raised my hand to identify myself.

The doctor kneeled on one knee. He looked me in the eye and began speaking in a soft voice. "I'm so sorry. Your wife arrived without a pulse. We worked on her for about thirty minutes, only briefly getting back a sign of life. But it was not sustained. We did everything we could, but she just could not be revived."

My head dropped into the palm of my hands. "No!" I said out loud in disbelief as I unconsciously began sobbing, my mind processing the unthinkable. My body went numb, and my head began to feel heavy. I slumped back in the chair with my hands covering my face, partially in shock and in tears.

"I'd like to talk with you outside before you leave," the doctor said to me. "Please take all the time you need with your family right now. Again, I'm so terribly sorry to bring you this news."

As the doctor left the room, Mandi's dad loudly wailed as he got up from his seat and walked into the corner of the room, staring at the walls. "Not Mandi! Lord, not Mandi," Pops said in a tone of grief I never wish to hear again.

Mandi's sisters, Amber and Abby, wept in stunned silence. Uncle Danny tearfully paced the room, acknowledging what he heard but not knowing what to do next. There were simply no words I could think of that would express any sense of how I was feeling. I was numb and in shock. I could only think of my beautiful wife, my best friend—gone at just thirty years old. And I never got to say "goodbye."

\*\*\*

Some time had passed, perhaps a few minutes, when I decided I needed some space. The private waiting room felt oppressive. Opening the door, I slowly walked through the public waiting room. I could feel the eyes of sorrow follow me; those waiting on their loved ones must have assumed the outcome of our circumstance as they almost assuredly heard the loud cries coming from behind the door.

I walked out onto the lawn in front of the hospital. I had no idea where I was going, I just needed to get away from that room. Still in shock, I pondered what had just happened. I felt so alone already. I thought about Kenzie, about how she may never really understand who her mother was because of her age and slower development. Most of all, I thought about my young wife and the life she would never get to live.

As I walked around in circles, I caught the appearance of a man exiting the hospital and coming toward me. My eyes were filled with tears, and I couldn't distinguish who it was from the distance between us. As he came closer, I could see the all-black clothing and recognized him as the hospital chaplain from the waiting room.

Head down and looking somber, the priest approached me. "Can I pray for you?" he asked softly.

"Yes," I replied in a barely audible voice. My faith in God was in serious peril at that very moment, but the comfort of somebody asking to help was something I could not turn down.

As the priest prayed for me, my mind was flooded with the images of the morning. Mandi lying on the floor, pale and gasping, begging the paramedic for help. Her unconscious state as they loaded her into the ambulance. Realizing I had to stay with Kenzie because that's what Mandi would have wanted me to do.

"Amen," the priest said.

I made the sign of the cross but had no idea what the priest said. I was frozen. Time was standing still, and the silence began to grow awkward.

"Father," I finally said in a hushed tone, "I feel cursed." Tears began flowing down my cheeks. "I feel like Job," referring to the biblical character who had endured great hardship as a test between remaining loyal to God and succumbing to the doubts of evil. Except, instead of my faith never wavering like Job, mine felt as though it was crumbling.

The priest looked at me curiously, as if he was trying to understand precisely how I was feeling.

"My life is unraveling," I said. "I lost my grandfather just nine months ago when he was killed in a hit-and-run. My cousin, who is like a brother to me, tragically lost his son not long before that. My daughter was born thirteen weeks premature, spent a hundred and thirty-three days in the NICU, and was diagnosed with a rare syndrome. And now my wife is suddenly gone, and I have no explanation as to what happened."

The priest seemed somewhat taken aback, but he found some words that offered a hint of comfort. "I'm so sorry, my son. Those are horrible events for you to have to face. God promises us eternal salvation after this time on Earth. Your faith will be important for you and your daughter moving forward."

I shook my head. I appreciated his prayer, but nothing and nobody was going to make this better. He gave me his card, and I watched him disappear behind the sliding glass doors. The world around me began to blur. People were moving, smiling, crying, embracing—and I had never felt more alone in my life.

*** 

"Mister Fisher?"

Looking up, I saw the doctor who had just informed me of Mandi's passing. I nodded at him.

"I understand it's a terrible time, and you are emotionally in a very difficult place right now," the doctor said. "But I would like you to go over the details of this morning with me again. We have an idea of what may have led to this, but nothing will be known for sure for a few days. Anything specific you can share will help point us in the right direction."

I knew what that meant. The pain of knowing she was gone was only surpassed by the pain of understanding they would have to do an autopsy to determine the cause of death. The thought of them cutting her open made me physically nauseous, and I tried very hard to put those thoughts out of my mind while we spoke.

"I told the paramedic that I thought it was a blood clot," I said to the doctor. "He replied that he didn't think that was the case, that she would be much paler than she was. However, her appearance was not normal to me, and I emphasized that to the EMTs. I'm not sure exactly why her back hurt, but her symptoms eventually presented to me as though she had a clot and could not breathe."

The doctor asked me to point on his back to where Mandi said it hurt. I poked a spot in his lower back on the right side, right around where the kidney would have been.

"The pain was so bad that she said her entire back hurt, but that's the spot she showed me and asked me to rub for her," I explained. "We initially thought it was a severe muscle strain. I put her into bed to rest, but then she threw up and was having trouble breathing ... she knew it was more serious than that."

The doctor confirmed that what I had described sounded like it could be a clot, but we would not know anything definitive for at least a few days. Before we finished the conversation, I had one other thing I wanted to share.

"The paramedic was extremely insensitive to my wife. He told her to take her hands off him when she grabbed his pant leg and pleaded with him to help her."

The doctor was a bit taken aback. But I felt he needed to know that, as well as the fact that precious minutes were possibly wasted at the house when she could have been in the ambulance. While I was grief-stricken and heartbroken, I still felt I was protecting Mandi. I wanted somebody to know I was pissed. Being angry wouldn't save her life now, but I wanted word to get back to Shane that he had disrespected my wife in her final moments, and I would not forget it.

"I will make a note of that and pass it along. You have my word," the doctor replied. With that, he walked away and disappeared through the emergency room doors to prepare for the next ambulance that had arrived.

*  *  *

Inside the private waiting room, the family was processing the news as best they could. Whispered anguish reverberated throughout the room. *Surely, this isn't real? Not Mandi. Didn't she just have a physical a few weeks ago? It isn't possible that she's gone.*

Slowly, the room began to disperse, and the family looked for safe places to grieve. Nobody left the hospital grounds. We just scattered to different parts of the hospital. Like me, some went outside and got away from the heaviness in that room. Others stayed close in case additional family members arrived.

Mandi's parents stayed in the ER area. They wanted to be close to their daughter. After some time had passed, they asked to see her and were led to a small area curtained off just thirty feet away.

I wasn't ready to see Mandi yet, so I remained outside. Struggling to make sense of it, I needed to talk with somebody. Typically, in moments of extreme emotion or difficulty, I turned to Mandi for comfort. Now who was going to help me make it through the most challenging time in my life?

I knew I needed to make calls and let people know before they heard about it through other sources, but deciding whom to call first was overwhelming. My parents, my sister, work associates? How do I tell anybody this unbelievable news when I didn't have any definitive answers as to why?

I decided my first call would be to my friend, Michael, whom I had just seen the day before at my house. As a life insurance agent and financial planner, Michael worked with me to prepare a better financial model after Kenzie was born. More than anything, Michael represented one of the few local friends I had in Mobile. So, before telling my family or coworkers, I wandered the lawn and dialed his number.

"Hey, man. What's up?" Michael said.

"I don't know how to say this," I started, my voice quivering. "I don't believe it ... and can't wrap my mind around it ... but Mandi passed away this morning." A few seconds of silence ticked by. "I don't know why she died. The doctors aren't yet sure ... I have no idea what I'm going to do."

"You're joking," Michael responded in disbelief.

"I'm serious, Michael. She's gone. We're at Providence Hospital's emergency room. Mandi's family is pretty much all here."

"I'm on my way," was all he said.

I let the phone slip away from my cheek. I dropped my head and couldn't believe what I was saying. I just told my good friend my wife had died. It's the kind of news you never expect to deliver, particularly so early in life.

\*\*\*

I saw more family and friends arriving, but I kept my distance from the door to avoid being seen and thus approached. I didn't want to be embraced and told it would be okay because I knew there was no way it could be. I didn't want the reality of the moment to find me. I knew I needed to tell more people, but after telling Michael—admitting for the first time that Mandi was dead—I couldn't fathom having to do it again and again.

But I did it.

Going through the motions, I left messages for Mandi's boss and my company's president, and then spoke to my mother and father. I talked to each of my parents for just a few minutes. Both were in shock, but they agreed to tell the rest of the family.

After I hung up with my parents, Duane called me back. Duane was more than my company's president and boss, he was a mentor and longtime friend of over twenty years.

"Jason," he said with a shaky voice, "I don't have the words to tell you how sorry I am. How are you doing?"

"I don't know, Duane," I said. The tears began to flow, and I held them back as best I could. "I guess I'm in shock. It doesn't seem real. She was fine early this morning."

I recounted the morning's event to Duane. He seemed to be in shock too. We talked for a minute or two longer before hanging up. "Call me anytime," he said. "Whatever you need, just let me know."

At that point, I felt I had made the most urgent calls. Mandi's work, my work, and my parents were informed. I had plenty of other people I would talk to over the coming hours and days, but I needed a break. And I knew I still had the most unimaginable undertaking to face—saying "goodbye" to my wife.

\*\*\*

With my head down, I hesitantly moved from the lawn and parking lot toward the hospital entrance, as if I were reentering a house of horrors. In many ways, I was doing just that. I knew I needed to see Mandi, but my mind told my body to resist at all costs. The thought of viewing her in that state, knowing I had just seen her healthy a couple of hours before, was piercing. I started shaking without even realizing it, subconsciously anticipating that I would never forget what I was about to see.

The automatic doors to the ER opened. Once again, I felt the eyes in the room shift toward me. The strangers in the public waiting room had seen a steady stream of Mandi's family walk through, distraught.

As I walked into the private waiting room, I heard the uncontrollable sobbing of Mandi's parents. Their entire life had been focused on protecting their children and loving their family, and now they were forced to deal with every parent's worst nightmare. And everybody who cared for them was powerless to stop it. I made my way over to them as various family members hugged me and said how sorry they were.

"You should go see your wife," Mandi's mother said. "She is all alone back there now."

"I know. I'm not sure I can do this, Gigi," I replied. Mandi's parents had requested we call them "Pops" and "Gigi," given that Mackenzie made them grandparents for the first time.

"This is going to be hard," she said. "But Mandi needs you with her now."

She instructed me where to go and after collecting my thoughts, I opened the door and took my first steps into the ER trauma area. There were makeshift rooms where they worked on patients. They weren't completely walled off but instead had curtains surrounding them for privacy. I pulled the dark-blue cloth and walked toward Mandi.

My chest felt heavy as I stood next to her. I couldn't believe this was happening. Pops and Gigi accompanied me for emotional support. I knew seeing her like this would be difficult, but I had no idea just how horrific and scarring it would be. My mind attempted to process what had happened and what it all meant, but I couldn't hold it in any longer.

"I ... I'm sorry, baby," I said between loud sobs. "I didn't know what was happening to you. I did everything I could."

Thoughts of the day raced through my mind. Her piercing scream for help. Seeing her lying on the floor. Her arm dangling from the gurney as they loaded her into the ambulance. It all felt like a bad dream, but it had become much too real.

The tears streamed down my face and slid off my cheeks onto the sheet that covered her. I had failed to protect my wife. I failed in my duty as a husband. Nothing anybody could say at that moment would make me feel otherwise. Not the doctors or nurses with their medical analysis. Not family or friends who knew the love we shared for each other. And not the chaplain who offered his thoughts and prayers.

I kneeled to kiss her forehead; the boulder of guilt overwhelmed my conscious mind. After a few minutes, I had to excuse myself.

Lost in a sea of grief, I was just in the beginning stages of feeling the pain of her loss. I was uncomfortably numb and having difficulty absorbing the shock of what had happened. I was beginning to physically feel the negative effects of all the adrenaline and emotions running through my body.

I didn't want to go back inside the waiting area and talk with anybody, so I just sat down in a chair next to the side entrance of the ER. That's where Michael found me some time later.

Our eyes made contact, but we didn't speak for several seconds. "Take me back to Mandi's parents' house," I quietly asked him. "I can never go back home again."

# CHAPTER 2
## Finding Mandi

On a relatively quiet Monday morning in October 2002, Bart Showalter stepped into my office and handed me a resume he had just received from our client email exchange.

"Hey, I think I might have found a good candidate for one of our center manager openings," he said with enthusiasm. Bart was in charge of the client software sales group for our direct marketing company, but like everyone at RuffaloCODY in those days, he was a team player and always looking out for other managers. "She's graduating from Southern Miss. They run a pretty good shop down there," Bart added.

"Great!" I replied. "I need some additional candidates for two potential clients."

I thanked Bart and glanced down at the resume, which listed the experience we were looking to acquire. I tucked it away in a folder for later that day and headed to my next meeting.

Part of my job as director of operations was to find, interview, and ultimately hire talented managers to run our professional fundraising call centers on college campuses. Our headquarters was in Cedar Rapids, Iowa, where I lived and worked at that point.

Cedar Rapids was essentially my hometown, about twenty minutes away from the small farm town of seven hundred people where I was raised. I had grown up in Van Horne, about twenty-five miles to the west. Surrounded by corn, soybeans, and hayfields as far as the eye could see, Van Horne was a close-knit community where everybody knew each other and looked out for their kids. It was a great place to grow up. There was enough to do outside to keep a kid busy, but you had to be very creative to get yourself into trouble.

Like most agricultural communities in the 1980s, Van Horne was hit hard by the farming recession. Almost all the job opportunities for young adults entering the workforce in the area were tied to agriculture. So, if you wanted to make a living doing something besides farming, you either moved to Cedar Rapids and found work in another industry or went to college. I did both.

I got my start at RuffaloCODY when I was eighteen years old. I worked part-time raising money for universities while attending the local community college. For a young man who came from modest means and paid his way through college, it was precisely what I was looking for in employment at the time. Better yet, the job had opportunities for advancement.

Many of my friends also worked the job, which made for a fun and competitive atmosphere. We jostled with each other nightly to determine who could raise the most and who could crack the best jokes. We had youthful, energetic leadership that was visionary in direct marketing and didn't mind taking chances on talent from within. Promotions were plentiful in the early years, though they were not necessarily easy to get. You had to learn to be patient, handle rejection with professionalism, and earn your way to the next opportunity.

Fast forward ten years, and I had moved up the corporate ladder. I loved my career, and I was on the verge of meeting the love of my life.

I didn't get a chance to call the prospective candidate until several hours after Bart dropped off her resume. *Amanda Cowart,* I said to myself as I read her profile. I was impressed with her qualifications and skill set. Indeed, it looked as though Bart had found a good candidate for me to consider. Not wanting to let an opportunity get past me, I picked up the phone and dialed her number. I spoke with a cheerful and enthusiastic young woman who told me to call her "Mandi." We set up a time for a quick phone interview the following Wednesday.

Throughout our thirty-minute conversation that next week, it was apparent that Mandi was knowledgeable about the job, well-spoken, professional, and extremely pleasant.

"I think you have many of the skills we are looking for and sound like a great managerial candidate. Would you like to interview for the job in person?"

"Absolutely," she replied.

"Good to hear!" I said. "Let me work out some details, and I'll get back to you soon."

Little did I know that the call I had just made, and the details I was about to iron out, would drastically alter the course of my life.

\*\*\*

I always made it a point to pick up all our interviewees at the airport when they flew in. It saved on a taxi or rental car cost, and it also provided an excellent touchpoint before the discussion started. So, on a cold morning, October 17, 2002, I gathered a few things in my office and headed for the airport.

Mandi was scheduled to arrive mid-morning from a connection in Dallas. As an early riser by nature, I was typically used to taking early flights to get to my destination as soon as possible. Not thinking it through, I cruelly booked her on the first flight out of Jackson, Mississippi—a 6:00 a.m. departure. Yes, it was usually the best fare on any given day, but in this case, I honestly wasn't thinking about the fact that college students are often nocturnal creatures.

I arrived early and had a few extra minutes to wait before her flight arrived. In 2002, social media wasn't a mainstream activity in life. I had no way to know what she looked like. Therefore, as with almost all candidates I interviewed, we traded descriptions of each other during the phone interview to know who we would be looking for in the waiting area.

"I'm about five feet, four inches tall with brownish hair," she'd said.

"I'm about five foot eight with brownish hair," I said. "I'll be the short guy staring blankly at the crowd of people, scanning them to try to find you. Look for the guy who is lost."

"Hey, you're taller than me," she said with a laugh. "And the Cedar Rapids Airport can't be that big, so I'm sure we'll be fine!"

As the deplaning passengers walked through the security checkpoint, my eyes locked with a young woman looking like she was ready for a job interview. She walked over to me with a calm confidence.

"You're Jason?" she said with a smile on her face.

"Yes," I said, extending my hand to introduce myself.

"I'm Mandi Cowart. It's nice to meet you."

There was something about Mandi that caught my attention. It's easy to see, looking back in time, but even then I knew there was something different about the way she carried herself. She had a bubbly, animated personality and a very confident demeanor. She was certainly professional, but she had the type of disposition and body language that made you feel you weren't meeting a stranger.

Mandi grabbed her checked bag from the carousel, and we walked to my car in the short-term parking section just outside the main entrance. The drive to the office was only about fifteen minutes, but that was plenty of time to ask how her day had been so far.

"Well, I was able to make it to the hotel in Jackson last night and still manage to get up this morning before the sun came up," she said, smiling with a smirk on her face.

"My fault," I said. "I probably should have booked you on a later flight so you didn't have to stay overnight in Jackson to catch your plane. I'm sorry you're so tired ... my bad."

"So, if I fall asleep in the interview, you won't hold it against me?" she retorted, still smiling.

It was already apparent Mandi had the gift of well-timed humor. She knew how to joke around, put people at ease, and still be professional. From my perspective, that is a skill set few have. There are Fortune 500 companies that train their employees how to handle themselves as Mandi did naturally. Her charm was disarming and allowed the conversation to be free-flowing.

Arriving at the headquarters, we set her luggage and briefcase in my office and proceeded to make the rounds. I showed Mandi around and introduced her to people she would be interacting with before breaking for lunch.

We spent the afternoon discussing the various responsibilities of the position, while Mandi elaborated on her background and experience. Frankly, I was sold on her skills and abilities within the first fifteen minutes of the discussion. But given that I had flown her up to Iowa at the crack of dawn and in freezing cold temperatures, I felt it would be best if I followed the agenda to make good use of the time we had scheduled.

Back in 2002, much of the growth of Cedar Rapids as a city was happening in the outlying communities. Our office at RuffaloCODY was located downtown, which was in the first few years of a revitalization plan. At the time, the city had a significant number of chain restaurants but only a few unique places to eat downtown. However, I had the perfect place in mind that was within walking distance of her downtown hotel.

Teddy's Steakhouse sat in the corner of the lower floor of the old Roosevelt Hotel, a landmark in Cedar Rapids named for President Theodore Roosevelt. The restaurant had a rustic feel to it: old horse saddles and bridles sat in the corners of the restaurant, and the lights were turned down fairly low to mimic what an old-style eatery might have felt like in 1905, lit with oil lamps instead of conventional light bulbs.

Mandi and I arrived at the designated time and were seated immediately. As I had learned, the more casual dinner was far better for getting to know somebody and their personality than a formal office interview. Given the light crowd that evening, the noise level was very low, and it was easy to have a comfortable conversation.

Following some introductory talk about how the day had gone so far, I jumped right into the question I most needed to know. "How do you feel about moving to Nashville or Colorado?" I asked.

"Both have their advantages," she said with a good level of enthusiasm. "Nashville would be closer to home, but Colorado sounds fun as well. And my dad loves the mountains."

I thought it was a toss-up at that point but let her continue.

"If I had my preference, Nashville would be my choice because it's closer to home," she added.

"Great," I said. "That's helpful to know, and I will keep you posted on the latest with our potential client there."

With that critical bit of information now discussed, we got back to the big decision at hand.

"Anything look good on the menu?" I asked.

"Everything!" Mandi replied with a laugh.

Mandi, I was discovering, could disarm a person and take the stress out of a formal conversation in a matter of seconds. I was trying to be professional, but I found myself becoming mesmerized by her gregarious laughter. She loved to laugh. That was apparent from the very beginning.

Our conversation was always professional, but we soon found ourselves laughing hysterically at each other's stories. The discussion and laughter were nearly effortless, so much in fact that the other patrons were turning their heads toward our table when Mandi laughed.

As we continued to talk and finish the main course, the waiter came back around to ask if we'd be ordering dessert. I glanced at Mandi and deferred to her. Typically, I decline dessert to wrap up the evening and allow the candidate to go back to their room. But I had a feeling neither of us wanted to end the dinner quite yet.

"I'll have the chocolate cake," Mandi said.

"I'll have the carrot cake," I said.

The waiter returned with our desserts as Mandi was telling me about her decision to switch majors in college and pursue a degree in mass communications.

"I was on the radio late at night," she said. "I had my own DJ assignment and had to report anything newsworthy that was happening at the time."

I was not surprised. Mandi had the personality of somebody who could host her own show.

"Mandi at Midnight?" I said jokingly. "That has a great ring to it!"

We laughed at the potential for the name of her show and talked more about her college experience. At some point, Mandi stopped to ask me how my dessert tasted.

"It's incredible!" I said.

Momentarily forgetting where she was and why she was there, Mandi reached over with her fork and cut a bite-size portion off the uneaten corner of my cake. As she put the cake in her mouth, she stopped, and her face went expressionless.

"Oh my God, I just ate off your plate," she said with a look of stunned disbelief. "I am so sorry!"

"Oh, it's fine!" I said, laughing. And I meant it. I was not at all bothered by her action. In fact, it felt like the moment happened in the normal course of two friends talking, not at a dinner interview.

I suppose if I had to pick a time that started us down our path together, Mandi eating directly off my dessert plate would be it. That magical moment created a sense of comfort, inviting both of us to let our guards down even more.

I knew there was something special about Mandi. Always the professional, I never let on that I was intrigued or captivated by her wittiness. But as I drove home that night after dropping her off at the hotel, I kept seeing her laugh and smile in my mind. She was not like any other candidate I had ever interviewed. I fell asleep that night thinking about this girl who turned an ordinary Thursday at work into something fun and memorable.

\*\*\*

Early the next morning, Mandi was standing outside her hotel with her bags when I pulled up. Having prepared for the high temperatures in the fifties, she wore a thin suit jacket that was more appropriate for a late fall day in Alabama than a cold October morning in Iowa. We had about half the day to tie up any loose ends before I needed to take her to the airport for her 12:30 p.m. flight.

I had already made up my mind that I would offer her a job if we could find a place she wanted to relocate, but my boss had instructed me to hold off on making any overtures until we had a signed contract from one of our clients.

So, we went through the specific job details again, covering anything we may have left out from the day before. After just thirty minutes, I ran out of questions and topics. We still had several hours to go before she needed to be at the airport, so I turned it over to Mandi.

"I've exhausted my questions, and I feel as though I have a pretty good idea of how you would fit in the organization," I told her. "Now's the time you can bring up anything you would like to discuss, and I'll be happy to answer any questions you have."

"Okay, so let me interview you!" Mandi said to me with an enthusiastic grin.

Pausing for a second, I smiled and got up from my seat, swiveled it around, and invited her to sit. Mandi jumped from her seat and sat in mine. I then made myself comfortable on the other side of the desk as Mandi composed herself momentarily and then began peppering me with questions.

"Mister Fisher, why do you think you would be good at this job?" she asked in a confident yet humorous tone.

"Well, I think I have the experience you are looking for and would be a great fit for your organization," I replied in a serious fashion.

"What would you say is your biggest strength?" she asked.

"I would say my professionalism and creative problem-solving skills."

Mandi took notes on a legal pad while nodding her head in approval. We went back and forth for another ten minutes or so. While we both attempted to stay in character, we caught ourselves straying from the impromptu interview and laughing aloud as the questions and answers started getting sillier.

Never before, and never since, have I had an interview experience quite like that. My memory of this moment is very vivid, given how different it was from the norm. And I can still see her crystal-blue eyes and exuberant smile as she sat behind my desk, having fun with the moment.

There seemed to be this harmonious energy flow between us. I usually get labeled as being a bit on the stuffy side at work since I'm always careful to present a professional approach. Yet, there was something about Mandi that disarmed me. And I allowed myself to relax and enjoy the moment as it went off-script.

As the clock moved closer to 11:15, our target time for departure to the airport, I felt slightly disappointed that my time with Mandi was nearly over. For the twenty-four hours Mandi was in town, I hadn't been stressed or concerned with what I needed to do before the weekend was upon me. I just enjoyed being present. And while I wasn't happy that our time was through, I had a distinct feeling I would see her again.

Typically, I thank interviewees for coming, drop them off at the entrance to the airport, and let them know they can call me if there are any concerns. But we were having too good of a conversation, so I parked the car and helped her with her luggage as we made our way inside the terminal. I made sure her flight was on time and she got checked in without a problem. We talked outside of security for a few more minutes before shaking hands and agreeing to connect again soon.

I walked back to my car knowing that whatever I had going on that weekend was suddenly not as important as it had been a couple of days before.

\*\*\*

About a month after Mandi interviewed, we signed contracts in both Nashville and Colorado. She was the first phone call I made after getting approval to hire a new manager. I gave her a choice to go to whichever location she wanted, with pay adjusted for any differences in the cost of living.

"I just can't leave home," Mandi said quietly over the phone. "That's the reason. It's not the job. It's not the company, the pay, or anything like that. I don't think I'm ready to leave home and move far away from family."

I wasn't completely surprised by Mandi's decision to turn down the offer. There's an old saying that you can take the girl out of the South, but you can't take the South out of the girl. Well, in this case, even a great job offer right out of college wasn't enough to convince Mandi to move hours away to either location. Mobile, Alabama was home to her.

While she had a sense of adventure, Mandi also had two younger sisters, and it was important to her that she watch them finish growing up. I respected that. Family was everything to her.

Of course, I was disappointed Mandi didn't accept the offer. She would have been a great program manager and, without a doubt, would have been successful. But for me, I was not wholly disappointed. We had maintained contact, and there was a hint that our friendship was blossoming into something more profound.

Every love story has a beginning. Ours was unique in many ways, for which we were thankful. When people ask me how I met my wife, I always tell them she turned me down for the job, but I still got the date.

# CHAPTER 3
# One Thousand Miles

One thousand miles is the approximate distance between Cedar Rapids, Iowa, and Mobile, Alabama. It represents about a seventeen-hour drive or at least two flights with a layover. In theory, it's possible to drive it straight through if two people took turns at the wheel. However, in reality, it's a two-day excursion.

Mandi and I didn't set out to date long-distance. But after she turned down the position for an opportunity closer to home, it seemed innocent enough to email her and offer to help with her employment search in Mobile.

We began exchanging humorous messages and discussed ideal jobs and interests. I sent her an announcement for our company Christmas party, teasing her that she could still go if she could make it back to Cedar Rapids. In turn, she sent me an invitation to her college graduation in Hattiesburg, Mississippi, more as a courtesy than an expectation that I show up. While we knew the chances of making it to each other's festivities were remote, the invitations signaled that the door was open for future opportunities.

Maintaining a connection with somebody such a significant distance away has its challenges. But the more we connected—through emails, instant messaging, texts, and phone calls—the more things seemed to fall into place.

In early February of 2003, I was scheduled to speak in Gainesville, Florida, to recruit potential fundraising managers during a meeting of the Southeastern Athletic Conference (SEC) schools.

At the time, nearly two months after she graduated, Mandi had not yet found a job in Mobile. I knew she maintained contact with her former coworkers and supervisor at the USM call center, and while Gainesville was not exactly a short drive from Hattiesburg, I recognized it as an opportunity to find a way to see each other again.

*Hey there! I'm going to Gainesville January 31st to speak at a conference,* I wrote in an email. *Think you might want to ride along with your USM colleagues if they attend the conference?* I asked.

*I would love to go!* Mandi quickly wrote back. *I need to make sure it will work on my calendar and run it by the family, but I will let you know ASAP!*

*Maybe we could grab dinner one night, and we can share a dessert again?* I joked, essentially asking Mandi Cowart out on a date.

It was a poorly disguised way to connect. Still, years later, I can admit that my primary intent for accepting the speaking opportunity was to get close enough to Hattiesburg so we could see each other again. Of course, I made a solid attempt at finding managerial talent at the meeting and did have several good leads from that conference, but having dinner with Mandi was my top priority.

*** 

It was just about February, which can be brutally cold in Iowa. Anyone who lives in the upper Midwest can attest that it seemingly takes forever for spring to arrive. Whenever I had an opportunity to travel to a warmer climate, I tried to take advantage of the schedule and find time to do something outside. So, before leaving Iowa, I went online and searched for golf courses in Gainesville. I located a decent-looking course close to the airport, called "Ironwood," and got a tee time for late morning.

Arriving on the first available flight the day before the conference began, I walked out of the Gainesville airport, rolling my suitcase behind me with my golf clubs slung over one shoulder. The weather was absolutely perfect, and a short time later, I checked in for my tee time.

I learned to play golf at about age fourteen. My buddy Wayne and I joined the school golf team and often practiced together, including away from the course. On his family's farm, we would hit old golf balls we found in the woods near our local golf course. The balls were in horrible shape and virtually unplayable for an actual round of golf, but they were good enough to practice our swings and hit them into his dad's nearby cornfield. In our moments of boredom, we'd occasionally aim at a cow grazing in the distance to see how accurate we could be. Although, cows are expensive assets on a family farm, and his dad didn't appreciate us using them for targets.

Having a competitive nature, I nearly always had a strong focus on playing my best. But on this particular day, I finished my round without a care as to what was on my score card. The sun was shining warm and bright, and I had Mandi on my mind.

\*\*\*

Mandi's former manager, Becky, agreed to bring Mandi along for the ride. This gave them both the comfort of having a friend along for the long drive and also allowed me to meet Becky, who was interested in a job with RuffaloCODY.

I admit I was nervous about seeing Mandi again, perhaps more so than I thought I would be. It had been several months of texting, emails, and occasional phone calls. Would the chemistry we both felt back in October still be present nearly four months later? Would she be as open and funny with her friend around as she was with just me those two days in Iowa? Those were the questions that danced in my anxious mind.

I watched the clock slowly inch forward throughout the afternoon hours. Mandi was scheduled to arrive around six o'clock if traffic was decent. We had planned to grab dinner with Becky but didn't make any firm plans beyond that.

Six o'clock came and went, and I got a familiar pit in my stomach. It was the feeling one feels when they have a crush on somebody and plans change. I was hoping this wasn't the case. I pushed the feelings down and tried to remain confident that everything was on track, and they were just running late.

A few more minutes passed by, and then a few more. Soon, it was 6:20, and I still hadn't heard anything. At that moment, I heard a soft knocking on my hotel room door. I jumped up, checked my clothes and hair in the mirror, and anxiously walked over to open the door.

"You made it!" I said enthusiastically as I greeted Mandi in the doorway.

"Yay!" she said as she reached her arms out to hug me.

Instantly relieved, a feeling of tranquility came over me. The chemistry was there.

"Sorry we were late. I dropped my stuff off in the hotel room and freshened up a bit. Ugh, that's a brutally long drive," Mandi said.

"I bet it was. I'm so glad you made it safely," I replied.

We knew our time together on this trip would be short, but we intended to make the most of our thirty-six hours together.

"So, what are your thoughts about dinner?" I asked.

"Anything is good for me," she replied. "There's a place I heard about in town that we might try if it's not too busy. They supposedly have the best barbecue ribs."

Barbecue ribs are about as messy as it comes. Did Mandi care? Nope. Not one bit. *This is a girl that is comfortable in her own skin*, I thought to myself.

We grabbed Becky from their shared room on the second floor of the hotel and made our way to the restaurant. After we were seated and ordered our food, the waiter brought us an entire roll of paper towels.

"You're probably going to need these and some wet wipes," he said as he laid down several packets of hand wipes.

Now, I'm a fairly picky eater. Ribs aren't my favorite, but I was willing to go with it so we could all enjoy dinner together. As we worked through our food, we talked about the long drive, what the Southern Miss call center was like, and Becky's background with the program. After all, she was essentially interviewing for a job, even though I considered the dinner a date with Mandi.

I felt as comfortable around Mandi as I did back in October, which was something I had hoped would happen. Nothing had changed. That night, Mandi proved that the trip to Iowa was not a show she put on just for the interview, but that her gregariousness and big laughs were who she was at heart. She was captivating.

Following dinner, we returned to the hotel where the ladies went up, and I returned to my room on the ground level. Mandi told me she would come down and see me as soon as she called her parents.

About thirty minutes passed before there was another soft knock at the door. I quickly muted the television, walked over to the door, and let Mandi inside.

"Hey!" she said. "Sorry it took so long. I had to call the parental units." She reached out to hug me and thanked me for dinner. But this time, she didn't let go. As we pulled back to keep talking, I found myself staring at the prettiest blue eyes I had ever seen. I was just inches away from her beautiful smile, but it was Mandi who leaned over and gently kissed me on the lips.

"I've been waiting for that for four months," I said with a big smile on my face.

The kiss was perfect and just as I had imagined it would be, though I thought I would likely be the one to initiate it. Ultimately, it didn't matter who kissed whom first. We both knew it was going to happen. We were just too interested in each other to let the moment pass.

We decided to stay in and watch a movie, given the time. I grabbed the channel guide laying on the hotel nightstand and thumbed through what was coming up at the top of the hour.

"What do you think?" I asked. "Comedy? Drama?"

"I'm okay with whatever," she said. "We can just watch regular television if there's nothing good on."

We spent the next several hours sitting on the couch, laughing out loud, and getting to know each other better. We talked a lot about her family, her mom and dad and her two younger sisters. Mandi was very close to all of them.

We eventually called it a night and agreed to meet in the lobby the following morning. I had to speak around 10:00 a.m., pitching employment opportunities with RuffaloCODY and seeking out talented folks who might be interested in a new career.

Saturday morning came early after a long Friday night. With only a few hours of sleep, I met Becky and Mandi, and together we walked the few blocks to the conference. When we entered the building, a crowd was gathered around a television, and everyone was eerily quiet. The news channel reported that the *Space Shuttle Columbia* had broken up while reentering Earth's atmosphere, killing all seven astronauts aboard.

The festive atmosphere at the conference was muted, replaced by a combination of going about the business of the day and circling back to watch that television. Mandi and I spent most of the morning watching the news coverage, except for the fifteen minutes or so I spoke to the group about available managerial positions.

With few people interested in talking fundraising, Mandi and I decided to leave the conference for the remainder of the afternoon and head back to the hotel. We grabbed dinner and then spent the rest of the evening talking and watching television. We did our best to tune out the day's current events and make our time together as happy as possible.

The clock seemed to be our enemy that Saturday night, continually moving forward while we wanted time to stand still and just be together.

"I'm going to miss you," I told her.

"I'll miss you too," she replied. "We have to find a way to get you back down here again soon!"

"I have frequent flier tickets accumulated from all my travel," I said. "Pick a weekend coming up, and we'll make it happen!"

Saturday night moved into Sunday when Mandi headed back to her room. As I turned out the lights to go to sleep, I thought about what the next day would bring. I knew I would have a difficult time saying goodbye, but I also had something to look forward to. We had a new trip to plan! This time, I'd be flying into Jackson and meeting Mandi in Hattiesburg for the weekend.

Early in the morning on Sunday, there was a familiar soft knocking on my hotel room door. I opened it to see Mandi, tears in her eyes, saying it was time for them to depart.

"I don't want to go," she said.

"I don't want to go either," I replied. "We've been looking forward to this trip for weeks, and now it's gone. I just hope the next month goes by quickly because I can't wait to see you again."

I hugged Mandi tight, looked into her eyes, and kissed her goodbye. "Please drive safe and let me know when you make it home."

"I will," she said. "You be safe on your flight, and come see me in a month."

We kissed once more, and then she walked away. As she went around the corner and out of sight, I let the hotel door slowly close by itself and sat on the edge of the bed.

"Ugh, this hurts more than I expected," I said to myself. I was missing Mandi already, and she had just left. It was going to be a long month.

\*\*\*

As the workers loaded the bags onto the plane, I sat resting my head against my hand and staring blankly out the window. Slowly, a tear formed in the corner of my eye. I was conscious not to let anyone see it, wiping it away as quickly as it formed. But it was unmistakable what I was feeling. My mixed emotions wreaked havoc on my mind. It had barely been two hours since we said goodbye. I was hurting from missing her and yet looking forward to planning another trip.

The plane lifted off the ground and headed toward the Atlanta airport for my connecting flight. I jotted down on my yellow legal pad some dates I thought I could get away, checking my calendar to make sure I had nothing else going on. I got out my laptop and typed an email to Mandi outlining the dates and times I thought would work best. I saved the draft and sent it once we landed in Atlanta, navigating to my next gate and simultaneously trying to find an open kiosk where I could connect to the internet.

My mood began to improve as I reviewed the past weekend in my mind. We had a lot in common, and I knew it. Better yet, I was confident Mandi knew it, and we were on the same page. So much of a good relationship is having confidence in your communication. In that regard, we hit it off extraordinarily well. We both enjoyed laughter, both could have a serious yet interesting conversation, and neither had any desire to control the circumstances. We just let our discussions take us wherever our minds wandered.

"How did the conference go?" Duane asked when I returned to the office the following week.

"Great," I said. "I'm pretty sure we have at least one good candidate and several more prospects that came from the visit."

At this point, I could have walked away from the update with Duane, confident he knew the latest managerial talent in the pipeline. But something told me the right thing to do was to tell him about Mandi.

"So, you remember Mandi Cowart, the woman I interviewed late last year?" I asked.

"Yeah," he replied. "She didn't take the job."

"No, she didn't," I said. "However, I saw her at the conference, and we hit it off pretty well. I'm going to find a weekend coming up and fly down to see her again."

Duane and I had built a good rapport over the years. I could tell him just about anything, and he would listen with a sympathetic ear. But we also liked to have fun at the other person's expense at times.

One year, when the Denver Broncos beat the Green Bay Packers in the Super Bowl, part of our friendly wager was Duane had to wear my John Elway jersey for an entire Friday. He hated the idea of wearing the orange jersey, but a bet was a bet. Like the honorable man he is, Duane wore the jersey for about two hours, then promptly declared he was taking a half-day off work and threw the jersey on my desk.

So, naturally, when I told Duane about Mandi, he saw an opening too good to pass up.

"Wait a minute," he started. "You're telling me that you're dating somebody that you interviewed for a job?"

"She never took the job," I quickly retorted. "I have no control over that."

"I think you sabotaged that managerial prospect on purpose," he said loud enough so the rest of our coworkers in the office could hear. He smiled, and I knew this wasn't going to be an easy one to live down.

I jokingly pled guilty as charged and walked back to my office. Duane obviously meant nothing by the ribbing he gave me. In fact, I'm quite sure he was happy for me, but he couldn't resist the opportunity to give me some crap about it.

* * *

Later that February, Mandi accepted a position as an implementation specialist with Computer Program Systems Incorporated (CPSI), a company in Mobile specializing in healthcare software administration. While the job itself had little to do with her degree in communications, Mandi was great at providing client services. With her personality and problem-solving ability, she could get things done quickly and professionally.

Mandi helped CPSI's clients learn their proprietary software after installation. Her position required a significant amount of travel in the weeks leading up to and after the software would "go live." While she spent a considerable amount of time on the road, Mandi was able to see much of the United States because of her newfound career. Within months, she had clients in Washington State, Idaho, Kansas, Minnesota, Chicago, and even Iowa.

Like Mandi, I also traveled extensively for my job. Over the years, I had attained a million-mile flier status on one airline, had executive privileges on several others, and racked up so many free trips that I routinely gave many of them away to family and friends.

Despite my generosity, I still had a large stash of frequent flier miles, which suddenly came in handy with Mandi in my life. I had already booked my first trip to see her. The plan was to meet her sorority sisters and friends in Hattiesburg on March 7, then she would show me around town, and we'd spend a couple of days finding fun things to do.

The days leading up to that trip seemed to go by slowly as I tried to keep myself busy at work. One eye on the calendar and one on my computer. Mandi and I stayed in touch regularly through email, mainly at night and on the weekends. During the day, I would send her emails she would read later that night. She would reply when it was her turn at the computer. The family shared one PC in the living room, and Mandi usually had to wait until her sisters were done with their schoolwork.

*Hey!* I would write. *I just wanted to tell you how much I miss you! Not long now. T-minus five days!*

*Oh my gosh!* she would reply. *I cannot wait!*

The littlest of things are so important in a long-distance relationship. Short emails such as those helped keep us looking forward instead of feeling down that we were not together. If there was one thing Mandi and I were great at early in the relationship, it was finding exciting and fun ways to keep the conversation going.

As March 7 approached, I repeated my routine from the month before. I found a golf course online that looked like a suitable place to play, made my reservations, and packed my clubs. Since it was a Friday, Mandi had to work until five o'clock in Mobile, then planned to leave and drive the ninety minutes to Hattiesburg.

When I arrived in Hattiesburg, it was still early and my hotel room wasn't ready. I grabbed something to eat quickly and headed to the golf course to make my tee time.

The southern United States in March is in a period of weather transition. It's not uncommon to see spring storms two to three times a week on average, depending on the weather pattern. Severe weather is also most prominent in the March and April timeframe. While it was a little chilly in the morning and the ground still a bit soggy from rain the previous night, the sun was out and the air warmed up nicely as the day moved forward.

Following my round, I found my way back to the hotel, where I checked into my room. The hotel was nothing too spectacular, but it was clean, the people were friendly, and best of all, it was free. I used points to reserve the room, so golf and food were the only expenses I had.

After showering, I took a quick nap to pass the time. With the sun fading for the day and anticipating Mandi's arrival, I heard a familiar soft knock on the door.

"Hey!" Mandi said as she gave me a big hug and a kiss. "Oh, I missed you."

"I missed *you*," I whispered back to her as our hug grew tighter.

It felt good to be in her arms again. It had been a long wait since we last saw each other, but I was happy we were finally together again and had around forty-eight hours to spend with each other.

"I want to stop by Marble Slab and introduce you to a friend," Mandi said.

"Okay," I replied. "What is Marble Slab?"

"You've never been to a Marble Slab before?" Mandi asked, incredulous.

"I have no idea what it is," I said with a shrug.

"Only the best ice cream you'll ever have! It's to die for. You have to try it!"

"Deal!" I said as I grabbed my golf pullover, and we headed out the door to my rental car.

While we were driving, Mandi caught me up on her day at work, giving me the details on precisely what her responsibilities were and the amount of training she was going through at the time.

"I'm going to be traveling a lot once I'm up to speed on the software. I think they have me going to Iowa later this spring."

"Really?" I said inquisitively. "Where in Iowa?"

"Somewhere by Omaha," she said. "I can't remember the name of the town, but we fly into Omaha and drive."

"Maybe I can drive out and see you if time allows?"

"Um, yeah!" she said. "You better if I'm that close!"

Mandi introduced me to her friend Cassie at Marble Slab. We talked with her for a while and then got our ice cream. Returning to the car, Mandi took the keys from me to drive and showed me around town, including the first dorm room she was assigned to as a freshman a few years earlier. We also drove by the call center where she used to work, and she described to me the atmosphere and how much fun she had at that job.

Saturday brought more of the same. She showed me a few more sights in the daylight when it was easier to see. And we did a little shopping as well, stopping by a furniture store so she could show me the new bedroom suite she planned to buy for her first apartment.

We walked around the store, chatting and daydreaming, talking about what we liked and imagining what our apartment together might look like someday. Sitting on a sofa she picked out for its coziness, Mandi shared many of her dreams and aspirations, then quizzed me about what I liked and disliked.

"Big wedding or small?" she asked.

"I'm agreeable to either," I said. "But I've always thought I would get married in a church with family and friends. So, I guess a decent-sized wedding, but it doesn't have to be a massive guest list."

"Okay, good," she said quickly. "We're on the same page then."

Mandi had class and style, but she didn't need to demonstrate a false sense of importance by having a large wedding. The furniture items she showed me were nice but practical. It was nothing too extravagant, and the prices were reasonable. She likely didn't think about it at the time, but she gave me the perfect glimpse into how she approached life.

Once again, the weekend came and went quickly. Sunday was soon upon us. Mandi had to head back to Mobile to get ready for work the next day, and I had a flight to catch. It was sad, of course. But this time was different. I knew we liked each other a lot. I knew she thought about a future with me. And I was more convinced than ever that this girl was far different than anybody I had ever met before.

*\*\**

Long-distance dating isn't for the faint of heart. It takes commitment and patience. The commitment was the simple part; patience is never easy when you're falling in love. But we pledged to make it work. The miles between us made it harder, and it took longer to get to know each other, but we utilized every opportunity to communicate.

Although we were living in two separate regions of the country, we managed to meet in places neither of us had ever been to before: Salmon, Idaho; Richland, Washington; Salina, Kansas; Denison, Iowa. We would find ourselves sharing schedules weeks in advance, circling dates on a calendar where we knew there was the chance to be together. Sometimes, it would be two weekends in a row if she were in a nearby city for her job. Other times, it would be a painful forty to fifty days if our schedules didn't match up. Each trip we took together would leave a lasting memory for us. And we managed to tuck away some memorabilia from each trip, items I still have in a memory box to this day.

By the fall of 2003, Mandi and I had totaled about seven or eight visits together. Even though our physical time together was less than twenty days total, we knew it was time to meet each other's families.

Mandi came to Iowa first, meeting most of my family in one weekend. Everyone loved her, of course. They saw what I saw: a girl with a bubbly personality and so full of energy and life that it was hard not to smile when she was around. And she blended into any conversation seamlessly.

Later that year, in December 2003, it was my turn to meet the parents. Mandi invited me down to Alabama to spend a few days between Christmas and New Year's Day. I admit I was a little nervous about meeting them. She had been apprehensive about telling her parents we had been dating, primarily because of our age difference.

Mandi was ten years and ten days younger than me. Most people we met never knew the age gap existed. They assumed I was older, but only by a few years. I had a baby face and looked much younger than I was at the time. And Mandi was an old soul in many ways; she looked her age but was also very mature. The age difference was never an issue between us in our relationship.

"Jason, this is my mom, Sheri, and my dad, Jerry. Mom and Dad, this is Jason," Mandi said quickly.

"Nice to meet you," her dad said. Jerry was his formal name, he added, but everyone who knew him called him "Skip."

"Jason Fisher, sir. It's a pleasure to meet you as well," I said, making a mental note to call him "Mr. Skip" in the future.

Mandi had schooled me on how to address her parents. As a measure of respect in the South, one uses "Mister" or "Miss" in front of the person's first name for anyone of significance, especially if they are older than you. The other Southern language reminder Mandi pounded into my head was the use of "sir" and "ma'am."

"Mandi has told us so much about you, and I know y'all have been talking for a while," Miss Sheri said. "Thank you for being so good to Mandi."

That first conversation with her parents put me entirely at ease. My nerves were calmed, and I quickly realized how tight this family was with each other. It wasn't a show for me. There was a lot of love and respect in the house, and everyone was sincerely interested in pulling in the same direction. They supported each other's activities and had a lot of laughs in the process.

I had been subconsciously searching for a close-knit family like Mandi's. I couldn't articulate it at the time, but I felt I was immediately accepted in the house and made to feel welcome. In many ways, I missed this in my childhood. My parents divorced when I was eight years old, and I have few memories of my family together under one roof.

I made several more trips to Mobile to see Mandi following the few days I spent with her family during the last week of 2003. I went down for Mardi Gras in February 2004 and again in May a few months later. With each trip or each call I made to their house, I grew closer to her family. I began to see how I fit into the bigger picture and felt just how effortless it was to be a part of Mandi's life.

Mandi's slight hesitation about telling her parents our difference in age never materialized into a concern. I believe her parents saw how much we cared for each other. There may have been some pause, wondering if I was set in my ways. After all, I was a single thirty-one-year-old guy. Was I flexible enough to accommodate Mandi's needs into my life? It would have been an understandable concern on their part. But I wanted what was best for us as a couple first. That was true from the first kiss until the last.

*\*\**

When I went back to Mobile in May 2004 to visit Mandi, I did so as a guy completely in love with a wonderful woman who had made my life so much more meaningful. While Mandi was still living at home, she was saving money and budgeting for her first apartment. Simultaneously, I was thinking about a life with her and what that might entail.

On a Saturday afternoon in mid-May, Mandi and I drove to a nearby apartment complex where she had been looking at a potential rental. The apartment was less than a mile away from her parents' house, but it would have been a place of her own. She enjoyed her family and loved being at home, but she was looking to start the next chapter of her life.

We had been talking for some time about what life might look like together, about every conceivable circumstance under the sun that could bring us together. We both wanted more than just a long-distance relationship, but figuring out how to make it happen was the key. Mandi and I wanted no shortcuts in our journey. It was essential for us to make the right decisions for the right reasons. What we didn't know was just how quickly those decisions would come.

# CHAPTER 4
# Arriving Home

There are times in your life when you just know a decision is the right one.

"Can the job be done from anywhere?" I asked Duane.

"Yes," he replied. "There's a fair amount of travel, but it can be a remote position."

He was offering me a job in a newly created division in the company. It came with the possibility of great success and also significant risk, but having the opportunity to work from home was worth a degree of uncertainty.

"If I can do it while living in Mobile, Alabama, I accept," I told him. "I've already checked out travel costs and cost of living, and they're nearly identical."

Duane agreed to the arrangement, so I began making preparations almost immediately. After a long eighteen months of long-distance dating, Mandi and I were ready for the next phase of our relationship.

"Babe, I got the job, and Duane just gave me the okay to set up my office in Mobile!"

"That's great! Oh, wow. Wow! This is really going to happen!" Mandi said. To say she was beyond thrilled was an understatement. I now had a job with enormous potential for growth—in her hometown—so our relationship would finally get the chance to grow in ways it never could dating long distance.

I had already sold my house to my cousin Danny the previous summer. He had been living with me for a few years when I offered to sell him the house. He needed a place to live, and I needed the freedom in case of a move. It was a mutually beneficial agreement.

Sitting at my desk in the finished basement of my cousin's house, I signed paperwork for the two-bedroom, two-bath apartment in Mobile we had originally looked at for Mandi. The apartment was on the third floor of a complex less than a mile away from Mandi's parents. It had a loft that would serve as my office, a perfect space that gave the rental unit an extra two hundred square feet and the feeling of a home.

When this consulting opportunity fell in my lap, Mandi and I agreed that it made more sense for me to rent the apartment while she stayed at home a bit longer to save money. We were very serious about our relationship, but we had no intentions of living with each other before we were married. Family would have frowned upon that decision, plus we didn't want to short-circuit the significant momentum we had going.

I called the property management office to let them know the rental agreement and the deposit were on their way. I was aiming for a June move and looking forward to a great summer for 2004.

\*\*\*

I was champing at the bit to get down to Mobile. I had about a month from the time I signed the lease until moving day in late June. In reality, I didn't need that much time. I was so motivated to make it to Alabama that I nearly packed my entire house into dozens of cardboard boxes in just one weekend.

While I was excited to begin this new chapter in life, I had to face the bittersweet reality of leaving Iowa for the second time in seven years. Unlike the first move to Georgia in 1995 for a three-year work agreement, I knew there was a decent chance I would not be coming back this time. I could see a new life in front of me, a life filled with the happy family Mandi and I had talked about wanting for the last year and a half. Unfortunately, I knew I had to leave behind my childhood home, family, and friends to realize our dream.

"Jesus!" my dad said as he caught sight of the twenty-six-foot moving truck I had rented. He motioned to the length of the truck and trailer. "You've got that much shit to fill up the back of this thing?"

"Dad, I'm only hauling about half the house," I said. "Danny's keeping some of the lawn and garden stuff because I'm not going to need it in the apartment."

"Jase, do you want to put the couch in next or wait?" Danny asked.

"The couch comes next and goes right up against the washer," I said, pointing out where I wanted it.

I reached in my pocket and glanced at the graph paper I was carrying with an approximate drawing I created of how all my things would fit. It was a bit like playing Tetris with your home furnishings.

"Are you gonna drive this big thing with that trailer on it?" Dad asked me, still in disbelief at the size of the moving truck and trailer.

"Yeah," I said. "Who else is going to drive it?"

"Well, I don't know," Dad said, laughing.

The truth was, I had no idea how to drive a twenty-six-foot truck, much less do so with my car on a trailer hitch attached to the back. I wasn't worried about navigating Cedar Rapids or even Mobile traffic. Rather, I was much more concerned about taking it through St. Louis and downtown Memphis.

Dad was just staring at the big yellow truck. Having grown up on an Iowa farm in the 1950s, he wasn't raised to show emotion or share his feelings, so I didn't expect much in the way of advice or long diatribes about the meaning of life. Still, it was undeniable that it was difficult for him to watch me leave again. He loved Mandi and wanted me to be happy, but like all parents who love their kids, he secretly hoped I would live a little closer to home.

"That's it," I said as I shoved the last box into the back of the moving van. "Now, I have to hook this thing up to the trailer and get my car on there."

Having Danny there was a huge help. He's very mechanically inclined and has the mentality of a problem solver. Schooled in the trade of tool- and dye-making, he is all about precision. He double- and triple-checked to make sure everything was properly locked down. Being about seven years older than me, Danny graduated and learned his trades before I even entered middle school.

While my memories of us hanging out when I was young were few and far between, Danny and I grew closer once I graduated high school. We became running partners, entering local races together and enjoying some friendly competition. But there was no mistaking who the better runner was. I'd be happy to finish in the top third of entrants, whereas Danny typically would compete for a high-end finish in his age group. I was going to miss living with him.

Night crept in, and it was time to say "goodbye" to my dad and cousin so I could get some sleep. I had a long drive ahead of me the next day. I wasn't about to try going the total seventeen hours, particularly in a moving truck and trailer, but I figured the long daylight hours would give me the chance to get pretty far down the road.

Rising well before dawn, I took a quick shower and got dressed. Staying quiet so I didn't wake up Danny, I went out into the humid air of the Iowa summer morning. I had been waiting for this day since I met Mandi twenty months earlier.

Still dark outside, I opened the door to the truck and climbed up into the driver's seat of the cab. The small interior light barely cast enough illumination for me to find the ignition with my key. I started the engine, put the big truck into drive, and steadied myself for the long road ahead.

\*\*\*

Driving by yourself in a twenty-six-foot truck that's towing a car on a trailer is quite the adventure. I had planned to split the drive into two days, getting far enough on the first day to arrive on Saturday around noon to meet Mandi's family, take possession of the apartment, and unload the truck. The weather for the first half of the day happened to be near perfect—sunny skies for most of the drive—and traffic flowed smoothly.

With nothing but cornfields as far as the eye could see, getting through Iowa and northern Missouri was simple. But the two places on the map I had been concerned about were St. Louis and Memphis. I avoided the worst of St. Louis traffic by taking the bypass around the city. Memphis, however, would pose the bigger challenge.

The bridge on Interstate 55 crossing the Mississippi River from Arkansas into Memphis was an older bridge with just two narrow lanes in each direction. Built before modern trucking and transport systems increased traffic on the roadways, the span over the mighty Mississippi made even the most confident driver pay very close attention to the road. A fully loaded moving van hauling a car trailer barely fit between the white lines. My hands gripped the steering wheel tighter than usual as smaller, more agile cars zipped by me on my left. A pop-up thunderstorm decided to unleash a torrential downpour at about the same time as I crossed into Tennessee and back onto land. The blinding rain brought traffic to a near standstill and made following the interstate signs much more difficult.

Having finally made it through Memphis by 3:30 p.m., I still had plenty of daylight left to drive. With the adrenaline and excitement running through me, I wasn't yet tired and didn't feel like stopping so soon in the day. I set a new goal of making it to Jackson, Mississippi, before calling it a day.

As the sun got closer to setting, I found a nice hotel outside Jackson that had a vacancy. I pulled the truck and trailer to an open space in the parking lot that gave me a good angle to get out the following day. Checked in and comfortable, I quickly drifted off to sleep.

Upon waking, I did some quick calculating. Jackson is about a three-hour drive from Mobile. Not needing to be there until noon, I could leave any time before 9:00 a.m. and still make it. But I'm an early riser by nature—I couldn't sleep past five—and being just a few hours away from my girl had me stir-crazy by seven. I couldn't loaf around the hotel for another two hours, so I decided to leave early and kill time in Mobile if necessary.

"Hey, babe. I'm just outside Mobile and will be in town around ten o'clock," I told her.

"Seriously?" she said in disbelief. "Oh my God, you're almost here!"

I laughed. "I couldn't wait around any longer, and there was no traffic in Jackson or Mobile to slow me down."

"I love you!" she said exuberantly.

Matching her enthusiasm, I told her I loved her too. "I'll call you as soon as I get to the apartment!"

As I snaked my way through the curvy roads on the western outskirts of Mobile, I looked at the surroundings and soaked it all in. I pulled the truck into the apartment complex I had seen just one time before and had the overwhelming feeling I was arriving home.

\*\*\*

They say when you meet "the one" that you just know. You know this is the person you were meant to be with forever. Well, from the very beginning, I was 100 percent confident Mandi was "the one." I was so confident, in fact, that I had been plotting an effort to discover Mandi's ring size and learn more about what she liked for designs.

A month before the move to Alabama, Mandi was in Cedar Rapids, visiting me while on a work assignment. We had just grabbed lunch when I made an intentional turn in the wrong direction away from home.

"Hey, do you mind if we stop into this store and say hello to my friend who works here?" I asked as we were driving.

"Oh, if it's that jewelry store, I don't mind a bit," Mandi replied.

Aaron, or "Arnie" as his friends sometimes called him, was a jeweler. He was just one of the many friends I hung out with on a regular basis. Playing golf or cards or watching sports, wherever Arnie was, there was going to be laughs. It was guaranteed. As funny as he was, Arnie was excellent at his job and knew his product line well. He prided himself on making sure his customers were absolutely satisfied.

"Aaron, this is my girlfriend, Mandi," I said. "She's the one I was telling you about the other day."

After I introduced the two of them, Mandi and I started walking around and looking at the displays. I could tell she was interested and not uncomfortable about the subject of engagement rings.

"Is there anything I could show you?" Arnie asked after a few minutes.

"Oh, yes," Mandi jokingly replied.

For the next forty-five minutes, the three of us wandered around the store, discussing what she liked about various rings and trying on a few under the special display case lights that made the diamonds sparkle brilliantly.

"Oooooh, I like this one," Mandi said.

"That's a great quality ring and very popular right now," Arnie said.

I watched Mandi as she proudly displayed the ring on her finger, and took a mental note of it.

We both knew exactly why we were there. Nothing had to be said that day. We knew for a while we were someday going to look for rings. This day just happened to be a great occasion to do so.

A few days later, I called Arnie. "Hey, it's Fisher. That ring that we were looking at Saturday? I want to come by and work out the details on a purchase."

"Excellent. I'll be here all day," he said. "Stop on over."

Part of picking out an engagement ring is finding the best quality diamond. There are variations in the grade of diamonds, ratings that measure the color and the stone's vibrancy. Arnie showed me the diamond rating system, explained how that would affect the cost, and started narrowing down the options for the center stone.

"See how this diamond gives off that fire?" Arnie said as he showed me the stone under the bright lights. "This one has great color and only has tiny imperfections. You can't even see them with the naked eye, they are so minor."

"This is the diamond," I said. "I love it. It's perfect."

Aaron and I discussed the type of cut Mandi liked, the ring size she would need, and the wedding band accompanying that ring design. I formalized the paperwork, gave Aaron my credit card, and left the store with his promise that the ring would be finished in about a week.

I knew I had wanted to marry Mandi for months prior to that moment. It was important she have a ring she cherished, one she would proudly show off. I took no chances when it came to her happiness about the purchase. And Aaron made sure every detail was covered. I picked up the ring the day before leaving for Alabama, placing it in my safe and keeping it with me in the cab of the truck.

***

"You made it!" Mandi exclaimed as she hugged me and kissed me.

I held on tight. "I'm so glad to be here with you, knowing I'm not leaving!"

There would be no more sad moments watching the other person walk through airport security to fly home. No more looking at the calendar to try to find mutually agreeable dates when we could see each other. The schedule was now going to be built around the two of us, not our locations.

As I opened the door to the apartment, I was stunned by how much work Mandi had already done. She and her family had already moved in her couch, love seat, a kitchen table and chairs, some art for the walls, and a lamp that sat on an end table. It happened to be the same furniture we had looked at in Hattiesburg when we were first dating.

I was appreciative of all the help Mandi's family had given us that day and the days leading up to the move. Unloading a moving truck is much easier than loading it. However, this was the end of June in Alabama. The air was hot and humid, and there were three flights of stairs.

"That's the biggest damn television I've ever seen," Michael said as he lifted my big screen TV.

Michael dated Mandi's younger sister, Amber, for a time in high school. I remained friends with him after they went their separate ways. At six foot seven with a big athletic frame, he was the go-to person for moving heavy furniture. I suppose it was unfair of us to expect him to pull the appliance cart the TV sat on up all those stairs, one at a time, but when you're easily the biggest and strongest person in the room, that responsibility is going to fall on you more often than not. Young and brimming with confidence, Michael wasn't afraid to show off his strength. In fact, he welcomed lifting the heaviest items as a challenge. It was as if he wanted to test how much weight he could tolerate hoisting in the hot June sun.

Once we got everything moved inside, Mandi and I opened boxes and scooted furniture to get the apartment set up just how we wanted it. All the texts, calls, letters, and instant messages had led to this moment. Since my relationship with Mandi had first evolved into something serious, I had daydreamed about this. And finally, we were together.

\*\*\*

With summer being a slower time for higher education development, my new job took a little time to build up the business pipeline. I started to travel with more regularity beginning in August 2004. Fundraising typically ramped up as students arrived back from summer break looking for jobs. I often was brought in as a consultant to help train the new student callers and provide general best practices. After struggling to get any business in July and early August, my September calendar rapidly filled up. I booked nearly every available day and easily met my goal for the month.

I had the good fortune of being in the right place at the right time from a career standpoint. I got in on the ground floor of a fast-growing company and worked hard to put myself in a position to succeed. RuffaloCODY was the undisputed industry leader in on-campus fundraising services, particularly in phonathon programs for higher education institutions. And when it came to phonathon programs and fundraising services, I prided myself on being among the best minds in the business.

While I majored in political science and business administration as an undergrad, nonprofit fundraising came along at the right time and seemed to fit my skill set. It was part science and part art. I could use my data analysis ability to break down numbers, spot trends, and build a plan for improvement. I created complex spreadsheets and statistical forecasting models that gave fundraising managers the tools they needed to raise more money. And I could find, motivate, and coach talented people. So, when the fundraising consultant opportunity came up, I was a natural fit for this first-ever position.

I built a good reputation in the industry. Soon, I was being asked to speak at conferences across the nation and was getting referrals from previous clients who saw significant increases in their results after my visit. I was beginning to make a considerable amount of money based on the volume of work I was doing. But there was a price to pay for my newfound success, and that was time. I'm confident I spent more nights in hotel rooms than I did in my apartment in the fall of 2004. And I was missing Mandi a lot during the week.

When I was out of town for work, Mandi would stay at the apartment. When I was in town, she would come over to hang out. Sharing the apartment wasn't just convenient, it allowed us to learn each other's living styles and iron out any differences before being together full-time under one roof. It ended up being one of the best things we did to help us grow together.

The spring of 2005 brought more of the same. My calendar was packed, and I even sold one client an entire month of my services on campus, meaning a month away from home. In some ways, it seemed as though I hadn't moved to Mobile at all. I spent so much time on the road that Mandi was living at the apartment full-time, and I was missing family events I wanted to attend.

I began to feel that moving hadn't changed much for me. I saw Mandi too infrequently for my liking, and while our relationship was solid, I was becoming a part-time boyfriend. Don't get me wrong, I wasn't complaining then, nor am I complaining now about the amount of business I could generate. I paid off my student loans early and wiped away all my debt in a year. But I missed my girlfriend and wasn't holding up my end of the agreement to put each other first.

\*\*\*

In the summer of 2005, I had lunch with a friend who worked in the development office at Spring Hill College in Mobile. She informed me that they had a major gift officer position that would soon be available and encouraged me to apply. My portfolio of prospects would be more local, and I could be home more often than I was with the intense travel of the consulting position.

I would have to take a pay cut and much of my flexibility of working at home would be gone, but in mid-August of 2005 I made the difficult decision to leave RuffaloCODY after fifteen years. I was essentially making a commitment to Mandi as much as it was a calculated career move. Because I was debt-free, I could afford the reduced pay and looked forward to reestablishing friendships in an office setting. I set my departure date for early September and readied myself for the significant career change.

Spring Hill College is a small, Jesuit liberal arts institution in the heart of Mobile. The Jesuits are wonderful teachers and believe strongly in the philosophy of service to others. These principles lined up well with my personal interests as well as my Catholic faith.

The job was an interesting change. I found myself focused more on the bigger picture and building long-term relationships versus analyzing short-term results. It was a simple enough adjustment, but truth be told, I missed the direct energy of annual giving and phonathons.

"We are down in donors," my boss Karen said in our weekly group meeting in early November. "Jason, I know you have a background in annual giving and wondered if you would take a look and see if you can discover anything obvious that we're missing."

"Absolutely," I said. "Happy to do it."

I dug into the results of the year to that point and studied the trends. It became apparent that donor retention was suffering, and we were in danger of losing a significant number of prior givers if we didn't increase our outreach methods immediately.

I recommended that I help get the phone program ramped back up and running at full speed, then return my focus to major gifts. In those days, phonathons were the dominant driver of annual contributions. It was a part of nearly every campus fundraising plan, and it needed to be emphasized more at Spring Hill College than it had been to that point in the year.

I created a statistical forecaster that showed precisely where I thought we could be at the end of the fundraising year. "I think we can set a record for donors," I told Samantha, the annual fund director.

"That's wonderful!" she said. "How soon can we surpass last year's results and get back on top?"

"Mid-February," I said. "But I need to be the one to run the program to make sure my suggestions are getting implemented properly. I can do major gifts in the day and phonathons at night for a few weeks to make sure we get off to a good start."

Samantha and Karen talked it over and agreed to the plan. I began working a few nights a week while I was hiring new callers and implementing my suggestions. Soon, the donors started to renew, and the dollars started rolling in. As the spring semester continued, we were on pace to set a record for donors and dollars to the Spring Hill College Fund, a critical general giving program that funds scholarships for deserving students.

\*\*\*

Working at Spring Hill College was a godsend in two main ways. First, it afforded me much more time at home with Mandi, getting to know our habits and reaffirming our commitment to a future together. Second, I had always wanted to run an Ironman triathlon race. It was a step up in terms of a personal fitness challenge, adding swimming and cycling to running.

"Babe, I want to run the Florida Half-Ironman race next May," I said to Mandi one day in the fall of 2005.

"Go for it," she said, likely not understanding the amount of training I would need to put in.

"It's a big race, Mandi. It's a combination of a one-point-two-mile swim, fifty-six miles on the bike, and a thirteen-point-one-mile half-marathon, all wrapped up into the same race."

"If that's what you want, I fully support you," she replied.

Mandi was as encouraging of a person as I had ever met. Still, the intensity would be such that I would need to train six out of seven days each week. Slowly, I had to build a base of fitness, then take it to another level in terms of distance and cardiovascular strength. I would train in the mornings before work, but the weekends would require significant time on the bike to make sure I got in long fifty- to sixty-mile rides.

I immediately dropped fifteen pounds within the first month of training, adding muscle, and increasing the intensity of my workouts. Family and friends said they had a hard time recognizing me because my body changed so quickly. The lean muscular tone I had during my marathon training had slowly begun to go dormant over time. Waking my body up and pushing it to a new limit took a tremendous amount of mental strength, perhaps even more critical than the physical training.

With the race in late May, my weeks consisted of an endless combination of swimming, biking, and running on different days. I trained in the cold winds of January, heavy rain of the early spring, and intense heat and humidity of late April and May. I would think about Mandi and the great relationship we had during the long runs and bike rides. On one such bike ride, I had an epiphany about how and when I would pop the question.

Throughout our several years together, I had filled three see-through plastic totes with all the meaningful items I accumulated from our relationship. On that bike ride, I decided to put together a scrapbook of memories that led us to that moment in time. Entitled "Our Story," it included early pictures, parts of her letters, the phone cards she used to call me long distance when cell minutes were still scarce, and memories of the move to Mobile. After putting the pages together, the last page simply asked, "Are You Ready for Our Future?"

*** 

In March 2006, I called Mandi's mom. "Miss Sheri, it's Jason. I was hoping I could find a time to come over and talk with you and Mister Skip for a few minutes on Sunday while Mandi is with her sisters."

"Sure, but is everything all right?" Miss Sheri said.

"Yes, absolutely. I just want to talk with you both in private for a quick minute."

I'm sure that all but gave away why I asked to speak to them.

A few days later, I went to the safe I kept in my office closet and got the engagement ring. I steadied my nerves, drove to Mandi's parents' house, and knocked on the door.

"Fish," Miss Sheri said affectionately, calling me by the nickname so many others used. "Come on in."

"To what do we owe this pleasure?" she asked after I got situated on the couch.

My heart began to beat a little faster, and I could feel my hands start to shake slightly. I had been thinking about how I would approach them for a considerable amount of time, but there's nothing that can prepare you for the moment you ask for their daughter's hand in marriage.

"I have enjoyed being a part of this family so much for the past several years," I began. "You have made me feel welcome in ways that I cannot describe." I took a deep breath and turned to Mandi's dad. "Mister Skip, I love your daughter so much and want Mandi to be a permanent part of my life. I would like your permission to ask her to marry me."

Her father took a thoughtful moment. "Are you sure?" he asked.

I remember thinking that this wasn't how I envisioned the conversation going. However, I knew precisely what he meant by the question, and I sought to reassure him the best I could.

"Absolutely," I confidently stated. "I'm 100 percent convinced Mandi is the love of my life. I have had the ring for a while now. I was waiting for the right time. Honestly, I wanted to make sure Mandi and I had the opportunity to build our relationship the right way before asking her to marry me."

I was not afraid of marriage or commitment. On the contrary, I respected it tremendously and wanted to make sure it would last. I had seen first-hand in my own life how failed marriages can impact children and tear apart families. From a young age, I had vowed that I would do this just one time, I would find the right girl and make sure I never rushed the process.

I knew that whatever hesitation her father had almost certainly came from a place of genuine concern for his daughter's future. I understood that completely.

Mr. Skip looked at me and smiled. "You have my permission," he said and got up to shake my hand.

"Congratulations, Fish. Welcome to the family, officially!" Miss Sheri said as she hugged me.

On a sunny Sunday afternoon, March 12, 2006, the family gathered under false pretenses. Mandi's parents had given the girls a reason to be there without giving away the real motive behind the event. As the family chatted in the living room, the moment I had been waiting so long for had finally arrived.

"I have a late Valentine's Day gift for you," I said to Mandi as I handed her a large box.

Mandi carefully opened the box and began reading the book I created. As she flipped each page of the handwritten story, I fidgeted in my seat and dug my hand into the pocket of my loose-fitting khaki pants to find the engagement ring box. She giggled and laughed at each page where I had pasted something from our history together, but I could sense she genuinely didn't know what was coming at the end.

As Mandi turned to the last page of the proposal scrapbook, I got down on one knee in front of her family. I looked her in the eyes and asked her the most important question of my life.

"Will you marry me?" I asked her, confidently and proudly and with a wide smile.

Mandi was so choked up from the question that she had difficulty replying. She moved her hands and fanned her face, trying her best to hold back the emotions so she could answer my question.

"Is that a 'yes'?" Miss Sheri asked her.

"Yes!" Mandi finally exclaimed between happy sobs.

I slipped the engagement ring on her finger. Her face lit up, glowing as bright as I had ever seen it. Ecstatic, we embraced for what seemed like ten minutes. I felt so comfortable and at peace, knowing I was committing the rest of my life to this woman. I couldn't have been happier with or more confident in my decision.

I also knew I wasn't just marrying Mandi. I was marrying into her family, who welcomed me with open arms. Without a doubt, Mandi's parents and sisters made my decision to ask Mandi easier because we had such a great relationship. They have a lot of love in their house. And it was precisely the type of family I saw myself building with Mandi.

***

I had always wanted to add a graduate degree to my portfolio, so prior to our engagement, I took the GRE and GMAT. In early 2005, I was accepted at Spring Hill College for an MBA and the University of South Alabama for a master's in public administration. I had also discovered an incredible program at the University of Arkansas: as the newest of the presidential schools at the time, The Clinton School of Public Service offered the only master's degree in public service anywhere in the world.

The curriculum at the Clinton School was especially unique. It was a sixteen-month program with a hands-on approach that emphasized fieldwork and internships, balancing them with classroom study for a complete student experience. While I have always had a large variety of career interests, I had long felt that public service was a calling. Whether it would be in my career or a volunteer capacity, I loved the idea of using my experience and skills to help others who were less fortunate than myself.

I had no ambition to move away from Mobile. I had made it my home and was very happy there. Mandi and I were doing great and building a life together. However, there was something about this program that intrigued me enough to tell Mandi I wanted to apply.

I worked on my references, application, statement of interest, and rounded up my transcripts. I was applying for the inaugural class and learned that one thousand candidates were seeking just sixteen student positions. Yet, the admissions office asked me for an interview. I was shocked.

"Babe, you're not going to believe this," I told Mandi one February afternoon in 2005. "The Clinton School wants me to come interview for a spot."

"That's great!" Mandi exclaimed. "But what happens if you get in?"

"I guess we sit down and talk about it," I said, realizing Mandi was fearful I would leave Mobile without a commitment to her.

"I trust you and want what's best for you," she said. "But don't forget about us." There was no chance of that happening, but true to her unselfish personality, Mandi wanted whatever made me happy.

I flew to Arkansas late on a Thursday evening; my interview was set for Friday morning. I was relatively calm and confident the morning of the interview. Truthfully, part of me felt like an impostor. A small-town Iowa boy from a blue-collar family who paid his way through college by working and taking out student loans, now a finalist for the inaugural class at the Clinton School of Public Service? I knew the competition would be strong for these sixteen spots, but I didn't let that deter me.

After an anxious morning prior to my interview, I left my downtown Little Rock hotel and walked the few short blocks to where the Clinton School was housed next to the Clinton Presidential Library. I entered Sturgis Hall, the school's only campus building at that point, and waited patiently for the staff to meet with me.

I was escorted down the hall into the school's small library where two people from the Clinton School admissions team met with me. The interview lasted about an hour, after which I received a quick tour of the campus and was introduced to staff and faculty members.

The entire staff who met me had been wonderful, professional, and gave off a warm welcome. I felt confident in my answers and that I could perform well at the school.

"How'd it go?" Mandi asked when I arrived home late that evening.

"I left nothing on the table and gave it my best," I said. "Now we'll see what happens."

"If you don't get in, there's nothing wrong with an MBA," she reminded me. "And you promised me a dog."

"Absolutely," I said to her. "I'll pick one of the other programs, we'll get a dog, and we'll start looking for houses."

I knew Mandi was getting a little antsy with my seemingly indecisive mentality. In truth, I had already decided I was going to ask her. I just had yet to do it.

Growing up as a child of divorce can affect you in many different ways. For me, I became extra cautious about relationships and took the commitment of marriage very seriously. Taking a little extra time on the front end to make sure it would work was worth it to me. I loved Mandi with all my heart and knew we belonged together. Still, I was admittedly a little nervous about the biggest decision I would ever make, which likely caused me to put off the proposal.

Around three weeks after I interviewed, I received a rejection letter from the Clinton School.

"Well, babe, it wasn't meant to be," I said, disappointed.

"I'm proud of you for trying," Mandi said sympathetically. "But an MBA or MPA is a great thing. Now marry me and let's get a dog."

Mandi's comment took some sting out of being turned down. Honestly, I was proud I had even made it that far in the process. But coming so close and falling short was still painful.

\*\*\*

Over the next few months, I made my peace with the rejection. I took the job at Spring Hill College that September of 2005 and decided I would start my MBA program in January. Mandi and I began to look at houses, and, as promised, we went to the city dog pound and picked out a puppy.

"I think she's a beagle," I said to Mandi as we held her in the noisy cages of the animal shelter to see if she would take to us.

"She's so cute and sweet," Mandi said.

I could tell by the way Mandi looked at me that this was the dog she wanted. I walked up to the gentleman who was helping us to inquire more about the puppy.

"It's twenty dollars to have her spayed," he said. "The adoption is free as long as you have the procedure done."

"I guess we're getting a dog," I said to Mandi as I looked over my shoulder, holding the puppy.

"Yay!" Mandi exclaimed as she took the dog from my arms and held her.

They say that sharing the responsibility of a pet is an excellent precursor to having children. That's likely not far from the truth. It took us a day or two to settle on a name, ultimately deciding on Gracie—named after Sandra Bullock's pageant character, Gracie Lou Freebush, in the movie *Miss Congeniality*.

It was late 2005, my job was going well, Mandi and I were happy, and Gracie was getting bigger. Then my phone rang one afternoon.

"Hey, you should apply to the Clinton School again." It was my friend and old consulting client, Susan. "I heard they are expanding the size of the second class and that you were very close to admission the last time. You shouldn't give up."

"I don't know, Susan," I said to her with a slight pause. "I don't know if I want to go through the process again and get my hopes up, only to be let down. Plus, my girlfriend and I just got a dog and are looking at houses."

"I understand," Susan said. "But this is a once-in-a-lifetime opportunity if you do get in. I know they were impressed with you."

After I hung up the phone, I quietly contemplated my options, ultimately deciding I would apply once again but keep it to myself. If I got in, I would talk it over with Mandi and determine what was best. If she didn't want me to go, I wouldn't attend. But if I didn't get in, nobody would be any wiser about it, and I wouldn't have to explain the second failure in a row.

A few weeks later, another phone call: "Jason, this is the admissions officer at the Clinton School of Public Service. You were accepted in the early admissions process as a student for our second class, starting in August 2006. Congratulations!"

I was stunned. I had been fairly certain I was going to be turned down again. Now I had to break the news to Mandi, which I was not looking forward to doing. Yes, I had my reasons for not telling anyone. But deep down in my gut, I knew they weren't good reasons. Fear of embarrassment should never have been why I kept this to myself.

"You applied again ... and you didn't tell me?" was Mandi's response to news of my acceptance.

"Babe, I'm sorry. I didn't want to be humiliated if I was rejected again," I said, ashamed. "I know it's a surprise, and I'm prepared to turn them down if that's what we decide is best."

Mandi was admittedly stunned. We had a plan. How could I deviate from the plan without discussing it with her?

Mandi supported me in just about everything I did. Whether it was going back to graduate school, training for a big race, or switching jobs, she always had my back. But this time, I could tell she wondered silently what this meant for us. No matter the good news I had just received, my relationship with Mandi was my priority.

I remained sensitive to the situation I had created. So, after I finally asked Mandi to marry me, I gave her a few scenarios I'd thought about before the proposal.

"We can either get married in December 2006 after my first semester is over so that you can continue to work, and we can have more time to plan. Or, we can get married this summer if we can find a venue and date, then move to Arkansas afterward. The entire experience can be done together, start to finish."

I was asking a lot of Mandi, and I knew it. I felt very guilty, but Mandi understood this was too unique of an opportunity to pass up. It was a very competitive program at the time, and getting in was not easy. It was an honor to be chosen.

Applying to the school the second time was a purely selfish decision I had made as a single man. I wasn't thinking about how it would affect Mandi as much as I should have. I vowed that would be the last time I would put her in that position.

"Oh, we're not waiting," she said in a funny but sarcastic reply. "We are getting married this summer, and I will make this work. I'm not letting you go anywhere without me."

# CHAPTER 5
# I Do

Finding a location to have the wedding we wanted in such a short timeframe proved a challenge. We both preferred a church wedding, if possible, but were willing to consider all options. We set appointments and visited a half-dozen churches, historic homes, and even a botanical garden in an attempt to find the right place.

My friend and colleague, Samantha, recommended St. Joseph's Chapel on the campus of Spring Hill College. I was initially hesitant. It was the perfect location and size, and it was beautifully renovated just a few years prior. However, I knew I would be leaving my job later that summer for graduate school, and I had not yet informed them of that decision. I felt guilty accepting the use of the facilities for our ceremony and then turning around and submitting my resignation a few weeks later.

I decided to walk down to the chapel on my lunch hour and take a peek. The chapel was breathtaking, both inside and outside. I stood alone inside the church, looked around in silence, and could easily see it was the perfect venue. More importantly, I knew Mandi would be thrilled.

Just a short walk away was Stewartfield, where many couples held their wedding receptions. While it was a little on the small side, the proximity to the church made it the logical choice.

After getting Mandi's approval, I contacted a staff member and walked through the list of available dates. Most of the weekends in the summer were already booked, but there were a few that remained available. I wrote down the dates and ran them by Mandi.

"It would be great if we could get married and go on the honeymoon somewhat in advance of needing to move," I said to her as we thought about the logistics.

"Oh, I agree. I do not want to be packing the apartment and preparing for the wedding at the same time," Mandi responded.

"Given the dates on the calendar, your work schedule and mine, there's really only one day that fits," I said as I circled the date on the calendar.

"That's our date then," Mandi said. "July 22, 2006. That's cutting it close, but I can pull this off. That gives me about four months."

Mandi's positive outlook on planning a wedding in just four months gave me confidence. Our guest list was approaching 250 people. Stewartfield would likely top out at 150, but we knew not everyone would attend the reception. As the RSVPs came in, we were confident the facilities would be more than adequate to cover whom we expected to show up.

\* \* \*

To be married at Spring Hill College, by rule, at least one person in the couple had to be Catholic. Being a confirmed Catholic myself, I had that part covered. Mandi was a practicing Methodist, but the difference in the religious denomination was not an issue for us.

Engaged Encounter—essentially a series of premarital counseling discussions in a group setting—is a mandatory weekend activity for couples in order to be married in the Catholic Church. It was held at an old monastery off Spring Hill Avenue in Mobile. We chose a weekend in April, the soonest available, to complete the program.

It ended up being a warm and sunny April weekend, the type of day you did not want to be inside participating in the requisite premarital counseling. But, knowing this was our ticket to getting married in July, we happily made the sacrifice.

Entering the monastery that Friday evening, there was a large lifelike statue of Jesus with outstretched arms near the door. The room was dimly lit, and I was not entirely sure Jesus was just a statue. Startled, I jumped back at first glance as Mandi laughed out loud, walking behind me.

Mandi and I were assigned to separate rooms with roommates of the same gender. Part of the weekend would be group activities, so they encouraged roommates to be conversational and help each other. Our assigned roommates were a Vietnamese couple who spoke very little English.

By this point in our relationship, Mandi and I had been dating for over three years. We communicated regularly and were very open about what our hopes and expectations were for our marriage. So, while this mandatory session was likely helpful for some couples, we frankly recognized it was going to be a bit boring.

As a Catholic, I spent many days of my childhood in quiet booths, confessing my sins to a priest. So, in keeping with that practice, I must now fully admit that I smuggled in an AM/FM radio and headphones to help make the time pass more quickly. That weekend happened to coincide with the professional football draft.

I grew up playing every sport imaginable, so the draft was an important event I wasn't about to give up to the Church. Mandi followed sports, but more as a hobby than as a personal passion. But we loved the buildup to the player selection process and were disappointed when we found out we would miss it.

On one of our first breaks of the day on Saturday morning, I retreated to my room, tuned in to the sports radio show, and put in my headphones. My roommate looked at me, puzzled, probably thinking I was the sinner he had heard about all morning.

I spent my breaks for the next several hours listening to the draft. I imagined this was how my dad had spent his youth on the farm, hearing static from an old AM radio as he listened to a baseball game.

Mandi knew I brought the radio and demanded to know what was happening. Unfortunately, I couldn't walk down to her room and tell her in person. To make matters worse, our rudimentary cellphones at the time were required to be shut off so couples could concentrate on the planned activities. But like two teenagers who couldn't stay away from trouble, Mandi and I placed our phones on silent and proceeded to exchange texts.

*The Broncos just traded up to get Cutler! Woohoo!* I texted Mandi. Being a Denver Broncos fan, I had been especially attuned to the news about the team being interested in drafting Vanderbilt quarterback Jay Cutler. The Broncos needed a quarterback badly.

*No way!"* she responded. *We need a TV in this place!*

*No doubt. Longest weekend ever! Love you!*

Needless to say, Mandi and I made the most of the Engaged Encounter experience. It was something we laughed about well after it was over. But that was a common theme of our time together: taking something less than desirable and finding a way to make it a positive.

*** 

The summer of 2006 was, in many ways, a blur. I had just run the half-Ironman race in Florida. Now, my focus was preparing for the wedding and making decisions regarding our impending move to Little Rock.

Even though I had left RuffaloCODY the prior fall, I was asked by my former colleagues to speak at their annual fundraising conference in July. Given my close ties with many of the staff, it was an easy decision to say "yes." The conference was in Las Vegas, and I looked forward to reuniting with old colleagues and friends for five days.

Considering the conference ended on Wednesday, July 19, the smart thing to do would have been to reconsider going and instead focus on what was bound to be a very hectic period. However, I had committed to RuffaloCODY, and I wanted to do my best to keep it.

"Babe, is the conference going to be a problem with the wedding plans?" Mandi asked.

"I plan to take a red-eye home on the nineteenth and be back at 8:00 a.m. July 20," I said.

"That's cutting it very close," Mandi said. "Remember, we have the rehearsal dinner on the twenty-first, and your parents are flying in the day before that." July 20 was also Mandi's birthday, but she was far more focused on the wedding events than she was on turning twenty-five.

Mandi likely didn't think the trip was the best idea, but she never expressed anything outwardly negative about it—and, fortunately, the conference went well and my flights were on time.

I arrived back in Mobile around 7:30 a.m. and was able to grab my bags, get my car, and be home by 8:15. I immediately unpacked my suitcases and started a load of laundry. Mandi had been staying at the apartment in my absence, cleaning and organizing for my family that would soon be arriving from out of town later that day.

Trying to save my family and friends some money, I had used frequent flier miles to fly a handful of people down from Iowa for the wedding. My mother and sister chose to drive, taking their time and seeing some sights in between. My dad, my stepmother Alice, and my cousin Danny all flew down on that Thursday.

Because of ticket prices and limited choices, all five family and friends using my frequent flier miles flew down to Pensacola, Florida, about an hour's drive from Mobile. Instead of renting a car, I decided to save them another buck and pick them up at the airport myself. Of course, they were looking at this as a vacation, but I was jet-lagged, so I tried my best to talk them out of being tourists for the day.

"Dad, I'm dead-tired and have several things to do before we get together tonight with Mandi's family," I said.

"You'll be okay for just a minute," Dad said with a slight guilt trip. "I just want to see it. I've never been to the ocean before."

"Dad, it's not an ocean. It's the Gulf of Mexico," I replied in a pleading voice. "If you call it an ocean down here, people will laugh at you."

"I don't give a shit what you call it. I just want to see it," he said with a laugh. "C'mon, Jase, we have time."

Hearing that my dad had never been to a saltwater beach just reinforced the notion of how fortunate I had been. I relented and drove the long way home through Gulf Shores so he could dip his toes in the water and check off a bucket-list item.

* * *

My parents and Mandi's parents had never met before due primarily to the long distance between Iowa and Alabama. In many respects, my family was very different than Mandi's. Different is often a good thing. It helps provide alternative views of the world that keep us all moving forward together. But sometimes different is awkward, and I was hoping to keep that possibility to a minimum.

Mr. Skip had booked reservations at Ed's Seafood Shed for Mandi's birthday on Thursday night. The day was losing its light when we sat down. The deck area where we were seated slowly began to come alive with the typical sounds of summer at a busy waterfront restaurant. Chatty patrons enjoyed intoxicating beverages and all seemingly tried to talk over each other while insects and wildlife provided steady background noise.

I introduced my mother and father to the large gathering, then introduced my cousin Danny, my stepmother Alice, and my sister Jill. Handshakes and hugs made the meeting official, and the group began to enjoy the conversation as I attempted to get as comfortable as possible in the outdoor metal chair.

The anxiety I was feeling about our families meeting had faded somewhat by the time the group ordered appetizers and drinks. It appeared that everyone was enjoying themselves. I did the best I could to remain engaged, but fatigue was settling in and it was all I could do to keep my eyes open.

My sister sat to my left, and I tapped her leg with my foot. I bent over to talk more privately and reiterated the prior instructions I had given her.

"If Dad starts getting salty with his language, I need you to kick him under the table," I reminded her with a nervous smile. "You're in charge of keeping him in line tonight."

"Okay, okay," Jill said while laughing. "You know that nobody can stop him from doing it."

"I expect it to happen," I said. "I'm just trying to keep it from going to the level of DEFCON 5."

My father does not know a stranger, and he can find humor in nearly every situation, regardless of whether or not it is appropriate at the time. And while I found his stories and conversational approach funny on most occasions, this was not the time nor place.

Dad grew up in the sparsely populated area of rural eastern Iowa, spending his early years on a farm and then moving into the small town of Van Horne when my grandfather took up work in a factory for better pay. After his basic training for the National Guard, Dad found work in the local factories of blue-collar eastern Iowa. He spoke the language of a factory man, not unlike his father. There was no shortage of colorful adjectives my sister and I learned growing up.

As it turned out, Dad only had one or two relatively mild infractions of our agreed-upon rules. The truth is, Mr. Skip and Miss Sheri are not very judgmental people, but I was nervous and wanted to avoid making any memorable moments for the wrong reasons.

As everyone finished their meals, the waitress returned to our table with a small dessert and placed it in front of Mandi, who was seated to my right. Immediately, the group began singing "Happy Birthday."

"Whose birthday is it?" I asked inquisitively to Miss Sheri as laughter began erupting from the table.

"Well, Fish, today is your soon-to-be wife's birthday," Miss Sheri replied.

I had already given Mandi her birthday card and a small gift earlier in the day. I had flown all night to make it home to be with her on this important occasion. But my sleep-deprived mind had temporarily rendered me incapable of recalling this critical fact before I opened my mouth and spoke.

Mandi just laughed. "Just in case you forgot this as well, we're getting married on Saturday," she said dryly. "If I need to call tomorrow to make sure you remember, I will."

*\*\**

Planning a wedding is no small feat, particularly if it's a sizable event. Planning a sizable wedding within four months while packing and getting ready to move out of state almost immediately thereafter is an amazing accomplishment. Sure, there were occasional hiccups that would typically frustrate a bride. Yet, Mandi seemed to take any setbacks in stride.

Mandi was a certified wedding planner, courtesy of an online course she took a couple of years prior. From beginning to end, she enjoyed the challenge. Whether it was catering, accommodations at the venues, or the guest list, she was on top of the details and did so with a steady hand.

Planning and executing your own wedding is challenging because you can't be in all places at one time. For that reason, Mandi asked her friend Laura to be the official wedding coordinator and help with all the essential details. Laura kept Mandi laughing, was a stickler for details, and allowed Mandi to relax more fully on her special day. Mandi's mom and sisters also helped, working with both Mandi and Laura on ideas, planning, and purchases. It was a complete team effort.

The wedding rehearsal may be just another detail to be checked off the list for some, but it was critical for me. I was wedding ignorant. I had never even been a groomsman in a wedding before getting married myself.

The steps in a ceremony and the order they are to be done were like learning a foreign language in a day. Our wedding photographer captured many of the moments in the rehearsal. At virtually no time did I appear relaxed. The last thing I wanted to do was make a mistake in my own wedding.

Fortunately, Father Viscardi, the Jesuit priest who was marrying us, was very familiar with St. Joseph Chapel. He gave Mandi and Laura various bits of advice; for example, how best to position the bride and the train of her wedding dress as they came through the doors. And our wedding party had many experienced groomsmen and bridesmaids. They took it all in stride and allowed me to follow along in hopes of having little difficulty.

Following the rehearsal, there is a customary dinner the groom's side is in charge of hosting. I wanted our friends and family to have a unique Mobile experience but not break my piggy bank in the process. As I reminded Mandi several times, we were about to be poor college students again. We would both be quitting our jobs at the end of the month, and only Mandi would have a job waiting for her in Little Rock when we arrived.

We held the rehearsal dinner at Wentzell's Oyster House, a Mobile original. There were roughly fifty people in attendance, and I distinctly remember fretting over the bill.

"It's over one thousand dollars," Mandi told me as she looked at the bill.

"Ouch. Was it fourteen or fifteen dollars a head?" I asked.

"Well, you have gratuity in there as well," Mandi gently reminded me. "Just pay the bill and don't count every head in the room, please."

"Okay," I said, feeling a bit guilty for fretting over the bill at that moment. "I'll be unemployed in about two weeks, so I'm just being cautious."

"You're just cheap," she said. "I love you, but loosen up. We're getting married tomorrow!"

Laughing, I knew she was right. But the stress of facing unemployment weighed heavily on my mind at that point.

Following dinner, I rounded up my dad, my stepmother, and my cousin Danny and we all packed into my car. Heading toward the hotel, I spoke aloud what I was thinking.

"This time tomorrow, I'll be married," I said.

"Big day," Dad responded. "It will be good. Everything is going great."

"So far, so good," I said.

With that, I dropped them off at the hotel, turned the car around, and headed back home to get some sleep. For thirty-five years, I had been a single man. And in less than twenty-four hours, my life would change. I was about to be the happiest man in the world, just one night of sleep away from forever.

\*\*\*

I awoke on Saturday, July 22, 2006, ready to be a married man. I was fully recovered from my sleep deprivation of the previous two days and had a few errands to run. I grabbed Mandi's checklist and headed out the door. It was early morning, but the day was already feeling especially tropical. Mobile's summers can be brutal at times, relentless in the heat and humidity on the Gulf Coast. And there's a chance of rain just about any day in the summer, given the air temperature and moisture saturation levels.

"Morning, baby. Happy Wedding Day!" I said to Mandi over the phone at ten in the morning.

"Yikes! We're gonna get married! I'm so excited!"

"I know it's bad luck to see each other before the ceremony, but I didn't think a phone call was against the rules," I told her. "I have a couple of things I wanted to run by you."

"Fire away," she said.

"Beer. How much do you think I should get? I don't want to run out before the night is over," I said as I stood outside Walmart.

"Hmm," she said. "What did we say? We're expecting two hundred, with probably 25 to 35 percent of them drinking one or two beers. So, maybe three or four cases?"

"Okay. I'll buy a few different brands," I said, walking into the store. "Next ... pictures. What if it's raining?"

"Hush your mouth," she said jokingly. "Seriously, if it rains, we have a backup plan. It doesn't matter anyway. We're about to be married!" she sang.

We were both giddy. Mandi was my dream girl, my soulmate whom I had hoped to meet in my life. I was hers, too, a man who loved her for her mind, body, and spirit. Our future was right in front of us.

After paying, I wheeled five cases of beer out to the parking lot, adding one extra just to make certain we were covered. The bottles rattled loudly as I pushed the cart over the rough pavement toward my car. Other shoppers and curious onlookers stared at me.

I smiled big. "Getting married tonight," I said to one of them as they stared blankly at my large purchase.

I drove to the reception area on campus to drop off the beer and then met Mandi's dad and uncle to put out signs directing guests where to go. Spring Hill College's campus is not that large, but there was no direct road between the chapel on one side of the campus and Stewartfield, our reception site, on the other. Signs were the best way to ensure guests knew where to park and how to attend both functions without frustration.

FISHER-COWART RECEPTION HERE! one sign read as I put the yard stake in the ground near Stewartfield. Mandi's sister Abby had used her artistic talents to hand-craft the unique signs.

"How many of these things do we have?" I asked Mr. Skip.

"Too many," he replied. "It's hot as crap out here."

The day was already heating up, and it was only 10:30 a.m. The temperature would eventually climb to higher than ninety degrees with significant humidity, which is just an average July day in Mobile. But even if you're prepared for the heat, it still saps the energy out of you.

"We're all going to need showers," Mr. Skip said. "We better hurry up and get this done."

Before driving back to the apartment, I glanced at my checklist. "Beer, check. Signs out, check. Just need to pick up the sandwiches for the groom's room, and we're good."

We had four groomsmen, including the best man, and four bridesmaids, including the co-maids of honor. There were three ushers, a ring bearer, a flower girl, and a person assigned to manage the guest registry. Mandi's friend from college was our vocalist, and we had two readers who would speak during the ceremony. There were countless others who had a part in our special day.

Because the space at Stewartfield was relatively small, the decision was made to have the bride get dressed at the reception hall before heading to the chapel. The groomsmen were to get dressed at Byrne Hall, the old library, which was recently renovated and just happened to be where my office was located. With a six o'clock wedding, the goal was to get everyone to arrive by two o'clock so we could be ready for pictures when it was our turn.

One of the best memories of the day was getting dressed and ready with my friends. Jokes were thrown back and forth as we all put on our tuxes. We wore black suits with peridot—green—colored vests and ties over white shirts.

"Fish, you getting nervous?" my friend Thad asked me as we were putting on our shirts and ties.

"I'm nervous that I'll forget the order things are supposed to happen, but I'm not nervous about getting married," I said as I tied my shiny black dress shoes. "I've been ready for this day for a long time."

"It's hot as hell outside," Thad continued. "I'm sweating already, and we're in the air conditioning."

"Quit your whining," our mutual friend and fellow groomsman, Chad, chimed in with half of a laugh. "This is Fish's special day."

"I'm just stating the fact that it's hot outside," Thad retorted quickly.

These two guys, Thad and Chad, had been my best friends for fifteen years. If there was fun to be had, the three of us seemed to find it. When I lived in Iowa, we golfed pretty much every weekend we could, whether it rained or was cold. Whenever we were together, we played poker and even played Yahtzee competitively for friendly wagers. We fished in the summer, went to various events year-round, and did whatever we could to find a laugh.

Thad seemed to enjoy playing the role of the gullible friend who fights back, with Chad and me starring as the instigators and poking fun at Thad whenever it seemed appropriate. If there were three amigos at any point in my life, the three of us would have fit that description.

Mandi's Uncle Jamie was another of my groomsmen. Ever the jokester, he also joined in the fun.

"So, how did the two of you meet?" the photographer asked as she clicked away.

"Prison," Jamie said without missing a beat.

The photographer looked up from her camera for a second to make sure it was a joke before laughing out loud and continuing the photoshoot. That photographer was amazing. I'm forever grateful for the 870 incredible photos she presented us with, for the memories they gave me long after Mandi was gone.

Our videographer, a high school friend of Mandi's, also produced great work, and his videos are true treasures I will cherish forever. A few years after Mandi passed, I had the DVDs he created for us converted to digital files, saving them to the cloud in two separate places and putting them onto flash drives. If technology evolves further and those tools become obsolete, I will convert them once again to whatever is universally considered the highest-quality product or service available. When it comes to my memories with Mandi, I take absolutely no chances with losing anything to a technical glitch.

***

After arriving at the church, the groomsmen and I gathered in the front entrance just outside the chapel. As the clock continued to tick toward six o'clock, I began to grow more anxious.

"Fish, are you ready?" Thad asked me.

"Of course he's ready," Chad cut in before I could answer. "Don't ask him dumb questions, Thad."

The familiar banter served to calm my nerves and make me laugh. Chad flashed his usual smirk as Thad insisted he wasn't trying to unnerve the groom at the last minute.

I watched the groomsmen and the bridesmaids connect and walk down the aisle arm-in-arm. Finally, it was my turn. I felt myself holding back tears. The emotions in me were nearly overwhelming as I turned at the altar and stood waiting for my bride. My eyes were fixated on the back of the church, and I felt a rush of adrenaline as the doors swung open, revealing my beautiful bride and her father.

Mandi was radiant in her elegant white dress. As she walked down the aisle toward the altar, we locked eyes and smiled at each other. Our day had arrived. We were about to be united in marriage.

"Take care of her now, Jason," Mr. Skip said in a simple but emotional moment as he handed off his girl to me.

"Yes, sir, I will," I humbly replied.

There are few moments in life where you truly understand the gravity of a situation as it is happening. This was one of those moments for me. I knew how much Mandi loved her father. And I knew how much Mr. Skip adored his daughter. I took every word he told me to heart.

*** 

"To have and to hold, to love and to cherish, until death do us part," I passionately and confidently said as I looked at Mandi and her beautiful blue eyes. Tears were beginning to well up as she shook her head gently back and forth in disbelief.

"I, Amanda Cowart, take Jason to be my lawfully wedded husband," she began. She gripped my hands tighter, silently saying to me how much she loved uttering those words in front of all her friends and family.

We had opted for a shorter ceremony that lasted about twenty minutes from start to finish. Every part of the service came off without a hitch. Like the bride standing in front of me, the ceremony was near flawless in my eyes. I was so in love.

My eyes were mainly fixated on my new bride. But I would sneak a peek at the audience or the wedding party every once in a while. My cousin Danny, my best man, seemed to brim with pride; the moment's emotions were evident on his face. Mandi's Uncle Jamie looked so happy for his niece, no doubt so proud of the woman she had become. Family and friends alike had smiles on their faces nearly every moment I gazed out upon them.

Our wedding was in every way precisely what I had hoped it would be. I married the most beautiful girl I could imagine, somebody who proved that unconditional love is real. Marrying her was the best moment of my life and a memory I will always cherish.

*\*\**

A light rain began to sprinkle the limousine's windshield as we made our way from the chapel to Stewartfield. We emerged from the car holding hands and made our way toward the reception area. The wedding party stood with their backs to the walls across from each other, lifting golf clubs in the air like swords. We walked under the makeshift swords toward the open dance area as the crowd began to applaud loudly.

Mandi had sent me one of her favorite songs in the early days of dating, burned onto a CD. "I'll Be," by Edwin McCain, was written in blue pen on the outside cover. After listening to the song and sharing our mutual love for the music, it was never a question that this would someday be our wedding song. Now, I took my new bride by the hand and pulled her close to me, dancing slowly.

Hugging close as we swayed to the gentle melody, Mandi wrapped her arms around my neck. We whispered to each other and began to laugh, sharing memories of all we had been through to get to that point.

"We did it, babe!" Mandi said to me.

"Can you believe it?" I replied. "You're my wife."

"And you're my husband," Mandi said as she emphasized the new word used to describe me. "Husband," she said again, shaking her head.

Some things are not subject to the erosive nature of time. Rather, they remain in their relative state of perfect forever. This was one such moment, dancing with my new bride and the love of my life. My soulmate in my arms, I did not want the song to end. It's likely to be the last memory to leave my mind or my heart.

*\*\**

The father-and-bride dance was as emotional as any part of the day. Mandi loved and admired her dad in unspeakable ways. It took just an embrace from his arms and the music to "Butterfly Kisses" beginning to play for the tears to start rolling off Mandi's cheeks.

The guests were focused on the middle of the room as the two danced while trying hard not to cry themselves. It was the dance every girl should have, embraced by a father who loved her with all his heart. Her mother was looking on with tears in her eyes, so proud of the girl she had raised into a beautiful woman and so thankful for Mandi's happiness.

As I looked on, I saw the full display of the love Mandi experienced growing up; the special relationship she had with her father made it possible for Mandi to be the person she was to all who knew her.

*\*\**

As the first few special dances came to an end, it was time to cut our wedding cake. Our guests gathered around the table that held the cake stacked three tiers high. Mandi and I grabbed the knife hand-over-hand, slicing down into the bottom layer of the cake and cutting off two small pieces.

In the weeks leading up to the wedding, Mandi and I had joked about smashing wedding cake in each other's faces. But my mother-in-law was very transparent in her feelings about this.

"If you mess up that beautiful bride's makeup or hair and ruin some of the pictures, you will be—"

"Miss Sheri, I'm only teasing," I quickly interjected. "I'm not going to do it. Do you honestly think I would be that dumb?"

"Well ... ." she said with a laugh.

"I promise," I said as I smiled at her and Mandi.

Miss Sheri and I always had a respectful relationship, breaking the myth that sons-in-law and mothers-in-law are like oil and water. We had our "circle of truth," as we called it. It was an oath to each other to always say what was on our minds but do it in a very reasonable manner. My first test as her son-in-law was at that cake table.

Mandi and I each grabbed a piece of the cake, steadying our outstretched arms. Looking over my right shoulder, I could feel Miss Sheri staring at me. I had a wry smile on my face as I looked in her direction before Mandi and I gently fed each other a piece of cake.

Next was the celebratory champagne toast. Mandi and I had secretly swapped out the champagne for a bottle of white grape juice. Our guests cheered us on and watched Mandi as she guzzled the entire flute within seconds. Acting stunned, I looked around the room in disbelief. Mandi asked for a refill and repeated the action. To my knowledge, nobody knew about the bottle switch. Everyone thought Mandi threw back those two flutes of champagne with such ease, likely wondering if they really knew Mandi as well as they thought. In truth, we had no intention of drinking any alcohol that evening. We wanted to make sure we remembered as many of the moments as we possibly could.

*  *  *

Stewartfield was an older, historic structure. And it was a beautiful reception area. However, it was not very energy efficient. The air conditioners did their best to keep up with the unrelenting heat of a July evening in Alabama. Still, the temperatures outside made it nearly impossible for a perfectly comfortable gathering on the inside. We knew the reception might be warmer than we wanted, but we expected enough people to be outside so the building could comfortably hold the guests who RSVPed.

Not too long after the reception began and everyone was inside, the heavens opened up and the rain poured down. Our plans for any outdoor activities were dashed. The ground was saturated as the water ran off the lawn and parking lot in sheets. The old building may have taken in the heat of the day, but it was unwilling to give it up at night, even with the rain-cooled air.

*\*\**

As our reception came to a close, some of our guests had come and gone but many remained. The rain had ended, but the air was still heavy with humidity. Our friends and family lined the sides of the stairs and walkway to give us a clear path to the open door of the limousine. Party favors and streamers went off all around us as we stepped hand-in-hand down the stairs.

In one of my favorite pictures, Mandi and her dad embraced one last time before the night ended. You could see the look of a loving father in that picture, saying "goodbye" to the little girl he raised while displaying how proud he was of the woman she had become.

"This was the best wedding ever!" one of her friends yelled out as we entered the limo. Cameras pointed and clicked as we waved our final goodbyes through the open window. We had made memories that would last a lifetime, just as we had planned. And while we were exhausted from the day's activities, we were charged with adrenaline at the future we would have together.

Willie, our driver, navigated his way to the downtown hotel, and I looked at my new bride with amazement. We had made it. Our dream had become a reality. All those days we had counted down until we could see each other again were behind us. All the notes, calls, texts, emails, plane rides, and rental cars had led us to this moment. The future was bright, and it was ours for the taking. We were finally husband and wife.

# CHAPTER 6
# That Was Utopia

Gatlinburg, Tennessee, had everything we wanted in a honeymoon location—seclusion, relative proximity to home, affordability, and fun activities. We knew a tropical honeymoon in July didn't sound very appealing or make a lot of sense for our budget, so we decided to rent a cabin for the week in the Smoky Mountains and relax.

"No obligation," the young salesman said as he approached us on the street and handed us a flyer. "We pay you one hundred dollars per person for two hours of your time for listening to our presentation."

Having just quit our jobs and already feeling the pressure of unemployment, I was intrigued.

"What's the presentation about?" I asked skeptically.

"This is a timeshare opportunity," the young man said. "There's no obligation to say yes. If you say no at the end of the two hours, we still pay you one hundred dollars cash on the spot."

I turned to Mandi. She had a look of helplessness on her face. She knew making two hundred dollars between the two of us would help pay for an entire day of honeymoon activities. She also knew we had to listen to a sales pitch for two hours when we were supposed to be enjoying our time together.

"What do you think, babe?" I said in as optimistic a tone as I could muster.

"I think we are on our honeymoon and could find better things to do with our time," she replied matter-of-factly.

"But it's two hundred dollars," I said with emphasis as I looked into Mandi's eyes.

She understood my point, and two hundred dollars was two hundred dollars. Still, I knew I'd probably pay for this decision in some way, shape, or form.

"Fine," Mandi said. "But you better not say yes to anything. And we're eating at the Hard Rock tonight with some of that money."

"Deal."

I can understand how some folks get talked into buying a timeshare. They make it sound lucrative, easy, and carefree. But I fended off the salesman's best pitch and stood firm.

"I'm sorry," I told them. "We're on our honeymoon, and we can't commit to anything financial given that I'm now unemployed."

Holding firm, I said "no" at least a half-dozen times before the gentleman brought in his manager for one final try.

"I think you're missing an opportunity here," the manager said.

"I think we sat through your presentation, listened politely, and made a decision," I replied. "We'll take the two hundred dollars now."

True to their word, we were handed two crisp one-hundred-dollar bills.

Leaving the building, I was proud of my financial gamesmanship.

"Told ya," I said as I handed Mandi the money.

"I'll never get that two hours of my life back," she said to me in an exhausted tone.

Mandi never let me forget the timeshare story. The event somewhat described our relationship as it had evolved over the years. I was always angling and trying to think ahead one step. Mandi lived more in the moment, looking for fun activities and enjoying the day at hand. In the end, we compromised like we almost always did. And sometimes, like this, she just gave in because she knew it would make me happy. That was Mandi.

*　*　*

Returning from the honeymoon, Mandi and I had about one week to finish packing, say our goodbyes, and move five hundred miles to Arkansas. We were very organized going into the wedding, which helped us tremendously as the final days in Mobile were upon us. Mandi still had to pack the many items she had at her parents' house, and I focused on my office. We tackled the kitchen and the rest of the apartment together.

I once again rented a twenty-six-foot truck and loaded up all our possessions. However, this time I left the trailer and had Michael drive my car to Little Rock and help us move our things into our new apartment. I then used my frequent flier miles to book him a one-way ticket back to Mobile.

As our August moving day approached, the mood began to shift within Mandi's family. The sadness of our upcoming move was starting to dominate the conversation. Mandi and I were eager to begin our new adventure, but I also knew how difficult it would be to say goodbye to her parents and sisters.

We spent our last night in Mobile at Mandi's parents' house and got up early the next day. The family exchanged hugs in the driveway.

"We wish y'all didn't have to go," Miss Sheri said with tears in her eyes.

Mandi was silent, but the emotions of the moment were not something I would soon forget. I was acutely aware of the tremendous responsibility I had for both my new bride and me. I was taking away their little girl. Granted, Little Rock is only a seven-hour drive from Mobile, but it might as well have been to the far side of the moon.

"We'll miss you too," Mandi finally said, the difficulty of the moment apparent on her face.

It was a bittersweet moment. Mandi and I were going on our first real adventure together. We had our whole lives ahead of us. But to have our moments to remember, we had to say goodbye to the comfort and family that surrounded us in Mobile.

\*\*\*

We were extremely fortunate that Mandi had found a job in Little Rock before we actually moved there. It allowed us to better plan and know we had one stable income to start our new life together.

Prior to our wedding, Mandi had been looking online for jobs and managed to set up an interview with a company in Little Rock for a day we planned to be in the city, looking for a place to live. So, in late May 2006, we drove across Mississippi, northeast Louisiana, and up through the southern part of Arkansas. As we neared Little Rock on Interstate 530, we crested a hill that gives you a perfect landscape view of the city.

"Look at that view," I said to Mandi, marveling at how far you could see from the top of that hill.

We had left early that morning, arriving in plenty of time for Mandi to freshen up and make her appointment that afternoon. We decided to check in to the hotel after the interview and concentrate on looking for apartments the next day.

As we drove through the western part of the city, we marveled at the scenery and the hilly terrain. Being a coastal city, Mobile is fairly flat. On the other hand, Little Rock sat at the foothills of the Ouachita Mountains to the west and southwest, and the Ozark Mountains to the north. The steep incline of many roads took us by surprise, but we were delighted to experience something new.

Finding the company's headquarters was relatively easy. I pulled into the parking lot and dropped Mandi off for the interview.

"Good luck, babe!" I said to her as she got out of the car. "I'm going to drive around a bit and get the feel of this area."

The interview lasted forty-five minutes to an hour. I was somewhere off Cantrell Road when Mandi called me and let me know she was finished. A few minutes later, I pulled into the parking lot and picked her up.

"Well, how did it go?" I asked.

"I would say pretty well," she replied. "They offered me the job making more money than the one I just left!"

"Wow!" I said, dumbfounded. "I didn't see that one coming. That's amazing! I'm so proud of you!"

Mandi would be working for a company in the same field as she had worked for several years, healthcare software administration. Having that experience, combined with her dynamic personality, convinced them to offer her the position before she left town.

Mandi and I felt as if we had hit the lottery. Things were starting to fall into place. A major stressor was now off our plate. Mandi had a job waiting for her when we arrived in August, allowing us to focus on the wedding details and making the physical move to our new home.

\*\*\*

Mandi and I spent our newlywed year in Little Rock getting to know new friends, mainly my classmates and her coworkers. We had a small apartment off campus and occasionally hosted a study session or small gathering of our colleagues. More often, we would spend our weekends outdoors. Mandi would take Gracie to the dog park to let out some energy, or we would go to Pinnacle Mountain State Park and run the base trails.

Mandi's new job was proving to be an excellent fit for her professionally. She was an immediate asset to the team and quickly picked up on the nuances of the software they used. For the first several months, Mandi stayed at home most of the time and rarely traveled. She learned the company history, client needs, and internal customer support mechanisms they implemented at sites around the country.

For me, I had a steady stream of classwork that kept me very busy. If I wasn't on campus and in the classroom, I might be attending one of the many public forums held once or twice a week in the Clinton Library or in the lobby of our campus building at the time, Sturgis Hall. But for the most part, I was home every night with Mandi.

We couldn't have asked for much more than to spend our evenings together building our family routine and enjoying the time we had to ourselves as a newly married couple. Unfortunately, before we knew it, the semester was over and our time away from home began to slowly increase.

Nearly half of the coursework at the University of Arkansas' Clinton School of Public Service was practical, hands-on fieldwork—the vehicles that delivered meaningful social change. And the concept of using my education and career to help others overcome obstacles was a significant draw for me. The summer internship is the pinnacle of this coursework.

Being one of the first thirty-five students admitted, I was fortunate to have great projects to pick from and a sizable stipend to offset any expenses. I could use that money to go anywhere in the world so long as my internship adviser approved my project. The vast majority of my classmates used the internship as an opportunity to study abroad, but I ultimately asked my adviser, Bob, if I could stay in the United States. Being newly married, I wanted to be close to Mandi and able to return home quickly should she need me. Plus, I still had my promise to her dad in the back of my mind. It was about what was best for the two of us and our marriage.

One of the first places I applied to was the Central United States Earthquake Consortium. Located in Memphis, Tennessee, CUSEC was founded to plan for, and mitigate the damage of, a devastating earthquake that was likely to someday occur along the New Madrid fault in lower Missouri. I was fascinated by the concept of public service in the form of disaster relief, having witnessed first-hand the needs of citizens and the community that arose from Hurricanes Ivan and Katrina.

As the end of April approached, I had not yet heard back from CUSEC. Other students already had assignments chosen and travel booked. I had nothing at that point and needed a second option to make certain I would not fall behind academically.

"I'm growing nervous that I won't have an internship selected and ready in time for summer," I told Bob. "Do you have any other recommendations?"

We went through a few possibilities, but at that point in the academic year, we knew I had to jump at the first reasonable opportunity or risk not having enough time to finish the full internship before the fall semester. Still, Bob tried to reassure me everything would work out. "Let me make a call or two," he said.

A day or two went by before I met up with Bob again in the hallway between my classes. "Jason, the Clinton Foundation is looking for another intern for the Alliance for a Healthier Generation program. I think you'd be a great fit for them."

I felt a weight lift off my shoulders. "That's great!" I said. "Let's make it happen."

Headquartered in New York City, the Alliance for a Healthier Generation was a partnership between the American Heart Association and the Clinton Foundation created to help curb the growing youth obesity epidemic in the United States.

Having traveled a fair amount to New York City for RuffaloCODY, I was familiar with Manhattan and the costs associated with living expenses. I looked through various websites to find an apartment, eventually locating one near Broadway and 140th. It was nothing fancy, but it was safe and had the basic comforts of home. As luck would have it, my classmate Dustin was interning with the Clinton Climate Initiative project. We decided to sublease the apartment together, helping to defray costs and benefit from knowing a familiar face in the big city.

The internship at the Clinton Foundation spanned about eight weeks in the summer of 2007. Unfortunately, the timing was such that I would still be in New York City, during our first wedding anniversary. Of course, missing such an important date was out of the question.

Whatever excitement I had going to New York for the summer had worn off after the first few days. I missed Mandi in a major way. All the things the city had to offer just weren't as enjoyable without her.

"What if you came to New York City and we spent your birthday and our anniversary here instead of me coming home?" I asked Mandi one evening in June. "I will be home for good just a couple of weeks later, and this could be a great chance to make a memory."

"Yes!" Mandi said decidedly. She immediately began making plans for what we would do together in the Big Apple.

"Let's see *Phantom of the Opera*!" Mandi exclaimed. "I've always wanted to see it on Broadway."

"I love it. Let's do it!" I said. "I miss you so much!"

Once again, all those frequent flier miles I had stashed away came in handy. "I can get you here on a flight through Chicago for twenty-five thousand miles, round trip. You'll arrive on the nineteenth of July and leave on the twenty-third."

"Do it," Mandi said in a funny, deep voice as she implored me to book the ticket.

As the days grew closer to Mandi flying in, I began to prepare all the details of our trip. Most of those details would be a secret I would wait to spring on her until she got into the city. Now we just needed the nineteenth to come quickly.

\*\*\*

"Babe, my flight has been delayed because of weather somewhere," Mandi said over the phone. "I'm going to miss my connection."

I dropped my head and rubbed my fingers on my temples, trying to relieve the pressure that had been building.

"Okay, did they automatically book you on the next flight?" I said.

"No, it's full," Mandi said as she let out a sigh.

All those years of travel between the two of us would help us on more than one occasion. Along with all those frequent flier miles came experience in just these situations.

"Let me look online and see what other options you have from Chicago," I said as I furiously scrolled through the website. "See if they will rebook you to Newark. They can pull your luggage if there's a seat available. I'm showing they have a few left. Newark is nearly just as close."

I could hear the gate agent in Chicago typing furiously on her keyboard. It was our last hope to get her to New York City that night.

"Yes, they have one. The agent is rebooking me now," Mandi said excitedly. "Oh, it doesn't get in until midnight."

"Take it. Tomorrow morning will be chaos trying to get out of there," I said. "If you can get to Newark, I will come and get you."

"Okay, I'm set. I will call when I land. Love you!" Mandi said, excited that her travel plans were back on.

"Love you too, babe. Be safe," I said as I hung up the phone.

As expected, Mandi's flight landed around midnight. Newark was largely closed down for the night, but there were still taxis looking for work.

"Babe, I'll take a cab to your apartment in the city. It's dumb for you to come out here and then ride back with me," Mandi said.

"I'm happy to do it to make sure you're safe," I said.

"I do this all the time. I got it. I'll see you in about forty-five minutes," she said.

I was never so happy as to see that cab pull up in front of the apartment. I looked out the second-floor window, watching as Mandi got out of the taxi and headed to the entry door. I rushed downstairs to meet her.

"I made it!" she said, her eyes looking groggy at one thirty in the morning.

"I missed you so much," I said. "It feels like forever. And you cut your hair!"

"Yes! That's my surprise to you. Do you like it?" she asked.

"I love it! It's beautiful and fits you perfectly," I said to her as I grabbed her luggage and toted it up the apartment stairs.

"Here, you're going to want these," I said, handing a set of earplugs to Mandi as we got into bed.

There was a liquor store located on the main level of our building directly below our apartment. They didn't close until 2:00 a.m. The owner and workers all spoke Spanish. Every night, regardless of the day of the week, they would blare loud music with a Latin flair until the liquor store closed. Between the taxi brakes screeching and the liquor store Latin music, I usually wore earplugs to bed so I could fall asleep.

"Are you serious?" she asked.

"If you want to fall asleep, yes. But it will only be like this tonight. Tomorrow and the rest of the weekend, I have a surprise," I said as I held my wife close to me for the first time in over a month.

\*\*\*

Mandi had purchased the tickets to *Phantom of the Opera* while she was in Little Rock. I had taken care of the rest of the weekend planning.

On her birthday, we dined at Tavern on the Green in Central Park, saw the play that evening, and checked in to a nice hotel on Fifth Avenue afterward. Over the course of the weekend, we saw a Yankees game in one of the last seasons they played in old Yankee Stadium, toured the Statue of Liberty and Ellis Island, explored Times Square, hung out in Central Park, and went to a variety of stores up and down Broadway.

Despite all my planning, one problem remained. Tradition holds that the top tier of the wedding cake is frozen for a year and then eaten on the first anniversary of the wedding. But the top of the cake was in a freezer at Mandi's parents' house. Fortunately, Mr. Skip came to the rescue and went all out for his little girl. He carefully packed the frozen wedding cake in dry ice and overnighted the box to our hotel.

"Mister Fisher, we have your package at the front desk," the night manager told me. "We are happy to deliver it to your room if you would like."

"Yes, please, that would be fabulous," I said as I hung up the phone.

The knock on the door came swiftly; the bellhop wasted no time. "Mister Fisher, your package."

"Thank you," I replied as I handed him a tip and brought the box into the room. Mandi and I were anxious to see if the package and its contents were in good shape. And we were curious, and perhaps a bit nervous, to taste the cake after a year.

Carefully opening the box, we quickly determined that Mr. Skip had packaged the top layer to perfection, and it made the journey without a problem. Now for the big test: Would it still taste good?

"It tastes just like it did a year ago!" Mandi said with a hint of shock and surprise after she took the first bite.

We each ate a piece, refrigerated the rest for later, and settled in for the night to look at the photos we had taken earlier that day. In truth, I'm not sure we could have had a better first anniversary celebration. While we weren't at home in Little Rock or with family in Mobile, we created lasting and wonderful memories in New York City—so many of which were captured by Mandi in pictures.

\*\*\*

In August 2007, after I returned from New York City, I entered the final semester of my sixteen-month Clinton School experience. Mandi's job was going well and with my graduation around the corner, we were looking forward to the next chapter in our marriage. We both assumed my new graduate degree would yield plenty of job opportunities in Little Rock, so we began conversations about possibly ridding ourselves of apartment living.

Mandi spent a considerable amount of time by herself while I was in New York over the summer. She used part of this time to get outdoors and enjoy Pinnacle Mountain nearly every day, weather permitting. But when at home, Mandi had the channel tuned in to HGTV and had begun to watch home decorating shows, programs about flipping houses, and shows about first-time homebuyers. She was eager for me to watch the home-buying shows with her, and we quickly caught the house-hunting bug.

We combed the internet, looking for properties within our anticipated price range, hoping something would catch our eye. At that point, we didn't know how serious we were about buying, but we were enjoying the process of window-shopping.

One afternoon in August, we grabbed a Sunday paper from the local convenience store and sat down to circle the open houses in our price range. We ended up with a list of about a half-dozen homes that were in the section of the city we wanted to live.

At the first open house we attended, we met a Realtor named Mike, who was the agent showing the house. To this point, our searches had been limited to what was open and available to view. But Mandi grabbed Mike's business card, and when we got back in our car, we spoke about the possibilities of bringing in an agent to help us.

"I didn't get the chance to talk to Mike. You liked him?" I asked Mandi.

"We need to work with this guy. He's very nice and knowledgeable. I got a good vibe from him," she replied.

"See if he has any recommendations on mortgage agents," I said. "We probably need to get prequalified if we're getting this serious."

"Agreed," she said. "I'll call Mike tomorrow and ask him about that and helping us find more properties."

Looking for your first house as a couple can be an interesting experience. Watching home shows had helped us decide what each of us liked. Mandi loved the concept of an open floor plan, and I was looking for something contemporary that could be spruced up, but not a major project. We needed a fenced-in backyard where Gracie could run and play. And, of course, it had to fit our budget and location requirements.

Buying a house is a very instinctual process. You can often tell whether you like a place within the first minute or two upon entry. It took Mike several attempts to get a feel for what we were looking for in a property beyond the square footage or floor plan. We did our best to help him narrow down the search even further, but it was clear we were picky. Mike was a consummate professional, though. He had lived in the area nearly his entire life, so he knew it well. He wasn't pushy, and he had an unquestioned ethical approach to his job.

One Sunday afternoon, Mandi and I went through the list of open houses in the paper and identified one that seemed to fit our needs. After touring the home, we thought it was nice, but not exactly what we sought. As we got back into the car to leave, we noticed a for-sale sign pointing down the street.

"Why not?" I said to Mandi. "We're close enough that it's worth a drive-by."

At the end of a winding, downhill road was a nice, relatively small brick and siding home with an open house sign. The house was on a dead-end street and surrounded by green space on two sides, with a large, beautiful weeping willow tree proudly standing in the front yard. The freshly manicured azalea bushes that stood outside the large living room windows seemed to greet visitors as they pulled into the driveway.

"Looks nice from the outside," Mandi commented.

"I agree," I replied. "Let's see what the inside looks like."

As we walked through the front door and into the living room, it became apparent that this house was different than the others we had viewed.

"This is the open floor plan we've been seeking," Mandi said.

"Everything flows in this house," I said, using a term I had heard on HGTV.

The 1,733 square feet seemed modest on paper, but the house's layout ensured no wasted space. It had a fireplace in the spacious living room, a covered patio, the large fenced-in backyard we needed, and it seemed to be in great condition.

We strolled through the house, carefully inspecting each room. When we arrived at the master bedroom, a large window facing the backyard greeted us. The amount of natural sunlight, which was also on our wish list, was stunning. The heavy curtains that hung in front of the window blocked nearly all the light when they were closed, ensuring we could sleep in an extra hour in the summer. It also served to keep the heat out during the peak sunlight of the day, giving our air conditioner a break and helping the house stay cool.

It was all too apparent that Mandi was in love with the house. This property was a bit hidden off the main road and likely didn't get a great deal of traffic because of the location. But with the condition of the home and the amenities it offered, we were both certain it wouldn't last long.

Mandi immediately contacted Mike and asked for a second, private tour the next day. We wanted to make a fast decision to avoid another potential buyer swooping in and stealing the property out from underneath us. This time, Mike came with us and gave us the comparable prices in the neighborhood and showed us a few extra items we did not catch the first time around.

As we drove back to Mike's office, Mandi had made up her mind.

"I love it," she said. "Let's put an offer in today."

"I don't know if we can talk them down any," I said. "It's slightly outside of our ideal price point."

Being budget-conscious, I was somewhat concerned it was outside our range. Mandi would have to qualify for the loan on her own because I had not yet graduated and found a job. Our credit was excellent, and I had some newfound income from the contract consulting I started doing on the side with RuffaloCODY after my internship. But that income stream was inconsistent and couldn't be used to qualify for a larger loan.

We came to a price we thought was fair and could afford, and Mike delivered the contract to their agent that same evening. We asked for a response within twenty-four hours. We went to bed that night, hopeful the owners would accept our offer.

When my phone rang the next day, I answered, hoping it was Mike. And it was.

"Jason, it's Mike," he said. "I have good news and bad news. The bad news is that they rejected your offer. The good news is that they countered, and it's not completely unreasonable."

"Okay, how much are we talking about?" I asked.

"A few thousand higher than you offered," Mike replied.

"Okay. Let me call Mandi, and I'll get right back to you," I said.

At this point, I was fairly confident Mandi and I were on the same page with how to proceed.

"Babe, they turned down our offer and countered three thousand dollars higher."

"Ugh. I don't think we can pass this up. I say we accept," Mandi said.

I wholeheartedly agreed. The payment difference was just an additional twenty-one dollars a month. "I was thinking the same thing! I'll call Mike back and ask him to convey our verbal agreement."

Mike called back a few minutes later. Conditional to a thorough home inspection, Mandi and I were now the proud owners of our first home. We compromised here and there on a few areas that may not have been our favorite features, but in the end, she and I were always willing to work together to get what we wanted.

The closing was set for October 12, 2007. We had about six weeks to give our notice at the apartment, plan the move, and officially take possession of the house.

When the closing day arrived, we went in, eager to get started. Mandi signed what seemed to be a mountain of paperwork, eventually becoming so numb to writing her name that she scribbled it in such a way that it was barely readable to a stranger.

"Here are the keys," Mike said as he dropped them into Mandi's hands. Her face lit up with excitement as she realized her days as an apartment dweller were officially over.

"I'm so excited!" she said as she hugged Mike. "Thank you for helping us!"

We drove over to the house, opened the door, and looked inside at the barren walls.

"It's not home yet, but it will be," Mandi said. "We'll get this place looking great in no time."

"And we're hiring movers," I said. "I'm all for saving a buck, but I'd rather save my back."

Mandi closed the house door, made sure it was locked, and walked back to the car.

"We did it, babe!" she said to me with enthusiasm. "Can you believe it?"

As we pulled away from the house, the willow tree's limbs blew gently in the breeze.

"Home," I said to her. "It already feels just like home."

*** 

I graduated from the Clinton School in December of 2007 and started looking for work almost immediately, despite knowing employers were unlikely to be hiring over the holidays.

Spring 2008 was an interesting time to reenter the job market. The competition for jobs in my field was strong, even with the newly minted master's degree and good recommendations from the Clinton School. I applied for positions I thought could build upon the experience I had and also allow me to use my skills in a new and exciting way.

The job search proved to be more challenging than I anticipated. I had many interviews over the first few months, but I always seemed to come up just short of receiving the offer. Many times, I had the education but not the direct experience needed. At other times, I had the experience but was missing a qualification that would have provided me a boost. I had so many final interviews that I could have collected runner-up trophies and filled the shelves of my home office.

Like anybody who has been rejected for jobs numerous times, I began to wonder exactly why I was struggling to get an offer. Having just graduated from a prestigious school with a stellar academic reputation, I expected to be pursued more aggressively after showing interest. Except, that wasn't what happened.

"You need to quit thinking that employers are just waiting to rain perfect job offers down on you from the sky," Mandi said with her typical funny, sarcastic tone. It was her way of telling me not to feel sorry for myself and to try seeing the bigger picture.

"I should have at least three or four offers by now," I replied, still convinced things were going to turn around any minute. "I don't understand why I'm getting turned down."

"Well, all I know is that I'm the one working full-time right now while you're moping around, waiting for the perfect job to come find you," she said succinctly. "Quit looking for perfect and realize the opportunities you have in front of you. Pick one and make it great."

Once again, Mandi was living in the present. My thoughts were either in the past or the future, depending on the day. I needed to see that the reality of the situation was the job market had changed since I entered graduate school. Employers began to tighten up their hiring practices, and the market was being driven in a different direction than it had been in the years leading up to 2008.

By March of 2008, I still had not found a permanent, full-time job in Little Rock that complemented my new degree. The market had slowed, and my prospects for landing a position with an employer in the public service field were growing more difficult to see.

At this point, I was three months post-graduation and feeling more pressure. I still wanted to find that perfect job, a job with exciting work, flexibility, and one that paid well. But my expectations were proving to be bigger than the availability in the market at that time.

I was still doing contract consulting work on the side for RuffaloCODY. It was a great part-time job, but I needed something full-time with a steady paycheck and benefits. I decided to call my consulting colleague to see if RuffaloCODY would consider making the position full-time.

With a new degree and some additional fundraising experience since I had left in 2005, I felt I was in a unique position. I had new insight into my old work and had ideas for services that could prove lucrative for both the company and its clients.

Fortunately, RuffaloCODY offered me a job as a senior consultant, starting in May 2008. They came through at precisely the right time for us. I knew if I worked hard, the chances were good that I could rise through the ranks and use many of my newfound skills. And I was happy to be back among the friends whom I had worked with for so many years. It had been less than three years since I left, but so much had changed for me during that time. My academic and personal growth had been tremendous, and I knew I could bring a unique perspective to the table the second time around.

\*\*\*

While I had been interning in New York City in 2007, I decided to take the LSAT exam and apply to law school. I wasn't 100 percent certain I wanted to go, but I wanted to keep my options open after graduating from the Clinton School. What I was certain of was that I loved the law school classes I took as part of my master's degree program and found the coursework both challenging and rewarding.

Following the LSAT test, I formally applied to the Bowen School of Law at the University of Arkansas at Little Rock. Shortly thereafter, I was accepted to start in the fall of 2008.

Convincing Mandi that I needed more education was always going to be my biggest challenge. She was not on board with the idea of me going to law school and made it no secret that she was ready to start a family. While she was diplomatic and respectful in pushing back, she simply had zero interest in waiting another three to four years for me to obtain a JD degree.

"You would be a terrible lawyer!" Mandi said, half-joking, as we discussed the idea in our kitchen one afternoon. "You cannot even win a debate with your wife over why you're applying to law school."

If you ever had the pleasure of debating any of the women in Mandi's family, you pretty much knew your fate when you got to this point in the discussion. They were not lawyers by trade, nor were they argumentative by nature. On the contrary, they are all very outgoing and respectful. They just articulate their points so well and concisely that it leaves the other person no choice but to stop and think. At that point, it's usually game, set, and match.

Stumped, I replied to Mandi with my typical reaction when she bested me in a friendly banter back and forth; I laughed and admitted she had a point. That said, I didn't feel that bad about the outcome. If the standard for attending law school meant one had to beat Mandi Fisher in a friendly debate, the world would have far fewer lawyers.

The truth was that Mandi had given up a lot for me already. She moved to Arkansas days after getting married, leaving behind her family and friends and starting a new life and adventure. She had endured me interning in New York City for eight weeks of our first full summer as a married couple. And she had been the only one of us who was employed full-time for the last eighteen months, waiting for me to add to the family coffers consistently. I knew in my heart it was time to set aside my plan.

"I can't disagree with your point," I said. "What if I defer for a year and reexamine where we are next year at this point?"

"That's perfectly fine," Mandi stated. "But if we start a family, I need you home with the baby and me, not in the law library studying like I know you would."

"I agree," I said. "I didn't think about it that way, but you're right."

Mandi knew I was disappointed with not being able to go to law school. But I made it clear she came first, it would be a joint decision, and I wanted and needed unanimous agreement before moving forward. Since she was opposed, I would not attend. Our marriage was paramount, and I would have it no other way.

I turned in my deferral form and was approved to start a year later. However, by then, I had a full-time job and was immersed in building our plans for a family. I decided to let my deferral lapse and closed the chapter on attending law school for the immediate future.

Although I occasionally think about it today, I don't regret the decision. It was the right choice to make at the time. The reality is that there are multiple paths available to you at most points in your life. When you're in a marriage, each person needs to make occasional sacrifices along the way. In this case, I put Mandi first, which was the right thing to do. Our goal was always to strive for a balanced relationship over time, ensuring we had each other's backs and our mutual happiness came first.

\*\*\*

Late one night in early 2009, Mandi flew into Portland, Oregon, for a work trip. She traveled a little more frequently than she did at the start of her tenure, with this trip scheduled to last several days.

A storm system off the Pacific Coast was producing high winds up and down the Northwest coastline. Flights were delayed, but those in the air were being allowed to land. As Mandi's plane approached the runway, the vertical turbulence increased significantly, and the passengers were greatly jolted in their seats. The flight landed without incident, but the experience left Mandi with some anxiety about flying again.

"I just had the most horrible flight," Mandi said to me on the phone after landing. "I'm still shaking, and I'm already at the hotel."

"I knew it was going to be rough, babe. I've been watching the weather all night. I'm sorry that it happened!" I replied.

Mandi had some time to think on that trip. She loved her job and enjoyed travel, meeting new people, and advancing her career. But I believe the bad flight was more jarring than a one-time experience. I think it made her even more committed to starting a family, sooner rather than later.

When Mandi and I were dating, we had dreams of three beautiful children and a dog named Bogey. While we were enjoying a relatively carefree life, something was missing.

"I'm ready," Mandi said convincingly after making it home safely later that week. "I want a family, and I don't want to keep putting it off."

"Okay," I said. "I'll look at the budget and start making plans."

"The budget is fine," Mandi said with a hint of sarcasm. "It's time."

I looked into her eyes and could see the passion in which she said the words. It was one of those times in life when you just instinctually know the answer without having to think. Mandi knew and was conveying to me to see the bigger picture—which I did. I nodded and smiled.

"You're right," I said. "I'm ready too."

With that exchange, our life changed forever. We were making a conscious decision to become parents. It was exciting and somewhat intimidating all at the same time.

*\*\**

"What's up, babe?" I said with my eyes still half-closed. "What time is it?"

"It's 4:15 a.m.," Mandi said. "Does this look like a plus sign to you?"

With the light from the bedroom lamp temporarily blinding my eyes, I squinted as I took a closer look at the pregnancy test that Mandi lowered into my line of sight.

"That looks like a plus sign to me," I said. "But it's very faint. I'm not 100 percent certain."

"Do you think it's the test?" Mandi replied. "Should we get a different brand?"

"We can, yes," I said, slightly ashamed. "We won't buy the cheap one this time."

A few days earlier, we had gone to the pharmacy together to pick up some items. Mandi wanted to shop for a pregnancy test. We looked at all the options, and I recommended we go with the pharmacy store brand because it was cheaper and looked similar to the more expensive brands. Note that this is not a recommendation I would make to other men in a similar situation.

"If we just spent the extra three dollars and got the name brand test, maybe we wouldn't be guessing as to whether or not this is positive," Mandi expressed with some early-morning edge.

"I know, I know. I'm sorry."

"I think I'm just going to talk to the doctor today and see what he thinks," Mandi stated.

Both of us had to work that day, but neither of us could get another wink of shut-eye. We knew there was a strong chance the test was positive, but we were afraid of a false positive because the lines were so faint.

Working from home, I had been thinking about the pregnancy test all day and wondering. I tried to take my mind off it, but there was too much anticipation that had built up. Mandi's appointment with the doctor was around the lunch hour, but she did not call or email me like I thought she might. Rather than bother her at work, I decided to wait until she got home to hear how things went.

I heard her SUV pull into our garage and the inside door from the garage shut. Gracie jumped around, excited that Mandi was home. I sat in my office, waiting for her to pop her head in the door with disappointing news. I had convinced myself that the cheap test we bought had given us a false positive.

"Yes," Mandi calmly said as she stared at me while I sat in my office chair. "We're having a baby!" Shocked but excited, I immediately got up and gave her a big hug. Just like the fathers who immediately become overly protective, I was careful not to press myself too much on her stomach, giving her a strong shoulder hug instead.

"Hug me, you fool!" Mandi said as she recognized my silly apprehension.

"I can't believe it. We're gonna be parents!" I said.

As we embraced in my office for what seemed like an hour, I thought back over our six-plus years together. This girl lit up my world, gave me a reason to smile every day I was with her, and now she was carrying our child. In a split second, our lives had changed.

\*\*\*

Mandi had been preparing for this moment since our wedding day. She immediately purchased two pregnancy books and rented a DVD from the public library on baby development. Similar to an eighth-grade health class film, the video first walked through a detailed description of how a sperm fertilizes the egg. It then described the cell division process in a science-like manner. Mandi was so excited that she practically rented everything from the library about pregnancy, firmly committed to doing everything "by the book."

The conversation about the baby pretty much dominated our discussions for several weeks. We would talk about what we wanted for the baby's room, whether we would use daycare, and if we planned on using only organic cotton for his or her outfits. We shopped at baby stores on the weekend, began gathering ideas for big purchases, and thought about how we would share the news with family and friends. At only six-ish weeks, we had another month and a half to go until we would feel comfortable telling the biggest secret of our lives.

Unfortunately for Mandi, pregnancy wasn't just talking about fun purchases and picking out baby names. Mandi was undergoing some pretty rough bouts of morning sickness. She was working remotely from home as she spent equal amounts of time at the kitchen table with her laptop and in the bathroom throwing up. The worst of the experience lasted only a week or two, but I still felt helpless watching her suffer.

"Do you want to go home to have this baby and raise it near your family?" I asked out of the blue one Saturday morning at the kitchen table. Mandi pondered the question, wondering if I was teasing or being serious.

"You're hesitating. Please don't think of what I want at this point. I need you to tell me what you see in your mind when you think about having this baby," I said.

Mandi paused before replying. "Ultimately, yes. It would be great to go home and raise a family there, but what will we do for jobs? Or daycare?"

"Don't worry about the logistics and planning," I said. "We have time, and I will make this work. It's important to raise this child around family. We can either go north or south, to Iowa or Alabama."

Being in Little Rock was great, but we were no longer honeymooners. We now had a baby on the way and would have to decide where we wanted to call home. I knew in my heart, Mandi wanted to be back in Alabama. And honestly, I missed it too. We never really had the chance to build a life there following our wedding. And while our intentions were good when we bought our house in Little Rock, the truth was that being a long distance from family wasn't easy around the holidays and other important dates.

"I'm serious about this decision," I reiterated. "I can do my job anywhere, and I'm confident that your company wants to keep you," I said. "They might allow you to work from home and travel as well. It doesn't hurt to ask."

Days before I asked Mandi about moving back to Mobile, I had already begun to plan for the possibility. I had researched home prices in both Little Rock and Mobile to learn about the markets, and I worked on a new household budget to make sure we planned for a worst-case scenario.

The previous fall, in 2008, Lehman Brothers had collapsed. The start of the financial crisis and the housing market crash made sales of existing homes come to a screeching halt while new policies were put into place to prevent risky lending. Existing homes in our price range were slower to sell, but inventory was still moving, both in Little Rock and Mobile. So, while we were excited about the prospect of moving back to Mobile, we were also realistic that it may not happen.

Our home was in good condition, and we had made modest upgrades during the twenty or so months we owned it. We also benefited from being in a desirable location at the end of the dead-end street with plenty of green space and zoned in one of the best elementary schools in the city. If a house was going to sell in this market, ours had as good a chance as any.

I fixed several items on the to-do list and then began detailing the kitchen and the bathroom. Having watched all the HGTV shows, we knew that little things made a big difference when selling a house in a tough market. I scrubbed the oven until it shined like new, organized our closest spaces meticulously, and shampooed all the carpets.

I then turned my attention to the Realtor. "Mandi and I are pregnant," I told Mike, "and we've decided to move back to Mobile if we can sell our house. We'd like you to help us."

"The market is tough right now, but you have the type of house that can still move," he replied. "I'll come over tomorrow, and we can discuss the details."

Mike and I set up our legal pads and calculators at the kitchen table. He liked what we had done with our decorations and improvements, giving us a high grade for paying attention to the right things. After looking at comparative houses that recently sold in the area, he gave me a price he would list it for and his strategy to help it sell.

"If that's the best we can do, then let's move forward. We trust you," I told Mike.

We chose a date in late April to put the house on the market, hoping to get enough traffic to identify a prospective buyer within a month or so. If all went well, we could move in July or August and still have plenty of time for Mandi to finish her pregnancy in Mobile.

On the day of the open house, I had to work in Memphis and Mandi spent part of the day at a friend's house. Around 5:00 p.m., as I was about to make the two-hour drive back to Little Rock, my cellphone rang.

"Hey, Mike. How did it go?"

"What would you say, Jason, if I told you I had two offers right now that are on the table, and you have twenty-four hours to decide?"

I was shocked but excited at this incredible news. Driving on I-40 back to Little Rock, Mike gave me the details of both offers. Both were lower than what we had hoped, but we had the chance to counteroffer the better of the two and come close to our targeted asking price.

While Mike was preparing the paperwork for a counteroffer, a third prospective buyer contacted him. They were the parents of a couple across the street and wanted to live close to their future grandchildren. After Mike told them we had two other offers on the table, the couple offered to pay our asking price—and in cash.

Stunned, I nearly had to pull to the side of the interstate. Somehow, in the middle of the worst financial crisis since the Great Depression, we managed to get three offers on the first day and sold the house in a cash transaction for our asking price. While home values were dropping precipitously all around us, we broke even. Our good fortune was continuing. We took it as a sign that we were *supposed* to be in Mobile.

\*\*\*

In the spring of 2009, H1N1, as it was known, had begun to circulate as a novel influenza virus. There was no vaccine that could prevent or lessen the symptoms at the time, given that it was a unique strain. I naturally worried about my pregnant wife and our unborn child. We were just in the first trimester, a very delicate time for a healthy pregnancy, let alone one where a mother contracts the flu.

As I packed the house on the weekends and prepared for the move, Mandi continued working and traveling. She limited her travel to only what was necessary and preferably by car versus plane. Our concern was that the H1N1 virus might spread more easily among the larger number of people in a jet.

"I'd like to come with you to the airport to pick up your rental car," I said to Mandi one Sunday afternoon as she prepared for a trip back to Alabama for business.

"Okay, but why?" Mandi replied.

"So I can wipe down the inside of the car with disinfectant and kill whatever viruses are in there," I said. "I don't want to take any chances."

I was already a proud and protective daddy-to-be and spouse. I didn't want anything to happen to my wife or our child. I knew I couldn't control everything, but I could do all that was reasonable to keep her safe.

During the mid-May trip, Mandi decided to tell her sister Amber about the pregnancy. They had tickets to a concert in Birmingham that had been purchased and planned for several months. We decided it would be okay for Mandi to go to the show so long as she kept her distance from people and used copious amounts of hand sanitizer.

Technically, our first trimester wasn't over until early June, but Mandi wanted to take advantage of the opportunity to tell her sister face-to-face. She delivered the news at a restaurant near the amphitheater where the concert would be held. Pictures from the event showed two happy sisters sharing a beautiful moment. The girls had a blast at the concert, and Mandi drove home to Little Rock excited that she got to tell her sister. However, we still needed to tell the rest of the family.

Mandi swore Amber to secrecy for the two weeks between the concert and Memorial Day weekend, when we planned to drive back to Mobile. It was undoubtedly difficult for Amber to contain her excitement, but she held true to her word and kept the news to herself.

Two weeks seemed to take forever. I was working on the house sale while Mandi was looking for a new home online and getting ready to tell her parents about our pregnancy. We took the day off work to get a head start and arrived at her parents' house mid-afternoon on the Friday before Memorial Day.

Earlier in the month, Mandi had heard about an idea she loved. She purchased a picture frame for her mom, dad, and two sisters. They were nearly identical replicas of each other. The outside of the picture frame said, "I Love My Grandma" or "I Love My Aunt." Inside the picture frame, Mandi wrote, "Photo Coming January 8, 2010."

Mandi wrapped each frame individually and handed them out as gifts once we arrived.

"Here, I got y'all a present," Mandi said to her parents as they were sitting in their living room recliners.

"You're not supposed to be buying us gifts," Miss Sheri said.

As they opened the gift bags simultaneously, it took a second or two for the message to register with the soon-to-be grandparents. The puzzled looks were almost comical to watch, knowing what was coming next.

"Is this ..." Miss Sheri started. Tears began to flow as she looked at Mandi, who was smiling and shaking her head in affirmation.

"I'm gonna be a Gigi," Miss Sheri said.

"This is wonderful news!" Mr. Skip said. He stuck out his hand and congratulated me.

There were hugs all around as the family celebrated. However, the festivities weren't done. The contract for the sale of our house in Little Rock had been signed earlier that day. Mike sent a copy to us via email. Seeing the message come through shortly after arriving, I had hurried back to Mr. Skip's office and printed out the signature page, returning to the living room with my secret literally in my back pocket. Mandi and I hadn't planned to tell them about the move until we were certain the house sale went through. But once I had that paper, the cat could be released from the bag.

"What's this?" Miss Sheri asked, still teary-eyed.

"It's the contract for the sale of our house in Little Rock," I said dryly. "We're coming home to Mobile."

"Oh my God, Fish! Are you trying to kill me?" Gigi said in a funny tone as she clutched her chest at the steady stream of great news. Not only was her baby having a baby, but we would be raising our child among family.

"We've got a list of houses in Mobile that we want to look at before going home on Sunday," I said.

Our goal was to be moved well in advance of the baby's arrival the following January. We wanted to establish OB-GYN care early, settle into our new house, and get into a routine before bringing the baby home. July 1, 2009, was our target date.

*** 

Finding a new house in Mobile proved to be more challenging than selling our home in Little Rock. As we went through the list of properties and looked at school zones, it quickly became apparent that it might take more than one weekend to find the perfect place to call home in Alabama.

After several open houses and private appointments, we hadn't found anything that didn't require either a tremendous amount of work or a property inside our financial comfort zone. With just one last house on the list, we found ourselves looking at a newly built home in a relatively new subdivision just outside the unincorporated area of Semmes, a neighboring community adjoining Mobile.

We did not expect to be in a position to buy a brand-new house. In fact, our list included only one new property. But with the housing crisis in full bloom, builders were motivated to sell their inventory quickly and meet their financial bottom line. Big houses were no longer in style, and owners of existing large homes were looking to unload their properties and downsize.

*Three beautiful kids and a dog named Bogey.* Mandi must have told me that a thousand times over the years. A big family was always what we had planned. Now we were staring at the perfect opportunity to buy a "forever" house where we could raise our kids with plenty of room—and at a price we could afford.

The house in Semmes was 3,025 square feet, which was nearly 1,300 square feet more than our home in Little Rock. We were both going to be working from home now, meaning we needed at least one, maybe two, offices. Fortunately, the house we were looking at was a four-bedroom with a large bonus room. It also had a front room that would be the perfect play area for our kids, along with plenty of storage space and a vast backyard that gave Gracie plenty of room to run. Most importantly, it was essentially move-in ready and available on the date we needed.

We made our offer on the property contingent that the builder enclose the backyard with a wooden privacy fence, add a refrigerator, install new blinds, and touch up a few areas where the contractors missed while working on the house.

To our surprise, the builder did not counter the offer. They accepted on the spot. Mr. Skip would act as our proxy while we were in Little Rock, ensuring that the builder kept their promises and had the property fully ready by the date of our move.

*\*\**

The month of June 2009 was our last full month in Little Rock. I spent that time working during the week and packing on the weekends. I also had a few minor home repairs to make on the house before closing.

I had contacted Michael to once again help with the move back home. He flew up to Arkansas to help lift the heavy furniture and get the truck packed for Mobile. For the third time in five years, I had rented a twenty-six-foot truck. This time, it would take all our belongings back to Alabama, plus a car trailer to pull my vehicle. I would have had Michael drive my car, but on the way to the airport to pick him up, my check engine light came on, and I did not trust it would make it to Mobile. Rather than risk it, I put the car on a trailer and had Michael ride in the cab with me. Not surprisingly, we ended up taking back to Mobile far more than we left with, a testament to the joys of homeownership and expanding your possessions to fit your new house.

I had cleaned the carpets for the new owners and prepared the final details to transfer the keys to our agent. Michael climbed into the cab of the truck while Mandi and I stayed behind for one last moment with our first home. We had lived there for less than two years, but it was everything we needed for the time we owned it.

Tears began to stream down Mandi's face as we closed the door to our home one final time. I pulled her into my arms.

"Baby, I know it's hard," I said as I squeezed her tight. "Part of me doesn't want to go either."

"It's our first home," she said in a whisper as she wiped away her tears.

"I know. It will always be special," I said. "We'll make more memories in Mobile. And you'll be coming back often to Little Rock because of work."

I was putting as positive of a spin as I could on a bittersweet moment. As excited as we were about going back to Mobile, leaving Arkansas was difficult. We could not have asked for a better three-year experience. It indeed was a utopia for us. We spent our newlywed years making new friends, meeting fantastic people, and growing together. We traveled, achieved great career success, and started a family.

We were also leaving Little Rock as a stronger couple than when we arrived. Naturally, coming home to Mobile would be another growth period for us. We would move into our new home, have fun family vacations, and continue to experience the career success we almost came to expect. At least, that was the plan we had in mind.

As we drove away from our house, we took one final look down the winding street we traversed so many times the previous several years. We were on to our next adventure, one that seemingly was falling into place perfectly. I was feeling optimistic about all that the world had to offer and was confident that the life I chose with Mandi was turning out precisely like the fairy tale I had envisioned when we met. All was going our way.

# CHAPTER 7
# Crisis Mom

Owning a brand-new house is exciting. To think that you're the only people who have occupied that piece of property is humbling. There's also a great deal of work that needs doing, even if the house is considered "move-in ready."

Our home had been built without an owner in mind, meaning the builders used the most basic beige paint, light-brown carpet, and simple plumbing that kept their cost down but increased our work should we have wanted any upgrades.

Given the cost of an interstate move, we once again unloaded the truck ourselves instead of hiring movers. Because Mandi was pregnant, she got the light duty in the kitchen, lining cabinets and cupboards and directing boxes to their appropriate room downstairs.

The second floor had a bedroom, bathroom, and bonus room that could easily serve one or two of the older kids as we expanded our family. For now, the bedroom would be my office, and the bonus room would convert to storage until we determined where we wanted everything to go.

One of the items we acquired in Little Rock was a nice oak desk for my office. The quality of the desk significantly added to the weight of the L-shaped corner unit. And while it came apart in two pieces, those two pieces were still extremely heavy—particularly to haul upstairs.

Michael was always our designated big furniture hauler. With his large frame, he could easily move almost any item in our house. However, his kryptonite appeared to be my office desk.

"I think I just gave myself a hernia," Michael said as he audibly gasped out loud halfway up the stairs. "I've got to put this down for a second."

Mr. Skip had the other end of the desk farther down the stairs, holding it in place while Michael caught his breath.

"Be careful not to hit the walls," I said with a grin as I supervised.

"Who cares about the damn walls!" Michael exclaimed. "I think part of my manhood might be laying on these steps somewhere!"

We learned it's hard to lift furniture when you're laughing. Michael's timely piece of comic relief kept us all from being too grumpy about moving in on a hot day in late June. We spent most of the rest of the day giggling and asking him about his manhood.

Mandi and I took a few days off after the move to get settled in and organized. Once the internet was functional, we got our offices set up and resumed working. This was Mandi's first experience working from home. I had been an at-home employee for about ten years total, so I had the routine down and knew how to limit distractions. But like everything else Mandi did on the job, she picked up on the nuances with ease and stayed very productive.

At night after work, Mandi and I would go for walks on a paved trail that encircled the local school a mile or so down the road. The path was approximately two miles long in a loop and served as a nice way to end the day, even if the heat and humidity of July in Alabama were at times oppressive.

"Are you okay?" I asked Mandi on one of our walks as she put her hands on her knees and bent over to catch her breath.

"I'm all right," she replied. "The heat is just getting to me. I feel a little nauseous."

At four months pregnant, Mandi was beyond any morning sickness that could make her feel nauseous. More than likely, it was just the heat of the day. H1N1 was still a potential issue, but the flu had diminished somewhat over the summer, and I was less concerned that she was sick with a virus. Still, Mandi reassured me she probably just pushed too hard on the walk and needed to rest and sit in the air conditioning.

* * *

Once we knew we would be having the baby in Alabama, Mandi switched to using her old OB-GYN in Mobile. She had seen this doctor for several years and was comfortable with his patient care.

I did my best to be as involved as possible during the pregnancy. I had the flexibility in my schedule to make sure I accompanied Mandi to each of her OB-GYN visits. From the first visit at ten weeks until the last visit before the baby was born, I didn't miss a single appointment. I wanted to be there to support my wife and understand as much about the pregnancy as possible.

By mid-August of 2009, Mandi was about five months pregnant. We had already had an ultrasound at ten weeks to confirm the baby's general health and get the initial vital signs. Any new parent who has gone into the ultrasound room holds their breath until they see their baby moving and the nurse notes the heart rate. At ten weeks, the baby registered a healthy heart rate of 150 beats per minute and was reported to be "very active."

As we approached our twenty-week ultrasound, Mandi and I had a decision to make. Did we wish to know the sex of the baby before it was born? There were pros and cons to knowing, but ultimately neither of us could contain our curiosity. We opted to learn the baby's sex before buying furniture, strollers, clothes, and more.

"Mandi Fisher," the nurse called as she stood with the door partially open.

Mandi squeezed my hand and smiled as we walked down the hall. She was giddy and could barely contain her enthusiasm. Within minutes, the OB arrived to ask questions and order the examination.

"We're scheduled to do the twenty-week ultrasound today," the doctor said. "Are we wanting to know the sex?"

"Yes," Mandi replied simply. "We are ready to find out what this baby's name is."

The subject of baby names had been on our minds since we found out we were pregnant. Mandi bought a book of modern baby names, and we started going down the lists to see which we liked.

After several weeks of searching and quizzing each other, we had settled on a boy's name. It would be Wilson, named after my great-grandfather. First names always get shortened by peers or relatives, so if he ended up being called "Will," we could live with it.

We were still in need of a girl's name. We both had a hunch the baby might be a girl; call it parent's intuition, I suppose. However, we had trouble being enthusiastic about the same name. By this point, it had been several months of back and forth.

"How about Carrington?" Mandi asked.

"I like it, but she'll end up being called Carrie for short," I said. "Carrie Fisher. Huh. Princess Leia ring a bell?"

"Nobody thinks like you," Mandi sarcastically replied. "Okay, what about Mackenzie?"

I stopped and thought about it. The only Mackenzie I knew was Mackenzie Phillips, the actress. Given that she hadn't been in the news for a long time, and Mackenzie had become a more common name, I gave it a tentative thumbs-up.

"Mackenzie Fisher," I said. "That flows pretty well."

"I agree," Mandi replied. She put a checkmark by that name and continued down the list. As we failed to agree on any other name on the list, we came back to Mackenzie.

"Okay, let's get that ultrasound started," the doctor said. "We'll know soon enough."

The doctor sent us with a nurse to another room for the ultrasound. I helped Mandi up on the table as she lay flat on her back. The nurse squeezed a small tube of jelly on Mandi's stomach, making her giggle because the gel was cold. The nurse then pushed gently and moved the wand in small circles to find the baby.

"Now, are you sure you want to know?" the nurse asked.

"Yes," we both said out loud simultaneously.

"We're ready," Mandi said.

The nurse moved the wand again, hit a few keys on the keyboard, and marked an "X" on the screen.

"This is your baby's private parts," she said. "And there is nothing there that would indicate it being a boy, so it looks like you're having a girl!"

"A girl," Mandi said softly, looking at me. Her eyes began to well with tears, and she squeezed my hand.

Like many fathers, I would often joke with Mandi that she was carrying our son. Despite my parental instincts telling me it was a girl, I had somewhat hoped for a son, partially so I could see my grandfather's reaction.

"Gramps," as we all called him, was in his late eighties at the time we were pregnant. He grew up in the Great Depression, along with his fifteen brothers and sisters. Large families weren't unusual back then, but sixteen total kids was still a significant number. I wanted Gramps to feel the joy of knowing we were naming our child after his father. I spent a great deal of time with him and my cousin Danny growing up, fishing and spending time outdoors. I knew it would mean the world to him if his great-grandson had his father's name.

Still, I had no feelings of disappointment when we found out the baby was a girl. I only felt an overwhelming love for my wife. Mandi was so happy. I leaned over and kissed her on the forehead as the nurse continued the ultrasound.

There were two nurses in the room. One was administering the test on Mandi, and another was watching the ultrasound and reviewing the vitals. Out of the corner of my eye, I noticed the second nurse subtly pointing to the ultrasound screen and making a gesture to the nurse administering the test.

"Is everything okay?" I asked.

"Yes, Mister Fisher. We are just looking carefully so we can share our thoughts with the doctor."

I wasn't reassured. The way the nurses looked at each other told me they saw something that wasn't typical.

"We'll get you cleaned up, and then the doctor will see you again before you leave," the nurse said as she wiped the gel off Mandi's belly and helped her sit up.

A few short minutes later, the doctor came in to see us. "I don't want to cause alarm, but we did see something on the ultrasound, and we want to get a better picture," he said. "We don't think it's anything major, but it's better to have it checked now rather than wait. We would like to send you over to another OB-GYN that has a different piece of equipment with an even higher resolution."

Mandi immediately began to cry. The doctor, who had likely had to deliver bad news many times before, seemed somewhat surprised by her reaction.

"Please don't be upset," he said. "It's just a precaution. There's something called a VSD, ventricular septal defect. Some people call it a heart murmur. It's not uncommon, and we just want to get a better view of it. Again, it's just out of an abundance of precaution."

Despite the OB displaying compassion and confidence, we left feeling like something was wrong. Mandi and I had planned to go to her parents' house after the ultrasound to share the news. We decided to keep that plan intact even though we each had a sick feeling in our stomach. As I drove the car leaving the hospital, I reached out and squeezed Mandi's hand with mine, interlocking fingers to make sure she knew we were in this together. Trying to keep the mood as positive as possible, I switched the subject and began to talk about the happy news of having a girl.

"So, it's Mackenzie then, right?" I asked.

"Yes, Mackenzie," Mandi said, doing her best to put on a happy face.

Arriving at her parents' house, we knocked on the door. Mandi's mother came to the door with a smile on her face. "Well, what are we having?" A mother's intuition is a powerful thing. She could instantly tell something was bothering her daughter despite Mandi's best effort to hide it. "Sweetheart, what's wrong?"

Mandi began to cry again. "They are sending us to another specialist because something may be wrong with the baby's heart."

Appearing calm and collected, Miss Sheri brought us into the living room, and Mandi told her about the nurse's reaction, the doctor's reassurance, and the need for us to visit a specialist within the next week or two.

"Well, that isn't the best news, but let's not borrow trouble just yet," Miss Sheri said. "I know you found out about the sex ... tell us what you're having."

"It's a girl," Mandi said, smiling.

"A girl! Congratulations!" Miss Sheri said. Mr. Skip had walked into the room by then to hear the doctor's update. Her parents were doing their best to keep Mandi in positive spirits.

"You seem upset," Mandi's mom said to me, alluding to the fact that I might be disappointed because it was a girl.

"Not at all! I'm thrilled about that," I said, giving her a hug. "It's just something about how the doctor told us the news that has me unnerved a bit."

"Look, guys. I'm sure he's just sending you there to double-check. Let's stay positive," Miss Sheri said.

We all agreed to table any notion of something being wrong until we had more information. The doctor they were sending us to was a high-risk OB-GYN at the University of South Alabama. But it was important for us to remember she had the better ultrasound machine. That was the primary reason we were seeing her for this follow-up appointment.

"I'll be glad when she's eighteen, and these worries stop," I said ignorantly while talking with Mandi's parents as we moved her sister Abby into her dorm at college the following weekend.

Mandi's parents began laughing and shaking their heads. "You have a lot to learn if you think worrying about your child stops at age eighteen," Miss Sheri said.

"You know what I meant," I responded as I thought about how dumb my statement sounded.

I wanted to fast-forward to the new ultrasound appointment and get the good news we needed so I could release my anxiety. Unfortunately, I was headed out of town the next day for work. Out of the country, actually. I would be making my third and final trip to Singapore for a fundraising consulting contract I had signed earlier in the year.

Given the news I had just heard at the doctor's office a few days prior, I was not in the best of spirits to make the week-long international journey. It was three flights and twenty-six total hours of travel—one way. And there would be plenty of time to think on the flight, which was not necessarily a good thing for somebody who has a penchant for worrying too much.

\*\*\*

Nearly two weeks went by before we were able to see the high-risk OB-GYN specialist. I had returned home from Singapore, taking my usual two days to recover from the extreme jet lag that a trip almost halfway around the world does to the body. Mandi had been busy working and continuing to unpack the moving boxes in our house, trying her best to keep her mind off the upcoming appointment.

The high-risk OB-GYN was an outstanding doctor. Her reputation was strong, and we were hoping that she would dismiss or downplay the concerns and give us back our peace of mind. It had been a long ten days between visits, and we were ready to get back to enjoying the pregnancy.

Throughout the spring and summer of 2009, Mandi had eaten well, exercised, and refrained from caffeine. She took acetaminophen for headaches only when absolutely necessary, and she had managed to stay illness-free. She quite literally did everything by the book and was determined to take the best care of her baby as she possibly could.

Mandi's parents accompanied us on the trip to help listen for information as the doctor talked. When you're nervous or emotional, it's easy to forget the details or misunderstand what the doctor tells you. They provided a source of comfort as we listened to the doctor outline what the visit would entail.

"We're scheduled for an ultrasound today to look at a possible VSD and also to check on your baby's growth," the doctor said.

Mandi and I looked at each other. We hadn't realized the baby measured small. We thought we were just there for a check on the potential heart murmur.

"Yes," I said. "Though we didn't realize the baby wasn't growing well."

"We'll take a look, and I can get you a more accurate reading for twenty-two weeks," the doctor said.

As a high-risk doctor, she saw many pregnancies with a variety of outcomes, some good and some bad. She had a very matter-of-fact style and owned it from the beginning, saying she was there to list out the possibilities and give facts. What she lacked in a warm bedside manner, she made up for in experience and information.

The nurses assisted the doctor as she performed the ultrasound. Once again, we observed the monitor and listened as the doctor rattled off statistics and information. Being thorough, the doctor went through all the possibilities based on her observations.

"Well, first of all, it should be noted that you two aren't the biggest people in terms of your size," the doctor said to us. "Mom, how tall are you?"

"Five foot four," Mandi said.

"And Dad?" the doctor asked.

"Five eight."

"So, right away, know that there's a good chance that the baby is going to be small to begin with," the doctor stated. "However, there are other possibilities. The baby is underweight and measuring small based on your gestation period. She should have gained one and a half pounds since your last visit, and she only gained a half-pound. I'm assuming you're eating like you should?"

"Yes, ma'am," Mandi said.

"Okay, good. We're going to put you on some high caloric and nutritious shakes to make sure the baby gets plenty of nourishment," the doctor said.

"Also, I did see the VSD the other OB-GYN saw. We'll have to watch it, but because she is measuring small, this could be any number of things. It could be Turner syndrome, which is rare, but I have seen it," the doctor said.

At this point, we were beginning to get nervous. We came in for a potential heart murmur and were now looking at a low-birth-weight baby and the possibility of Turner syndrome, something we had never heard before.

"I'm going to put you down to come back in ten days and see me again," the doctor said. "We'll draw blood today, and we'll have Mom give a urine sample to test for gestational diabetes and a few other things. We'll go over the results at the next appointment and do another ultrasound."

Leaving the appointment and driving home, I tried to analyze the situation and look for the positives.

"The doctor is just going through the possibilities," I said to Mandi as I drove.

We both were unnerved by this visit and had to absorb a lot of new information.

"Why was she so quick to jump to Turner syndrome?" Mandi asked rhetorically. "Doctor Doom didn't give us anything positive to consider."

The nickname stuck. Mandi didn't intend to be mean, and we never said it outside of our circle. It was just meant to decrease the tension and nervousness we felt having to go to a high-risk doctor and absorb bad news. We had spent twenty weeks thinking about baby names, what color to paint the nursery, and trying to guess the baby's day of birth and weight. Now, all those conversations shifted to things that could potentially be wrong with the pregnancy.

Ten days went by slowly, and we once again returned to see Dr. Doom.

"The bloodwork came back with markers that are showing the possibility of three things: early delivery, spina bifida, or preeclampsia," Dr. Doom said as she got right to the point. "Now, there's a one-in-fourteen chance of one of those things happening, but it's not a guarantee."

One in fourteen seemed like long odds. There was no sign of any of those things at the moment. We thought this might be a worst-case scenario that was being presented to us.

Once again, Mandi lay on the observation table and had the cold gel squirted on her belly. The doctor carefully moved the wand, looking for any signs of Down syndrome or other possible markers of low birth weight.

"Well, Mackenzie has grown just three ounces in ten days. She should be way over that at this point. I assume you're drinking the shakes as prescribed," Dr. Doom asked.

"Yes, every one of them."

"I see no thickening of the neck or clubbing of the fingers or toes," the doctor observed as she continued the ultrasound. "This does not look like Down syndrome."

Relieved, I looked at Mandi's mom and smiled. Ignorantly, I thought that would likely take us out of the possibility of rare genetic disorders. Down syndrome was one of the most common disorders. If it wasn't Down syndrome, there was a good chance we were out of the woods on genetic disorders. Or so I thought.

Over the next four weeks, Mandi and I visited Dr. Doom a total of three more times. She performed ultrasounds each time and sent us home with instructions to consume more calories in order to increase the baby's weight, get plenty of rest, and report any unusual issues. We were now in a wait-and-see mode.

***

We awoke to a typical Sunday morning in October. Mandi had been on bed rest per the instructions of the doctor, who suspected preeclampsia, so I brought a load of laundry into the bedroom to fold and keep her company. She complained that her pulse was racing and her chest hurt. I grabbed the blood pressure monitor I had purchased earlier in the week and took a reading. Her blood pressure was extremely high—150 over 100. She also was in considerable pain, and it didn't seem to be improving with rest. Dr. Doom had asked us to look out for these specific symptoms. Taking no chances, we decided to go to the University of South Alabama's Children's & Women's Hospital.

The causes of preeclampsia are not very well known. What is known is that the only cure for this is the delivery of the baby. If left untreated, the lives of both the mother and the infant could be in danger due to high blood pressure or the risk of stroke. Rest is usually prescribed to keep the blood pressure as low as possible.

After arriving at the hospital, the nurses checked Mandi's blood pressure and immediately hooked her up to a series of machines that monitored both the baby's and Mandi's vitals. Ironically, as high as Mandi's heart rate was, the baby's heart rate was much lower than it should have been. With several decelerations, the doctors and nurses grew more concerned that the baby was in distress.

Following several hours of tests and evaluation, it was decided that Mandi would be admitted for further monitoring and evaluation. The goal in this situation isn't to cure the preeclampsia, it's to manage the symptoms as much as possible and keep from delivering the child too soon. At just twenty-seven weeks and two days, the doctors were doing everything they could to avoid premature labor or being forced to perform emergency surgery to save the baby and Mandi.

I asked the nurse how long they expected Mandi to be there.

"It could be just one night or several nights, depending on how she and the baby are doing," the nurse said. "There's no way to know for sure with preeclampsia."

Having rushed to the hospital, we didn't make arrangements for the dog to be let out or for any longer-term accommodations. Mandi needed her cellphone charger and her laptop if she were going to be staying at the hospital for any considerable length of time. Luckily, Mandi's parents had joined us at the hospital in the afternoon to provide support.

"I don't feel comfortable leaving tonight," Miss Sheri said. "Why don't you go home and get some sleep? If we're still here tomorrow, you can stay, and I'll go home. We'll do this in shifts."

Reluctantly, I agreed. It didn't feel right leaving Mandi, but I knew Miss Sheri would take care of her and let me know if anything was out of the ordinary. Besides, if we were going to be there several nights, I would need help with taking care of the dog, swapping out clothes, and making sure Mandi had everything she needed.

I kissed my wife on the forehead and told her I would see her in the morning, bringing back her charging cord, laptop, and anything else she wanted or needed.

On my way out the door, Miss Sheri handed me a piece of paper. "What's this?" I asked.

Miss Sheri said nothing, just motioned for me to read the note.

"Chapstick, phone charger, camera. Camera? Why do we need the camera?" I naïvely inquired.

Glancing up, Miss Sheri looked me in the eyes and silently mouthed a sentence. "Bring the camera, just in case."

Mandi was asleep by that point, but Miss Sheri took care not to say anything too loudly to wake her up.

"Okay," I said begrudgingly, thinking she was just a nervous mother. "I'll see you in the morning. Call me if anything changes."

*＊*

On Monday, October 12, morning arrived earlier than expected. My cellphone rang out, startling me. I quickly looked at the clock and then stared at my phone for a second, slightly disoriented and trying to determine who was calling.

"Hello?" I said in a groggy but nervous voice.

"Don't hurry or panic. Bring your things and come to the hospital as soon as you can," Miss Sheri said in a very calm, clear tone. "Mandi and the baby are fine, but they are making comments that the time for Mackenzie to arrive may be coming sooner than expected."

I was stunned into near silence. Mackenzie coming early? Surely that isn't the case. I had gathered the items on the list the night before, packing an overnight bag so I could get up early and relieve Miss Sheri at the hospital. I left the house quickly for the twenty-five-minute drive to the hospital.

A hint of storminess was in the air, and the humidity was high for an October morning as I arrived. Turning and entering Mandi's room, I made eye contact with Miss Sheri. She stepped in my direction and met me before I got to Mandi's bedside, pulling me out into the hallway to talk.

"How is she doing?"

"She is stable, but her blood pressure is still high," Miss Sheri stated with a soft but purposeful tone. "The baby has had a few heart rate decelerations that have given the nurses a scare. They are going to be watching her very carefully to determine if they need to take Mackenzie early."

"Has the doctor been in yet?"

"She's due in any minute," Miss Sheri replied.

Mandi was fading in and out of sleep, exhausted from a long night in the hospital. Almost immediately after we stepped back into the room, the doctor on call that morning arrived. She had just been at the nurse's station, reading the report and watching the baby's vital signs on the large computer monitors attached to the wall.

Mandi woke from her sleep as the noise level in the room became elevated. I reached out and held her hand, gently squeezing it to tell her I was there.

"Are you Dad?" the doctor asked me.

"Yes," I replied.

"I'm Doctor Reese," she said. "Kiddo has to come out. Her heart rate is decelerating too low and too often. I don't like what I am seeing. We need to deliver her now."

Stunned, I turned to look at Mandi. Tears were welling in her eyes as she realized her worst fears. "It's too soon," she said, sobbing.

Just shy of seven months pregnant with our first child, Mandi was now facing an emergency C-section. Immediately, the nursing crew entered the room and began giving instructions as they prepped for surgery.

"Only one person can go back with her," the nurse said. "Dad, will that be you?"

I looked at Miss Sheri. I knew she was very concerned, and I had the utmost respect for what she and Mr. Skip might also be feeling at that moment. I was also in shock. But I understood Mandi was the person who would be the most nervous, and I thought it was appropriate to defer to her wishes on this important question.

"Babe, what do you want?" I asked Mandi.

"I want you to be there with me."

The nurse handed me a set of yellow scrubs and told me to get dressed for surgery. My hands were trembling with fear of what I would see. I asked for assistance to help tie the gown in the back. Securing the mask last, I flashed the thumbs-up sign as Mr. Skip had the presence of mind to take a picture of the moment. Our first child was on the way. But while it was a scary time, capturing the memory would be a blessing to reflect upon someday.

I tried to display confidence in the room so Mandi would be as calm as possible. On the inside, I was scared out of my mind. I was not mentally prepared for this possibility and was still reeling from the news the doctor just had delivered.

Mandi, shaking with anxiety, was being prepped by the nurses. A catheter had to be inserted while she was still awake and alert. Miss Sheri held Mandi's hand as the staff worked quickly.

"Mother of Pearl!" Miss Sheri exclaimed as a more appropriate substitute for what Mandi likely thought as she gritted her teeth through the stabbing pain.

It did not take long to fully prep Mandi. The hospital staff went from calm and patient to a focused frenzy within a matter of minutes. I walked alongside Mandi's bed as the nursing staff wheeled her through the door, down the hall, and into the operating room. There, a team of nurses and the doctor were waiting, gowned up and ready. They wasted absolutely no time beginning the procedure.

I sat on a stool next to the bed facing Mandi, with the doctor to my left and Mandi's head on my right. I held Mandi's shaking left hand as the doctor started the procedure. The nurses had inserted a cloth divider so Mandi could not see the doctor working. She was still awake, though numb from the nerve block they had given her.

The cloth divider also obstructed my view. That was most definitely for the best. I could have stood up to watch the delivery, but I chose to remain seated. I had no idea what to expect. My wife was undergoing a major procedure, and the baby's prognosis was anything but certain.

I was terrified my baby would not cry, and I would see my child stillborn. Unnerved beyond comprehension, I stayed sitting down, glancing up occasionally to watch the suction machines whisking the massive amount of blood away from the hole they opened up in my wife.

"I'm so scared," Mandi said, trembling as she was still awake as the doctor started cutting.

"I know, baby. So am I," I replied to her as I squeezed her hand. "Everything is going to be okay."

My hand stayed in constant contact with Mandi's the entire duration of the procedure. I spoke to my wife, showing her my best calm and collected face while the panic stirred inside me.

Dr. Reese continued to work, giving instructions to the four or five nurses in the room gathered around the table. I stayed focused on Mandi, talking to her and telling her I loved her.

"I got her," the nurse said. Several seconds of a pause went by as they clamped the umbilical cord and separated the baby from Mandi. Nurses began to scurry around the room as the doctor handed Mackenzie to the NICU trauma nurse for evaluation.

I listened intensely for any sound that would assure us of a positive outcome. I stared at Mandi and counted in my head—four, five, six seconds. Finally, the sound of a tiny baby's cry filled the room. Incredibly, at twenty-seven weeks and three days, Mackenzie's tiny lungs seemed to work well beyond their expected capability.

"Is that her? Is she okay?" Mandi said, holding back tears and fighting the sedation they had given her after the baby was born to put her to sleep and close her up.

"Yes, sweetie. That's our girl!" I exclaimed. "She's crying, and they said she's doing well."

"Want to see your baby girl?" the nurse said as she held Mackenzie out.

A blue-striped hospital baby blanket was wrapped around Mackenzie's fragile body. The nurse held her head as they showed our daughter to us for the first time. Mackenzie's dark eyes were wide open. She let out a piercing cry as she seemingly locked eyes with her parents for the first time.

I felt Mandi's hand instantly relax as she knew Mackenzie was alive and doing well. She closed her eyes with a sense of relief and peace that all was going to be okay. I stayed by her side while the nurse quickly read the vital signs out loud for another nurse to chart.

"Seven hundred fifty-six grams," the nurse said. "Thirteen inches long."

Mandi began to drift off as the anesthesia caught up with her adrenaline. I continued to hold her hand while the doctor finished the C-section, and the nurses began preparing to take her to the recovery room. I kissed my wife on the forehead as she lay sleeping before I stepped back, thoroughly exhausted.

The NICU nurses quickly placed Mackenzie in a warm incubator and rolled her toward the elevator. They paused at the door to the hallway to allow Mandi's parents and sisters the opportunity to see her for the first time. With her eyes still wide open, Mackenzie let out another series of loud cries before the nurses hurriedly moved her into the elevator and took her up to the neonatal intensive care unit on the second floor.

As I exited the operating room, I felt both a sense of relief and enormous anxiety for the future. Mackenzie was here, though she was very early. It appeared her condition was good, but she was incredibly small. I knew virtually nothing about the NICU or what to expect going forward—except that I was a proud father, and my wife was the bravest soul I knew.

\*\*\*

With Mandi in the recovery room and Mackenzie in the NICU, the family gathered in the general waiting area for news on both. We were all feeling the effects of a dramatic morning, and at just 10:30 a.m., the better part of the day was still ahead of us.

The NICU nurse told us it would take some time to stabilize Mackenzie and complete her post-birth observation. When she was ready, visitors were allowed, but only two at one time could go through the NICU doors, and one of the two must be a parent.

After taking a few minutes to regroup, I decided to make a few phone calls and inform my family of the news.

"Dad, Mackenzie's here," I said matter-of-factly as I stood outside the hospital.

"What did you say?"

"Mackenzie is here," I said again. "Dad, she's alive and in the neonatal intensive care unit. Mandi is in the recovery room after having an emergency C-section. I don't know much beyond that at the moment. I'm supposed to be seeing Kenzie soon, and I will call back with more details."

Dad was in disbelief when I hung up the phone, promising to share the news with my aunt and other family members. I then called my mom and repeated my news. She was also in shock but offered to catch a flight and come down.

"That's not necessary, Mom. Kenzie and Mandi need some time to recover. I don't know anything more at this point. Give me a bit, and I will call you back with an update."

Feeling helpless, my mom did the only thing she knew how to do in such a situation: she forged ahead with her travel plans anyway, letting me know later that she would be arriving that night.

My mother is from the "old school," as they say. As the middle child in a family of seven, she experienced the difficulty so many of her generation endured: money was tight, and times could get rough as my grandparents tried to provide for a big family.

My maternal grandfather was a laborer and worked for many years in a quarry, driving a truck, and as a janitor. My maternal grandmother was a seamstress in addition to a homemaker. Times were not always easy, but the family was scrappy. Mom learned the value of working hard and earning her way, and these were attributes she attempted to pass along to my sister and me. She also learned that the surefire way to overcome adversity was to keep fighting through it and never quit—a pull-yourself-up-by-the-bootstraps mentality that was particularly strong when I was young.

Mom is not the sentimental type. That personality served her well in so many circumstances growing up and then later providing for two kids, but at times, it made it difficult for her to connect with me. In my youth, I seemed to be more sentimental and empathetic than other boys my age. Whether it was the death of a pet, the trauma of losing a friend or relative, or even the standard ups and downs of dating, many of my experiences were met with a tough-love approach from my mom. She knew how to overcome adversity her way but had difficulty relating to the way I approached getting past pain and learning how to deal with loss.

During the morning phone calls to my mom and dad, I had asked both of them to tell my sister Jill the news that Mackenzie had come early. She, in turn, would help tell other members of the family. With three people circulating the same information, most everyone would be covered without the need for me to call everyone individually. Having wrapped up both brief phone calls, I went back into the hospital and walked to the waiting room where Mandi's family had gathered.

"Any updates?" I asked.

"No, we're still waiting to hear," Miss Sheri replied.

Soon after that, one of the NICU nurses approached us in the waiting area. We had gathered in the corner of the room so we could have our privacy.

"Are you Dad?" one of the nurses asked me, seeing my bracelet.

"Yes," I said.

"Mackenzie is stable and on an observation table," she said. "You can visit her if you're ready, but we ask that you go in by yourself first and then take your family members back one at a time. When you get off the elevators on the second floor, head around the corner toward the double doors, wash up and put on the yellow gown and mask, and pick up the phone on the wall. We will come to get you and walk you back to Mackenzie."

Distracted and anxious, it took me a minute to process the instructions. My mind was racing, and I was thinking about both my wife and my daughter. I turned and began to walk toward the elevator.

"Jason," Miss Sheri said. "Are you okay?"

"Yeah, I'm all right," I replied. "I'm just processing everything I heard."

"It may not be easy to see what you are going to see," she said. "Just know that we would go with you if we could, and we'll be with you in spirit. Stay strong for your little girl."

I nodded, then pushed the button to summon the elevator as I tried to emotionally prepare for what was ahead.

Before entering the NICU, all visitors must wash their hands thoroughly and put on sterile gowns and masks. It's a routine but critical process to keeping the babies of the NICU healthy. Any bacteria or virus introduced from the outside can have terrible consequences. A simple cold for an adult can be deadly to a premature baby or a child with a health complication.

I followed the nurse's instructions, washing my hands and gowning up. I used the excess material on the gown to cover the handle to the phone before I picked it up so I would not get any germs on my hands.

"NICU, can I help you?" the nurse said through the phone.

"I'm Jason Fisher. My daughter was just born and brought up here," I said nervously.

"Okay, please enter and go left toward Pod 2," the nurse said. "Somebody will meet you and take you to see your daughter."

The double door automatically began to open as I hung up the phone. A nurse approached me as I gazed at the walls, looking for directions.

"Mister Fisher," she said. "I'm Nicole, and I'm taking care of Mackenzie. You can follow me."

Any parent who has experienced the NICU will recall the first time they walked into a NICU pod. The NICU is not a quiet place where babies sleep. It is a maze of observation tables, incubators, monitors, IV towers, wires, and digital technology. Nurses are constantly in motion tending to the babies, watching the monitors, and performing their tasks.

Entering Pod 2, there were four to five babies on each side of a wide aisle. The monitors and alarms were beeping and dinging loudly, indicating to a nurse that a baby's vital signs were above or below a set threshold for that child. The collective sound coming from the pod was nearly overwhelming to a new parent. But there was also a futuristic feel to the room, a blend of science fiction and medical beauty.

We walked down the aisle and stopped at the second table on the right. A small sign was freshly taped onto the observation table with Mackenzie's name, weight, date, and other essential information. Perched waist-high, the table was tall enough to see her easily but short enough for the nurses to have full, quick access if something went wrong.

As I approached my daughter for the first time, Nicole gave me a short briefing on what I would be seeing. "Now, Dad, Mackenzie is doing very well. I was in the delivery and operating room when she was born. She's been very stable, and we've had no problems so far." Nicole was an experienced nurse with many years spent in the NICU. She was sharp, extremely engaging in conversation, and very comforting to a new NICU parent.

"She's so small," I said with a slight pause in my voice.

"She weighed seven hundred fifty-six grams at birth. That's about one pound and ten ounces. Very tiny," Nicole replied.

"But she's doing okay?" I asked, taking in the seemingly endless array of wires attached to her.

"She's doing well so far, and we are constantly monitoring her. The tubes in her mouth are for the ventilator that helps her breathe. The wire attached to her toe measures her oxygen saturation rate. This wire attached under the mesh cap she has on her head is the temperature sensor. Babies born this early have trouble regulating their own body temperature." And she kept going. This wire measured her heart rate; another measured her breathing; this was for fluids; a central line for medicines would likely be added as well.

I tried to soak in as much information as I could. "What is the shiny substance on her skin?" I asked.

"That's petroleum jelly, which helps her skin stay moist under the UV light. Mackenzie needs to tan because her bilirubin number is low. She is a little jaundiced, but that is very normal with a child born this early," Nicole replied.

My anxiousness had worn off a bit as I became more used to the noise and realized Mackenzie was under superior medical care. My questions to Nicole became more specific as I learned more about her condition.

"So, an APGAR score of eight out of ten at birth is not bad?" I asked.

"That's very good for her gestational age. She got a point deducted for jaundice, but that is very treatable. She was at a nine out of ten just a few minutes after birth."

"Help me understand the monitors. What am I looking at here?" I asked.

Nicole walked me through each monitor attached to Mackenzie and what the indicators meant for each of them. She told me which numbers would be considered too high or low and what would set off the alarms. Also, because her lungs were so premature, they had inserted a tube and put Mackenzie on the mechanical ventilator to help her breathe while she learned to adapt outside of Mandi.

"This monitor is for apnea and bradycardia," Nicole said. "We call them the 'As and Bs.' They are essentially times when Mackenzie might stop breathing or pause too long, or when her heart rate does not stay above one hundred. We've given her some medicine to help with this, but she's still tiny, and her neurological function is immature, so she has the As and Bs fairly often. We will just rub her back and wake her up, which stimulates her to breathe again. Right now, the ventilator is doing most of the work, but if she improves, then she will come off the vent and will need to breathe on her own."

The concept of a child this small breathing on her own was almost too hard to comprehend. Mackenzie's skin was nearly translucent; it was so thin and fragile. Yet, here she was, her tiny heart beating on its own, and she seemed to be doing very well.

I stayed for another ten minutes, talking to Nicole and gathering information. Other than times during periodic nursing shift changes, I could come back whenever I wanted, up until 8:00 p.m. I thanked Nicole for taking care of our baby and walked back out the NICU doors.

It had been less than twenty minutes since I put the yellow gown on and entered a new world. The NICU had already changed me. I saw my daughter up close for the first time, her pale skin connected to a maze of wires and monitors.

I was presented with more than a dozen new terms I needed to remember and absorb so I could tell the others what to expect. And, most importantly, I was introduced to an amazing nurse caregiver who seemed to exude a quiet confidence in a room full of fragility.

***

After taking Mr. Skip and Miss Sheri back to see Mackenzie, I visited Mandi in the recovery room. She was in tremendous pain, as one could imagine, coming in and out of the fog of sedation and pain-relieving drugs. I told her Mackenzie was doing well, I loved her, and I would be there all day until they kicked me out. Mandi insisted I spend as much time with Mackenzie as I could, giving her updates until she could make it to the NICU herself.

I continued to inform family and friends of the latest news as much as I could. Mom, who had boarded a flight to Mobile, was due in at 7:15 p.m. She insisted we go right to the hospital, but I told her we would arrive too late to visit Mackenzie, and Mandi was recovering and needed as much rest as possible.

As Monday, October 12, wound to a close, I visited my new baby girl one more time, kissed my wife goodbye, told her I would be back in the morning, and went to the airport to pick up my mom. I had pledged to stay Monday night and trade places with Miss Sheri, but my mom coming into town changed that plan. Miss Sheri was more than happy to stay with Mandi again, but I couldn't help feeling like I wasn't there for my wife during a critical time of healing.

I awoke early Tuesday morning and showered quickly. I wanted to be at the hospital as soon as possible to get any updates. They had moved Mandi from recovery to her room on the third floor, where she would stay for three nights while recovering.

During my visit to the NICU, it was recommended that a family member with the same blood type, A positive, give blood for Mackenzie if she needed a transfusion during her NICU stay. Feeling helpless, I jumped at the chance to do something to help my newborn daughter.

After taking Mom back to see Mackenzie, I headed out to give blood. I hurried to and from the blood bank in West Mobile about twenty minutes away, making it back in time to see my wife as she awoke in her room from a short nap.

Expecting to find my wife groggy and in pain, I was instead greeted at the door by her parents and the chief neonatologist, Dr. Eyal. A grandfatherly man with a deep passion for his job, Dr. Eyal introduced himself and shared his purpose for the visit.

"Mackenzie has had a small Grade 1 intraventricular hemorrhage," he said in a sympathetic tone of voice.

I instantly knew what that terminology meant; Mackenzie had a blood vessel rupture in her brain. However, I wasn't familiar with the classification of how they graded these episodes and the severity of the outcome.

"She has had a very small brain bleed due to the pressure differences outside of Mom," he continued. "These are very common in extremely premature babies. A Grade 1 hemorrhage is the least serious. The brain often absorbs them, and there are generally no complications."

I listened as attentively as possible, but my stomach was in knots. I'm usually very good about understanding the nuances of medical diagnoses and finding the silver lining. Still, I learned that there was a major difference in how I processed and absorbed information when my baby girl was being discussed.

"So, her prognosis is good?" I asked the doctor.

"We think so, yes. But we'll have to watch to make sure there are no complications."

Instead of taking the good news and running with it, I focused on the negative. I thanked the doctor, turned away, and walked out of the room. At the end of the hallway, I stared out a window to the parking lot below. I could no longer hold back the grief. The shock of the past two days was beginning to wear off, and I felt the extreme effects of anxiety.

I kept asking myself if this was a dream. Just seventy-two hours before, Mandi was doing okay on bed rest, and we were optimistic that we could make it to thirty-two weeks, the target Dr. Doom had given us when she suspected preeclampsia. Now, Mackenzie was fighting for her life in the NICU, and Mandi was recovering from a difficult emergency C-section.

Tears streamed down my face as I peered outside as best I could through my watery eyes. I had a few minutes by myself before my mother came to try to comfort me.

She offered her best advice. "You need to stay strong for Mackenzie and Mandi."

"Mom, I just need a few minutes. I'm overwhelmed right now." I continued to stare out the window.

"You're going to need to toughen up, Jason," she stated with a sense of parental entitlement.

My mom did her best to be there for me. She knew I was hurting and feeling lost. But I was in no mood to hear a lecture about my supposed shortcomings in how I dealt with emotional trauma.

I stared out the window in silence and wiped away the tears as they came; I felt helpless.

"Maybe you can get through to him," I heard my mom say to Mr. Skip as he walked into the hallway.

I was already hoping Mr. Skip would come over to talk to me. I needed his calm demeanor and words of wisdom. He was and still is a father figure to me, and I value his thoughts, particularly at a difficult moment like we were facing.

"I can't handle her attitude right now," I said as he placed his hand on my shoulder.

"She means well. She's a lot like my mother was. Her advice is pretty straightforward, and the delivery isn't easy to hear, but she just feels helpless like the rest of us," he said.

I knew he was right, but what I needed was for somebody to tell me it would be okay, to listen quietly to whatever I was willing to share, and then respect the fact that I was not in control of my emotions at that moment. Whatever power I had over my ability to hold back the tears slowly eroded. I was exhausted, and the bad news delivered with a slow drip was wearing me down. The trickle of anxiety transformed into a river of emotions, and I was unable to stop it. I wanted to stay strong for Mandi, but I could no longer hide the fear that was welling up inside me.

***

The nurses had promised Mandi that she could visit Mackenzie on Tuesday if she could get up from the bed and into a wheelchair with a reasonable level of assistance. Mandi's physical pain was intense, and I was sure it was unquestionably beyond what I had ever felt in my life. Yet, when it came to Mackenzie, there was absolutely nothing that would keep her from seeing her child.

"Okay, are we ready?" the nurse asked.

"Let's do this," Mandi said as she slowly slid her feet off the bed, wincing in pain with every slight movement. With help from the nurses, she was guided into a standing position.

Mandi then maneuvered her body 180 degrees and slowly descended onto the seat of the wheelchair, using her arms to take as much pressure as she could off her core.

Grabbing the handles, I turned Mandi's wheelchair toward the elevators. Every small crevice or doorway threshold we rolled over felt like a giant set of railroad tracks to Mandi. She gripped the armrests of the wheelchair, holding her breath from the pain.

"Can you please slow this down and pay attention to where you're going?" Mandi said to me emphatically. "Or get me another driver that doesn't hit every bump!"

I agreed to proceed with more caution, though truthfully, I'm not sure I could have been more careful. I can only imagine what I would have said had it been me in that wheelchair with a stomach full of staples.

As we reached the NICU doors, I helped Mandi wash her hands and put a gown over her while she remained seated. I then picked up the phone, spoke to the nurse, and waited for her to buzz us in.

The doors opened, exposing Mandi to the sounds and experience of the NICU for the first time. I slowly pushed her wheelchair around the corners into Pod 2, rolling her gently up to the edge of the observation table where Mackenzie lay on her tummy in a curled-up position under the UV lights.

"Hi, baby girl," Mandi said as tears formed in the corner of her eyes. "Hi, Mackenzie." Mandi reached out her hand, gently touching her newborn baby whom she had carried so lovingly. Mackenzie moved slightly and responded to her mom's gentle caressing.

Mandi gathered herself and mustered up all the energy she could find to ask Nurse Nicole questions.

"She's doing great," Nicole said. "These UV lights are helping with her jaundice, and Mackenzie is wearing a mask to protect her eyes."

Nicole gave her the brief rundown of the equipment that surrounded Mackenzie's observation table, explaining what the main monitors tracked and how each functioned. Mandi, still under the influence of strong pain medication, did her best to take in all the information.

Seeing Mackenzie for the first time motivated Mandi to heal and get better so she could spend even more moments with our daughter in the coming days before being discharged. It had been only thirty hours since Mackenzie came into this world unexpectedly. Little did we know how much time we would spend with Mackenzie in Pod 2 in the weeks and months to come.

\*\*\*

Mandi was discharged after four nights in the hospital. In what is undoubtedly one of the hardest moments I've ever seen her experience, she had to leave the hospital without her daughter. That is a feeling no mother ever wants to experience.

Our days and evenings going forward were primarily spent at the hospital with Mackenzie, from the time the NICU opened until the moment it closed.

Like many new parents, we were sleep-deprived and anxious. But unlike most new parents, we could not lay eyes on our baby in the middle of the night. Instead, Mandi would often call the hospital in the early morning hours while pumping breast milk to get an update.

About two weeks went by, and we had settled into a mini-routine. Mackenzie was stable and making steady progress, including no longer needing to be intubated and on the mechanical ventilator. Since Mandi and I were both off work, we visited the NICU in shifts so Mackenzie was never alone during visiting hours. Early one morning in late October, the phone rang.

"Missus Fisher, this is the nurse from the NICU. We don't want you to be alarmed, but Mackenzie appears to be sick, and her oxygen levels and vital signs have been a bit erratic this morning."

"What?" Mandi said in an exasperated tone. "I just called you a few hours ago, and she was fine!"

"Yes, ma'am," the nurse replied. "She just started showing symptoms in the past hour or two. Doctor Eyal is here, and they are looking over Mackenzie as we speak."

"We'll be right there."

I was already dressed when we received the call, but Mandi wasn't completely prepared to head out the door. She was still moving slowly after the surgery, but she didn't want a moment wasted without one of us being there.

"Go. I'll be right behind you," she told me. "Call me as soon as you know something."

Speeding down Moffett Road to the hospital, I weaved in and out of traffic to gain every second I could. Upon arriving, I was told Mackenzie was stable but needed to be put back on the ventilator and wasn't breathing well independently.

"We believe Mackenzie has a staph infection, but we aren't sure what type it is," Dr. Eyal said. "We are going to treat her with a combination of powerful antibiotics and wait for her culture to grow."

Staph infections are unfortunately common in hospitals. They can also be deadly, particularly for a premature baby the size of Mackenzie. If your child acquires a staph infection, you hope and pray it isn't the type of bacteria that is resistant to antibiotics.

"Also, when we were reintubating her, we noticed she had a very narrow v-shaped cleft palate. It's very tiny, so we missed it during her first intubation when she was first born."

Stunned, I tried to absorb the news now being shared. Mackenzie was not only fighting for her life, but she also had a birth defect that somehow went unnoticed when she was born.

*How in the world am I going to tell Mandi this?*

I walked outside the hospital entrance, down the stairs to the parking lot below, and called Mandi's cellphone.

"Babe, they think it's a staph infection, and they started her on three strong antibiotics. She's stable, but she's back on the ventilator." I updated her as calmly as I could, though I did not feel at all calm. "One more thing … the doctor discovered that she has a small cleft palate when they reintubated her this morning."

"What?" Mandi practically shouted into the phone. "I can't even process what you're saying. I'm going to start crying, so I need to let you go."

She and her mom pulled into the parking lot a few minutes later. I immediately walked to her car.

"A cleft palate?" Mandi said with frustration. "How in the world are we just finding out about this now?" Tears were welling up in Mandi's eyes as she started walking toward the entrance.

Having a child in the NICU is a roller coaster experience. You can go from extreme highs to extreme lows very quickly. This illness was the first, but unfortunately not the last time we would ride on that train.

"This is my fault," Mandi said. "If we hadn't held Kenzie yesterday, she wouldn't be sick now."

"Babe, we don't know that. We took every precaution, and we had to hold our baby at some point. Mackenzie needs her mom and dad," I said, trying to deflect her self-punishment.

The nurses and doctors all but dismissed that Mandi was responsible. A pic line inserted as a medicine port was more likely the cause, but Mandi was hearing none of it. She vowed not to hold Kenzie again until she was much bigger and less fragile.

The doctor returned to relay the latest to Mandi. "We still don't know whether the infection is gram-positive or gram-negative, which will dictate how well it responds to the antibiotics. We hope for gram-positive bacteria, as they respond better to the antibiotics. If that's the case, she should start responding to the antibiotics in the next few hours. Once we get the culture back, we'll be able to verify what we are dealing with."

We looked down at the observation table. Mackenzie looked horribly sick, with a ghost-like complexion, and she was unresponsive to the nurse's touch like she usually had been. Weighing just one pound and twelve ounces at the time of her sickness, it was apparent she was in a fight for her life.

Mandi and I clutched each other and cried big tears. I felt a hollow feeling in my chest, just like the day Mackenzie had been born. This time, I had Mandi with me. But we were both in the same mindset, feeling helpless and wondering why these bad things kept happening to our baby girl.

Several hours passed before we received the next update. Unfortunately, there was no change in Mackenzie's condition. The ventilator continued to do the breathing. The nurses occasionally adjusted the supplemental oxygen levels they gave her, raising it higher and higher to stay at a place where her breathing was not labored. Her oxygen saturation levels needed to remain above 90 percent. An IV tower hovered over the observation table, dangling several bags of fluids and an antibiotic cocktail. The fluid slowly dripped into the thin line that was inserted into one of Mackenzie's tiny veins.

Mandi and I continued to be with Mackenzie every minute the NICU was open. During nursing shift changes, we would go down to the cafeteria to kill time until the hour was up, and they would let us back in. We were scared to leave Mackenzie's side for fear that something would happen, and we wouldn't be there.

In the early evening, Mackenzie started showing signs of responding to the antibiotics. The nurses were turning her oxygen down, returning to more reasonable levels. She was becoming more active and showed signs of the fighting spirit that would come to define her medical history.

A short time later, Dr. Eyal came in and shared news from the lab.

"Mackenzie has a gram-positive staph infection, and we think she is responding to the antibiotic cocktail we gave her. She still has a fight on her hands, though."

Relieved inside, I still had to ask the question for clarification. "So, you're optimistic about her prognosis then?"

"Yes, but she is not out of danger. She's very tiny. But the gram-positive infections are easier to treat than the gram-negative infections," the doctor reiterated.

We absorbed the welcome news. Mandi and I had been riding a roller coaster of emotions all day and needed to hear something that would lift our spirits. Given Mackenzie's condition, the nurses allowed us to remain past 8:00 p.m., when the NICU was typically closed to parents. They only allowed one of us to be back with her during this time, so we took turns watching over her while the other one slept in the waiting room or the car.

The next morning, Mackenzie had improved enough to be removed from the ventilator. She was breathing independently, and her oxygen levels increased to the point where a nasal cannula was sufficient treatment. Like a couple of weeks prior, when she was born, Mackenzie showed that she had a strong and instinctual will to live despite the significant medical adversity she faced.

\*\*\*

Mandi and I made a habit of looking at Mackenzie's chart every day when we came into the NICU. The nurse from the previous night would weigh Mackenzie and make notes on how she was progressing. Mackenzie had hit two pounds in November, nearly a month after she was born. She continued to make steady gains almost every day thereafter. In the NICU, they measure progress in ounces and grams. Every premature child is different in how they gain weight, but two pounds in total weight is a magical mark.

Mackenzie had been steadily gaining weight through December and had begun to make considerable progress. She had been moved to a different wing of the NICU assigned to more medically stable babies. Aptly nicknamed "The Fat Farm," it was a place where young preemies would put on some pounds and march toward eventually being discharged to their parents.

On a cold morning in early January, we received another unexpected call from the NICU nurse. Mackenzie's oxygen levels were decreasing, and the doctors weren't sure why it was happening.

Like the reoccurrence of a bad dream, we jumped in the car and headed to the hospital. Running up the stairs instead of taking the slow elevator, we quickly walked to the hand-washing station, gowned up, and went through the NICU doors.

"Have you run any tests to rule out infection?" Mandi asked.

"No, we're just observing right now," the neonatologist said. "We don't feel that she is sick."

"You don't know that for sure, though. You haven't run any tests. Can we run a CBC to rule out another staph infection?" Mandi asked.

Seeing that this momma bear was not going to back down, the doctor ordered the tests. They understood Mandi to be serious, and I sensed that the tests were as much for peace of mind as they were for diagnosis. Fortunately, the complete blood count test came back within normal limits, and it was determined that Mackenzie was not fighting an infection.

While we were relieved she was not sick, we still didn't know why her oxygen levels were dropping. The doctors decided to get an X-ray of Mackenzie's lungs to determine if they could see any abnormality that might be causing the sudden decrease in oxygen saturation. It did not take long for the results to be confirmed.

"Mackenzie is retaining fluid," the doctor said. "We are calling in a cardiologist to evaluate her and starting her on furosemide to eliminate the fluid."

Mackenzie was born with an atrial septal defect (ASD)—a small hole in the wall of her heart. This was almost certainly what had been showing on the ultrasounds that sent us to Dr. Doom. But once again, it evaded precise detection until after she was born. As she grew bigger, so did the ASD. At that point in time, it was six millimeters in diameter and had reached the point where her heart could no longer pump enough fluid efficiently to keep up with her oxygenation needs.

"Mackenzie is technically in congestive heart failure," the cardiologist said.

"Congestive heart failure?" I was sick to my stomach and felt as if the floor suddenly dropped out from underneath me.

"Yes, technically," the doctor replied. "Once we give her the furosemide, she will pee off the fluid she is retaining, and it will take the pressure off her heart."

Mandi was in stunned disbelief. She stood silently while I spoke to the cardiologist. I had no doubt in my mind she felt the sudden drop of the NICU roller coaster we rode together.

After a day or two on the medication, Mackenzie lost a noticeable amount of weight, but the fluid was largely gone. Her oxygen had returned to its previous level, and she eventually was breathing room air again.

***

I spent a considerable number of nights in the NICU, just staring at my baby and thinking about life. When I was in the NICU alone, I would sit in the rocking chair and watch Mackenzie's monitors or read her a book. She couldn't hear me or understand, but it made me feel I was connecting with my daughter.

Mackenzie's vitals would grow more consistent over time to be within the threshold limits. Outside her illnesses, she could go an hour or two without an apnea or bradycardia event. During this time, the NICU could almost become hypnotizing, particularly in the evening when most parents were gone for the day.

At times, I would stare into Mackenzie's incubator, studying every part of her tiny thirteen-inch frame. Whose eyes did she have? Was her hair color changing? I might ask these questions as I was silently looking at my baby girl and contemplating this new life.

However, over time, her eye and hair color weren't the only things I noticed. One night, I studied the number of "stork bites" she had on her face and neck, realizing they were actually quite extensive when you looked closely. Stork bites are benign cosmetic birthmarks that often fade with time, but Mackenzie sure did have a lot of them. And then there was the "ear pit" she had on her right ear cartilage, a tiny hole that was barely noticeable but can sometimes be an accompanying marker for incomplete ear formation.

By this time, we had already known about the other birth defects Mackenzie had; the atrial septal defect, the small cleft palate, and an umbilical hernia that was thought to be part of her prematurity. But if you included the numerous stork bites and the ear pit, Mackenzie had three known birth defects and two additional markers of concern.

Having idle time on my hands and a smartphone, I would look up these appearances or markers to learn more about them. How common were they in isolation? Did they accompany other issues, or were they common in some syndromes? The more I researched, the more questions I asked the medical staff. I was most definitely the "Internet-Searching Dad" the NICU nurses had affectionately nicknamed me.

"Did you ever notice the small hole in Mackenzie's right ear?" I asked Mandi one day. "It's called an 'ear pit,' and it's sometimes associated with birth defects involving ear formation."

"Quit finding things wrong with our baby girl!" Mandi said. "Just enjoy her and stop studying her."

Was I paranoid, or did these smaller but noticeable traits with Mackenzie mean something bigger was at play?

I brought my concern to Dr. Eyal. He recommended we contact Dr. Martinez, a local geneticist who had an excellent reputation among the staff in the NICU. He was known to be extremely thorough and very knowledgeable about premature babies who exhibit signs of genetic abnormalities.

The following week, I had planned to be at the hospital while Dr. Martinez was observing Mackenzie, but he arrived early, and I was unable to make it there in time. The doctor had completed his review and was heading out the door when I arrived, but I was able to stop him and ask the questions on my mind.

"I think she is fine," Dr. Martinez said reassuringly. "She just has the preemie look."

"What about the ear pit? The umbilical hernia? The heart murmur?" I asked. "Were those all coincidences, or is there a chance that they are connected?"

"I don't believe they are connected to any syndrome I have seen. But we will run genetic testing so that when you get this question in the future, you can say with confidence that she is fine."

*Thank God*, I thought. We needed to hear his positive analysis. A highly respected geneticist reviewed Mackenzie's file and personally gave her a thorough checkup. Mandi and I breathed a sigh of relief, hugged, and felt we could finally relax. I was never happier to be wrong in my life.

Exactly one week later, on a Monday morning in mid-January, the house phone rang. "The doctor has Mackenzie's genetic test results, and he wants to review them with you and your wife."

"Can't you just tell us over the phone?" I asked.

"No, we don't discuss test results over the phone. The doctor will need to visit with you in person to go over the results."

I could see where this was going. There was no reason to call us to give us a clean test result. The doctor could have waited until we came in later that day, knowing we never missed a day to visit Mackenzie. But he didn't.

We gathered our things quickly and headed to the car. In yet another long drive to the hospital, neither of us said a word. We were sick to our stomachs, wondering what was possibly wrong with our baby this time.

We arrived, scrubbed in, and entered the NICU. Dr. Eyal saw us and asked us to follow him to his office. Upon entering, there was a medical encyclopedia on the table. It was open to a page that had several sketches and also a lot of medical terminologies. Instantly, I knew that what we were dealing with was rare. I silently said a prayer while I pulled the chair out for Mandi and helped her sit down.

The doctor sat next to us at a small circular table. "It appears that Mackenzie has a very rare chromosomal deletion of the short arm of the eighteenth chromosome. There can be significant prevalence of seizures and neurological dysfunction. And it is also likely that there will be some level of cognitive impairment."

Mandi instantly began to sob. I placed my arm around her and squeezed her close to me. I then turned to the doctor and asked a series of questions that immediately came to mind.

In a quiet, subdued voice, I asked, "Is it compatible with life? Does it have a high mortality rate?"

"Based on what I am reading and what I have researched, some of these children do quite well," he said. "It is not always bad. In my practice, I have told mothers before that their child would be cognitively impaired, and they turned out to be fine. One never knows in these rare syndromes just how things will play out."

He was obviously trying to comfort us and paint as optimistic a picture as possible, but Mandi and I both realized it was likely we would be raising a special needs child.

"I don't want the kids to make fun of her," Mandi said tearfully as she absorbed the emotional news.

Mandi's comment nearly broke my heart. I know kids can be brutal to other children at times. While it's better in today's society than when I was growing up, it still happens way too frequently.

"Babe, Mackenzie will grow up with two parents who love her. We will give her every chance to succeed and be happy." In truth, there was little I could say that was going to provide comfort.

The doctor informed us that Dr. Martinez would be at the hospital the next day to go over the specifics of the genetic test.

The news we just received was more than overwhelming. It was suffocating. The nurses had all been informed of Mackenzie's diagnosis before we arrived, so when they saw us exiting the doctor's office, they offered the best words of comfort they could. Still, we both needed a minute to compose ourselves before going to see Mackenzie.

"We can take you to the conference room," one nurse said. "You can have some privacy and talk things through. We'll take good care of Mackenzie."

Mandi and I headed out the NICU doors, took off our gowns, and walked thirty feet to the hospital staff conference room. There, with the door shut, we openly sobbed in each other's arms. We cried for our dreams. We cried for the future that had once again changed so drastically. And we especially cried for our baby girl, whose own future was suddenly much more cloudy and obscure.

After some time, we decided we needed to relay the news to our immediate family. Our first call was to Mandi's dad. We agreed it would be best to talk with him first and allow him to help break the news to Mandi's mom.

"Dad ..." Mandi began. Her emotions welled up inside her, and she had a difficult time getting the next words out. "Mackenzie was diagnosed with a rare syndrome. The doctor said she could have seizures and be cognitively impaired." We clarified what the doctor told us and gave him what little information we had.

Like the little girl who had hugged her father and wept during their wedding dance, Mandi seemingly clung to her dad through that phone call. His heart breaking, Mr. Skip calmly and carefully chose his words like he always did, steadying his daughter in her time of crisis and reassuring us both.

"We will do whatever we have to do to get her to her A-game," he said. "We don't know where that is right now, but we'll do all we can as a family to make sure she is healthy, loved, and has the best life possible."

Mandi's parents told us later that Mr. Skip went home early that day to tell Miss Sheri in person. She had been shocked to see him walk through the door, but she immediately knew something was wrong with Mackenzie and feared the worst had happened. After hearing the diagnosis, she felt a slight sense of relief that Mackenzie was still with us and that whatever lay ahead would be tackled as a family.

Mandi and I placed subsequent calls to my parents. My dad processed the information and did not have much to say. My mom said she wasn't surprised and had suspected something might be wrong with Mackenzie, though she offered no specifics. We left the conference room emotionally worn out and went back into the NICU to spend time with our girl.

The next day, we met with Dr. Martinez to go over the details of the genetic test. He had a sympathetic bedside manner, honed over years of sharing difficult news with families. We met in the conference room Mandi and I had shed tears in the day before.

Dr. Martinez carried with him a binder and an envelope containing two pieces of paper. These were the genetic results of Mackenzie's blood test. One piece of paper had medical data on it while the other was a karyotype image of all twenty-three pairs of Mackenzie's chromosomes. As he handed them to us, I immediately noticed that the syndrome name was different than what the doctor told us the day before.

"This says '18q-,'" I commented to Dr. Martinez.

"Yes, that's correct. Mackenzie has a terminal deletion of the q, or long, arm of the eighteenth chromosome."

"The doctor yesterday told us that it was 18p-," I replied. "What's the difference?"

Dr. Martinez paused for a few seconds before continuing. "I'm sorry you were told that. While on the same chromosome, this is a different syndrome with a different possible outcome."

Once again, Mandi and I were stunned. We had spent the night researching a syndrome Mackenzie did not have! I had to rein in my frustration so Dr. Martinez could tell us more about the correct diagnosis.

"I have only seen one other child with this syndrome in my career," he stated. "Based on my initial research, this particular syndrome appears to have a wide range of outcomes. Some are more severely challenged and have greater physical disabilities than others."

"So, is this a fatal condition?" I asked.

"Based on my research and knowledge of the previous patient, there's nothing to indicate that. It is very rare, so not much is known about these outcomes."

Dr. Martinez offered his business card and asked us to follow up with him if we had any questions. He pledged to stay in touch with us and do some research on his own. Since the syndrome was so rare, there was little medical knowledge or data available. Forced to absorb this new information, there was virtually nothing we could do other than return home and study this new condition online.

Following the meeting, we once again made a quick trip into the NICU to see Mackenzie before heading home. The smiles that typically accompanied our trips to see our daughter were replaced by sadness and fear. It was impossible to hide our pain and confusion. Leaning over the edge of Mackenzie's crib, Mandi and I cried together, trying to make sense of this latest plunge on the NICU roller coaster.

\*\*\*

The diagnosis was yet another dagger in our hearts. The shock and fear accompanying her birth, the staph infection that nearly took her life, the diagnosed congestive heart failure, and now the syndrome diagnosis. We were up, and then we were back down. The NICU roller coaster is not for the faint of heart, and it was not over yet.

Mackenzie still struggled with feeding and consuming all her calories orally. Her cleft palate, while small, still did not allow her to generate suction properly to nurse. We had tried a modified bottle, researched feeding techniques, and even attempted to use the in-house NICU transition room to simulate a home environment in hopes of getting Mackenzie to drink her allotted calories for the day.

Without progress, we were looking at the likelihood of Mackenzie needing to go through surgery to place a gastric feeding tube. A "G-tube," as it's commonly called, is a small, plastic peg-like device surgically implanted directly into the stomach through the outer abdominal wall. Essentially, it's made to bypass the mouth and esophagus and allow direct nourishment and liquids through the tube into the stomach.

When we were forced to consider the option of placing a G-tube in Mackenzie, we were told that the surgery was relatively straightforward but, there would be a recovery period of several days, and there were always risks. We were also informed that this was our only realistic ticket home, Mackenzie could not stay in the NICU indefinitely, and the G-tube would be her best chance to gain strength and grow, given her feeding problems.

Mandi and I both steadfastly refused to allow them to perform what we considered to be an unnecessary surgery on our daughter. We had no appetite to tempt fate with all that had already gone wrong and introduce another invasive procedure into the mix. We would keep trying until Mackenzie learned to feed from the bottle. At some point, we reasoned, her instincts had to kick in and allow her to eat normally.

Like we would discover time and time again, things were not simple or straightforward when it came to Mackenzie. Mackenzie's a zebra, not a horse. In other words, she looked and acted like a typical premature child in so many ways, but her "zebra stripes," in this case, her rare genetic makeup, set her apart from the typical pediatric NICU patient.

Mandi and I continued to try the bottle at every feeding in hopes that Mackenzie would eventually learn to take the entire contents and save us from a difficult decision. We would chart her progress with the nurses, who were as dedicated as we were to making sure Mackenzie got home without another procedure. But for every step forward, we would experience a setback that challenged our sense of optimism.

During many feedings, I noticed Mackenzie would turn red and scream. Other children happily took their bottles, but Mackenzie seemed not only to refuse but be extremely uncomfortable. Once again, I turned to the internet. *This study talks about reflux in premature babies. I wonder if this is what is happening?*

We were determined to show the nurse what we thought could be the answer to our prayers. After all, we could treat reflux! Mandi and I had spent weeks attempting to introduce the bottle to Mackenzie. We knew full well that if we could not get Mackenzie to eat, a G-tube placement would be the only solution.

It was well after 7:00 p.m. when the nurse came over to watch as we fed our daughter. "See how she's arching her back and screaming?" I told her. "That could be reflux. Based on published research, the 18q- babies have lower muscle tone, which could mean she's unable to keep the contents in her stomach."

The night nurse agreed to ask the charge nurse that evening to come and look while it was happening. She returned with a report I was not interested in hearing.

"She said she was busy, and that she would bring it to the attention of the neonatologist tomorrow," the nurse said.

After nearly four months in the NICU, we were tired of the roller coaster and wanted off at the first stop. Frustration set in, and I'd had enough of my observations being dismissed. "You tell the charge nurse that unless she and the medical team want to hear from my attorney, she'll do her job and come out and watch what one of her patients is going through as it's happening."

The nurse turned and again walked to the back office. This time, the charge nurse returned, visibly frustrated herself, and motioned Mandi and me to the conference room in a hasty fashion. The night nurse shut the door behind us, and the charge nurse instantly raised her voice and began to point her finger in my direction.

"You have no idea what I was doing in that office!" she said in a hostile tone. "For your information, I was working on another patient's case when you called me away for something that can wait until tomorrow."

At this point, I had reached the limit of my patience. I don't consider myself a confrontational person, preferring to listen, reason, and collaborate if possible. But that clearly was not going to be effective at this point, and I was not about to put up with any of the attitude being displayed.

"First, don't point your finger at me. You had an opportunity to see a patient exhibiting symptoms that could very well be causing a major issue with her feeding. I'll be damned if we're going to put our child under the knife before we exhaust every possibility that could help her. If you want a lawsuit, you keep going down the road you are and ignoring your professional responsibility."

I was visibly angry and extremely direct. Mandi was emotionally exhausted at the end of another long day. Upset, she was crying at the circumstances but having none of the excuses either.

"We have sat in this hospital for nearly four months," Mandi said. "I'm tired of being here, and I will not put my child through an unnecessary surgery without knowing if something as simple as reflux is causing her feeding problem. Run the test, or we'll be back tomorrow with legal help."

I'm confident that other words not suitable for children were used in the discussion. In fact, I later apologized for my choice of language but not for being upset and certainly not for advocating for our daughter.

The next day, Dr. Eyal called us into his office upon our arrival. "We will perform the reflux test," he said. "But let's not threaten the staff with legal action. They are only trying to do their jobs."

Mandi and I had decompressed from the night before and came into the NICU ready to collaborate and not argue. Ultimately, Dr. Eyal agreed to try ruling out reflux as a major problem.

"I apologize for last night," I said. "I rarely have that reaction. However, I'm serious in trying to exhaust every possibility without another surgery."

Dr. Eyal agreed and ordered the twenty-four-hour test. Ultimately, he knew we were prepared to do whatever it took to take care of our child. And we knew the staff was doing the best they could. They were good people. But sometimes, emotions will get the best of you. I had to speak up and protect my child if that was necessary. And I had no plans to abdicate that responsibility to anybody else.

The results of the reflux test were inconclusive. There were signs that reflux was present, but it was not a clear-cut case. Thankfully, the doctor ordered acid-reducing medication to help with any pain Mackenzie was experiencing. We were hopeful that would make her more comfortable and lead to better feedings. But while we saw progress, we did not see enough improvement to avoid placing a G-tube. Feeling defeated and out of options, Mandi and I reluctantly agreed to the surgery to be scheduled as soon as possible. We wanted to take our baby home.

The day of the surgery arrived quickly. We dreaded thinking about handing Mackenzie over to the surgeon and letting them put her under anesthesia and on a ventilator once again.

The nurse from the surgical team soon appeared at Mackenzie's bedside, unplugged the monitors, and began to push the crib into the hallway toward the operating room. There are few feelings as overwhelming as knowing that your child will be put under anesthesia and cut open. It's a feeling Mandi and I had felt several times. I can attest that it never gets easier.

Mandi and I each kissed Mackenzie on the forehead and held her hand for a minute. The nurse waited while we said our prayers and begged God to keep her safe, then wheeled Mackenzie down the long corridor; our eyes were fixated on the crib the entire time until they entered a side hallway and disappeared out of sight.

After a nerve-wracking hour of waiting, a nurse came out to tell us that the procedure was a success, and Mackenzie was moved back to Pod 2 as part of her recovery plan. She would remain on the ventilator until the anesthesia wore off, and she could maintain appropriate respiration independently.

"Thank God," Mandi said as she put her hands over her face to cover her emotions. Finally, something had gone according to plan.

As Mackenzie began to wake up, it was evident she was in considerable pain. Her heart rate continually exceeded the upper threshold limit, and her monitor continued to ding as she cried out in a painful voice.

The nurse watching Mackenzie felt she needed pain medication to manage the discomfort and come off the anesthesia more easily. She consulted with the head nurse, who could approve prescription orders and obtained a dose of morphine administered through the IV that had been placed in a vein in Mackenzie's scalp before the surgery.

With the pain medication pumping throughout her system, Mackenzie calmed down considerably, and her heart rate dropped to within normal limits. However, she was not able to come off the ventilator due to her breathing rate remaining low.

"When can we pull the ventilator?" I asked the nurse.

"When Mackenzie begins to breathe on her own and starts fighting against the machine, that is when we will pull the ventilator tube and go back to the nasal cannula," she replied.

Unfortunately, Mackenzie was not showing any signs of increasing her respiration rate. The nurses continued to adjust her oxygen to keep her within normal limits, but Mackenzie was not responding as expected.

As time continued to go by slowly, it was apparent that Mackenzie was having difficulty with the morphine given to her. Her tiny liver and metabolism rate could not break down the narcotic fast enough to clear her system. The nurse said Mackenzie was "snowed," a term used to indicate she was not responsive due to the reaction to the morphine.

Over the next six to eight hours, Mackenzie required more and more oxygen to maintain her saturation rates. Room air is approximately 21 percent oxygen. Mackenzie was at a 25 percent oxygen rate after the surgery. By the time the clock struck midnight, she had needed well over 50 percent oxygen and was still headed in the wrong direction.

Mandi did not leave Mackenzie's side the entire time. The nurses allowed us to stay overnight in the NICU against typical rules. Feeling sick from worry and lack of sleep, I occasionally dozed off in the reading chair next to her observation table. It was not a restful sleep by any means. Mackenzie's oxygen levels continued to be too low. The alarm would sound, indicating to the nurse she needed to turn the levels up to keep her blood oxygen saturation levels within appropriate limits. My eyes would open, and I would instantly check to see the oxygen levels she was registering.

Nearly twelve hours after the morphine was administered, Mackenzie's oxygen levels began to stabilize. It was near 6:00 a.m. at this point, a full seventeen hours since her surgery. Mandi had been up the entire night, refusing to sleep until she knew Mackenzie was safe, and the ventilator could be pulled. While I had dozed off in the rocking chair a few times, I felt sick and sleep-deprived.

Around 7:30 a.m., Mackenzie began to wake up and fight the ventilator. The nurses asked us to leave while they pulled out her endotracheal tube. When we returned a short while later, Mackenzie had her eyes open and appeared to have no ill effects from the morphine scare. Mandi still refused to go home, staying with Mackenzie until noon while I went home to get a few hours of sleep and let the dog out. Absolutely exhausted, she was determined to see it through and know her baby was safe and recovering before she left.

\*\*\*

Mackenzie slowly began to heal and improve following her surgery. She was gaining weight and progressing at a rate that would have us home in a matter of weeks. Still, using the new feeding tube was very intimidating for two parents who were still shell-shocked from the entirety of the NICU experience.

The nurses showed us how to hook up the feeding tube to the "button" in Mackenzie's stomach. It eventually became second nature, but it was a task to learn in the beginning.

After hooking up the tube and connecting the large sixty-cubic-centimeter syringe, we poured formula or previously pumped breast milk directly into the tube, plunging down the contents slowly so the milk directly entered the stomach.

The first time I attempted to feed Mackenzie solo, I neglected to cap off the syringe quickly enough, and milk poured into her stomach at a very fast rate. Mackenzie could not handle being "flooded" with that much liquid at one time, and she immediately began vomiting up the contents through her mouth and nose. Choking, she squirmed in her bed while the milk spilled on her blankets and down the crib.

Shaken, I immediately called for help. Chuck, the night nurse, surveyed the situation and quickly fixed my error. But the psychological damage was already done for me. I was worried I had just aspirated my child by missing one of the steps. How was I supposed to feed her with confidence at home if I could not do so in a supervised medical environment?

The entirety of the NICU experience was weighing on my shoulders. My daughter had a hole in her stomach with a peg sticking out. She could not suck from a bottle like a typical child and was still extremely tiny, around five pounds nearly four months since her birth. I had undeniable self-doubts about my ability to care for my own daughter.

Over the next several days, we intensely watched the nurses as they fed Mackenzie through her G-tube. There were a series of steps we needed to master so we could do this independently at home. Right now, it was a two-person job at best. Mandi and I wanted to bring home our baby girl as soon as possible, but we also silently worried we may not care for her well enough to ensure her good health.

Slowly, I began to get the hang of the feedings. The first step was to overcome any apprehension about touching the button and causing her physical pain. Once her wound had sufficiently healed, I had more confidence I could handle this task without hurting my baby. The nurses in the NICU were extremely patient with the parents. They understood we were not medical professionals. With Mackenzie starting to thrive again and having reached her targeted weight, the schedule was finally set for us to go home.

On the morning of February 22, 2010, after 133 days in the NICU, Mandi and I loaded the car with our new car seat, blankets, and anything else we needed. Arriving at the hospital as we had for the previous four-plus months, we climbed from our car, ready to finally go home with our little girl.

Mandi and I had spent the weekend preparing for the arrival of our baby girl, deep cleaning every room and installing hand sanitizer stations throughout the house. We even brought yellow gowns home to ensure that whoever held Kenzie had an extra layer of protection to keep her from getting sick. We were ready!

The nurses had prepared Mackenzie's area for the departure. Many of her regular nurses had worked that day or chose to be there. It was bittersweet. They were instrumental in Mackenzie's NICU journey and had been there through the most challenging moments of her stay. We adored the staff at the University of South Alabama Children's and Women's Hospital and were thankful for the good care they had given our daughter.

Mandi and I signed the discharge papers from the NICU. The nurses detached most of the monitoring equipment from Mackenzie, except for the portable heart rate monitor that would alert us if Mackenzie had any apnea episodes while she was home. Premature babies are at a higher risk of these events than typical children, so Mackenzie would wear the monitor for over a year at home to ensure her safety.

Mackenzie finally got her first look at natural sunlight as we stepped outside into the fresh air. Mandi picked up her tiny girl who was securely tucked away in the baby carrier, gently clicked her into the car seat base, and made sure every fastening was properly adjusted before closing the door.

We waved goodbye to the only home Mackenzie had ever known. We were excited, yet apprehensive. We genuinely wondered if we were up to the task. The safety net of the NICU and the immediate proximity of dozens of medical professionals who cared for Mackenzie was now gone. Like a young child learning to ride a bike, the training wheels for Mandi and me were now officially off.

*My beautiful bride-to-be soaking up the moment at her wedding shower. June 27, 2006*

*Mandi's infectious laugh and outgoing personality were on full display during our wedding reception.  July 22, 2006*

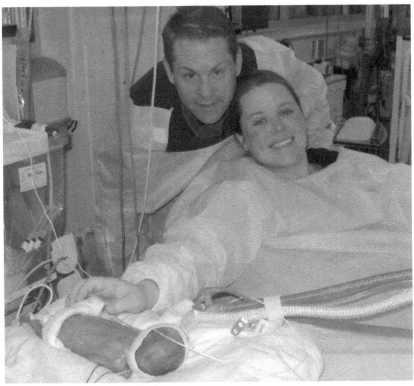

*Mandi meets Mackenzie for the first time after birth. A micro-preemie born at twenty-seven weeks and three days, she weighed just over one-and-a-half pounds at birth, and spent 133 days in the neonatal intensive care unit.  October 13, 2009*

*Newlyweds. My best friend and soulmate. Mandi's radiant beauty always seemed to light up the room.  March 31, 2007*

*The Fishers take their first family photos with Mackenzie at home.*
*May 8, 2010*

*Nearly a decade after Mandi's death, I still reflect daily on our time*
*together. Despite my struggles, I have come to find a measure of peace*
*and solace in the many wonderful memories.  November 16, 2021*

*There's nothing easy about raising a child with a disability. However, the reward of seeing your child persevere and the love you receive back from them is limitless. December 1, 2016*

*Mackenzie and I walk the pier that her mother first took me to eighteen years prior. Time has marched forward, but we still feel Mandi's unconditional love every day. November 16, 2021*

# CHAPTER 8
# Team Fisher

The solid relationship that Mandi and I had was never more evident than in the difficult moments of the early part of Mackenzie's life. Having a special needs child adds an element of stress to a marriage that can test even the strongest partnerships.

The phrase *Team Fisher* started early in our marriage. Mandi liked to use it to signify we were in the same boat and rowing in the same direction. It also provided a reminder that when we got married, we shed the absolute individualism that brought us to that point. We still had our unique personalities, interests, and individual goals. But we knew the best way to accomplish our happiness was to go through life working together to achieve it.

I am enormously thankful I had somebody in my life who "had my back." It was not an unprincipled commitment to staying together no matter what because we were forced to but rather a way of living our life for each other. "I take care of you, and you take care of me," we would often say. And we practiced what we preached.

Mandi and I also had a saying that helped us keep things in perspective. We would often say, "Ones and twos, babe," which meant that on a scale of one to ten, with ten being the most critical, these minor occurrences ranked very low and didn't warrant an exaggerated response. By communicating effectively and understanding how to trust each other's reactions, we made it through some pretty rough times when decisions involving Kenzie had to be made jointly. I'm confident this was part of the reason we stuck together like glue on those issues.

Mandi and I truly learned to keep things in perspective from the early stages of our relationship when we were dating long-distance. When you cannot see the other person's expressions, disappointments, or misdirected anger at relatively minor frustrations, it could lead to significant issues. At that point in time, phone conversations, texts, or emails were "in essence" all we had at our disposal to communicate. We couldn't afford major blowups over minor things. Almost instinctively, we learned to handle the minor inconveniences before they could grow into difficult issues.

\*\*\*

*Team Fisher* may have been used prior to Mandi's pregnancy, but it was never tested as rigorously as it was in the two-plus years Mackenzie was home, and we lived as a family.

While it can be done, raising a special needs child with medical concerns is, ideally, not a job for one person. The myriad of specialists Mackenzie saw, the number of doctors' appointments that were necessary, and the amount of therapy time devoted to helping her were just several aspects of our new, highly stressful lifestyle.

Mandi and I would share the responsibilities of Mackenzie's daily care. We each had areas we focused on individually, but we also made sure we understood what the other person was doing so we were both involved in the parenting process. We tried to make it as fifty-fifty as possible. However, I must confess that Mandi's motherly instincts automatically meant the scales were tipped toward her handling many of the child development issues.

Mackenzie's nursing remained problematic. We continued to feed her exclusively through her G-tube four times each day; at night, we would place her on "continuous feeds" using a feeding pump machine. Because of Mackenzie's gastric reflux, this was the only way we could meet her caloric needs and help her grow.

We could not place Mackenzie on her back in the crib for the first few months for fear of her vomiting and choking. The reflux test may have come back inconclusive in the NICU, but we did not doubt the validity of our concern once we were home. Mackenzie frequently coughed and vomited after a sizable feeding. Therefore, Mandi and I took turns sleeping in the recliner at night while holding Mackenzie upright, the small feeding pump attached and making continuous noise as it slowly pumped breast milk or formula through the tube and into her digestive system.

Mackenzie's daytime feeding cycle was regimented. Every four hours on the dot, she would get fed a bottle of breast milk or formula in a "bolus" fashion, meaning all at once. Every day at 8:00 a.m., 12:00 p.m., 4:00 p.m., and 8:00 p.m., we fed her in this manner. She needed to lay in our arms in an upright position, allowing gravity to help with the digestive process.

Mackenzie's reflux was so severe in the beginning that it was not uncommon to have two or three significant episodes of vomiting each day, which was making it practically impossible for her to gain weight. The gastroenterologist assured us she would likely one day just stop vomiting, as if there were going to be a magic moment when her esophageal sphincter muscle would suddenly work as the body intended. We hoped and prayed for that day to come quickly, though we had doubts that the reflux spigot would abruptly turn off.

Surprisingly, after she turned fifteen months old, the reflux episodes suddenly ceased. Mackenzie was growing larger and stronger over time, and the appearance of her low muscle tone gradually disappeared between fat rolls that are a common sight for a baby not yet walking.

"What is this fat baby doing with a G-tube!" a nurse said jokingly as we visited an orthopedic specialist when Mackenzie was eighteen months old.

"She's living large!" Mandi said without missing a beat.

The room erupted in laughter. Some parents might have been offended. But we found it amusing. We did have a fat baby! Nobody had ever told us that before because Mackenzie had always been less than the first percentile on the growth chart, meaning she was usually the smallest child for every one hundred girls her age.

*\*\**

One of Mackenzie's medical conditions wouldn't get better on its own over time. We had been thinking about the cleft palate repair since the day it was discovered. For an entire year, we knew we were going to have to endure another surgery.

In preparation for the procedure, I made the mistake of watching a video that showed an actual cleft palate surgery. I felt that the additional knowledge could only help me make decisions down the road. Of course, watching the surgery ahead of time also allowed me to see exactly what they would do to my baby.

Mackenzie had a narrow but complete cleft of the hard and soft palate. Essentially, the roof of her mouth and the soft skin at the back of her throat had a v-shape hole that completely separated the two sides. Her uvula, the small piece of tissue that hangs in the back of the throat, was in two separate symmetrical pieces. Her palate was never completely fused in utero.

Before leaving the NICU, the doctors and nurses gave us referrals for the specialists we would need to see once we departed. On the list was finding a plastic surgeon who would repair the cleft palate. Typically, the surgery is done anywhere from ten to eighteen months after birth.

The plastic surgeon whom the hospital referred us to practiced in Mobile. Mandi was working on a project that required her undivided attention at the time, so Gigi went in her place to help with Mackenzie and allow me to concentrate on what the doctor had to say.

The doctor was an older man, perhaps in his late fifties or sixties, thin in stature with a small sliver of a mustache that outlined his upper lip. He wore reading glasses and rarely looked up from the papers he was holding. Following a quick review of Mackenzie's charts, he asked to lean her head back. He shined a small flashlight into Mackenzie's mouth after opening it gently with a tongue depressor. He peered inside for about five or ten seconds before he turned his chair toward us.

Like a scene from a strange movie, an extended pause hung over the room. A solid minute of silence dominated the moment as the surgeon appeared to gather his thoughts. Becoming uncomfortable, I glanced over at Gigi, who was holding Mackenzie. She gave me a puzzled look, which I returned with an equal look of confusion.

"I believe I can do the surgery," the doctor finally said. "It looks pretty straightforward."

I felt immediately apprehensive given his hesitant response. "How many of these procedures have you done?"

"Oh, I would say maybe a dozen or so," he told me.

Well, that settled it. I was not going to risk putting Mackenzie's health and happiness in the hands of a surgeon who had only performed twelve cleft palate repairs in his long career!

"Well, thank you," I said, attempting to find a way to politely bring the conversation to an end. "I appreciate your time."

As we walked toward the car, I turned and looked at Gigi. "So … he won't be doing the surgery."

"I'm so relieved you said that," Gigi said as she laughed. We shared a few jokes about the doctor's mannerisms on the drive home, and I left determined to get as many opinions as it took to find a doctor we trusted.

After doing some research, I came upon two doctors in close proximity who seemed to have great reputations for performing cleft palate repairs. One doctor was in New Orleans, and the other was in Birmingham. Even though New Orleans was closer to Mobile, we chose to visit Birmingham first, setting up the initial consultation in the summer of 2010.

Dr. Grant practiced plastic surgery at Children's Hospital in Birmingham. An experienced surgeon with an excellent reputation, he instantly instilled confidence within us. A relatively young man in his thirties or forties, Dr. Grant wore Mickey Mouse neckties that seemed to reflect his colorful personality. He smiled much of the time and was very engaged in the discussion of Mackenzie's specific condition. The combination of appropriate humor and knowledge of his craft brought out a calm, confident demeanor.

Given our experience with the last surgeon we interviewed, I came prepared to our first meeting with Dr. Grant, ready to ask questions to make sure he passed "the parent test."

"Does Mackenzie's case present as typical, or do you see anything that gives you pause?" I asked after his initial evaluation.

"Mackenzie is very typical of a complete bilateral cleft of the hard and soft palate. It's not exceptionally wide, and I'm confident it will take just one surgery to repair."

That was music to our ears, but I stuck to my plan and asked additional questions. "So, I understand that patients can sometimes develop a small hole in the repair that requires additional surgery. How often does that typically happen, and how does your rate of occurrence compare to other surgeons?"

"You're describing what we call a fistula. The typical average is that 2 to 4 percent of patients will develop a fistula," Dr. Grant said. "My rate is half of that, about 1 to 2 percent of the time."

I nodded my head in acknowledgment and looked out the side of my eye toward Mandi. Her facial expression told me we were on the same page about Dr. Grant.

We traded a few more questions and answers, giving background on Mackenzie's syndrome and NICU stay. Finally, I exhausted our list, so we shook hands and said "goodbye" to the doctor. A small team of nurses immediately came into the room to discuss potential dates for the procedure, the pre- and post-op surgery particulars, and to answer any additional questions we had.

Leaving the office and walking through the waiting room to the clinic, we observed many other children Mackenzie's age. Suddenly, I didn't feel so alone in this journey. These families faced the same challenges we did. While I hated to see any child face the prospect of surgery, I took some measure of comfort in the sense of connection I felt with the other parents.

"I'm sold," Mandi said as we exited the hospital and stepped out into the hot, humid July air. "I liked him. I think he's the one."

"When he told me that his rate of a fistula developing was half that of typical surgeons, he had me," I replied. "He is confident but not cocky."

The good news was we found our surgeon. The bad news was it would be November before they could get us on the schedule to perform the procedure. Don't get me wrong, I was in no hurry to see Kenzie go through this surgery. But I wanted this behind us, marking another milestone we could use to work toward being a typical family. We were tired of feeding our child through a port in her stomach when other kids her age were past the bottle and onto solid foods.

*\*\**

The time between July and November 2010 seemed to fly by. The level of anxiety in our minds rose tenfold the closer we got to the date of the surgery. We were attempting to prepare ourselves mentally for the experience but often found ourselves ruminating on our worst fears about the sedation or level of pain Mackenzie would experience.

As the date of the surgery approached, I felt myself getting tense. Little things were quickly frustrating me, and my mood shifted to feeling very nervous and apprehensive. I knew we needed to go through with the surgery, but I dreaded it as much as anything we experienced in the NICU.

A few days before the surgery, the prep nurse called me with questions that needed answering before bringing Mackenzie to Birmingham. Each question seemed straightforward, except I found myself explaining every level of detail I could to ensure they understood Mackenzie as well as we did. What should have been a fifteen-minute discussion turned into forty-five minutes.

"Mister Fisher, does Mackenzie have any known allergies?" the nurse asked.

"None confirmed by a test, but we believe she may be allergic to shrimp based on family history. Also, she had a bad reaction to morphine after a previous surgery, so we are asking that it not be given to her as a painkiller, that we find another drug that can serve as a substitute."

"Okay, but she's not allergic to morphine, correct?"

"For purposes of this surgery, yes, she is. We do not consent to the use of morphine."

Our thinking was clear on this. If you don't spell out precisely what your feelings are on a particular issue, there is room for interpretation, and we wanted no confusion. The last time Mackenzie had morphine, she required high oxygen levels and was "snowed" for hours. We weren't about to take any chances of going through that again.

Given Mackenzie's surgical history, her still-sensitive premature lungs, and the rare syndrome, the doctor wanted to keep her two nights following the procedure. There was a chance of her going home the next day, but it was likely we would be staying both nights and leaving forty-eight hours after surgery. Staying an extra night was fine by us. Even if we hated hospitals, we knew she was in a great place with highly trained professionals.

We booked a hotel room in downtown Birmingham for the night before. Mandi and I both planned on spending the night in the hospital room with Mackenzie after surgery, so we only reserved the hotel for one night.

Mandi's parents made the four-hour drive up from Mobile, and my mother drove a long thirteen hours from Iowa. Arriving the day before the procedure, we all got together and had dinner the night before. It was good to have family there to provide a distraction, but it did not take away the anxiety we were feeling.

The surgery was set for 7:30 the next morning. Check-in was 5:45 a.m., with plenty of time built-in for surgical preparation. We had given Mackenzie a bath the night before the surgery and attempted to get as much sleep as possible before our 4:00 a.m. wake-up call.

I was restless most of the night. We had placed Mackenzie between Mandi and me on the queen-size bed. There wasn't much room to maneuver without waking everyone up, so I spent a good portion of the evening staring at the ceiling and thinking about the events of the next day.

My alarm sounded at four, and I rose to take a quick shower. I was feeling sick to my stomach from the lack of sleep and the anxiety that had caused it. Mackenzie was comfortably resting in the middle of the bed where Mandi had surrounded her with pillows, making a small fortress so she could not accidentally roll off the mattress and fall onto the floor.

"Babe," I said softly as I gently rubbed Mandi's arm. "It's four thirty. You asked me to make sure you didn't sleep too long so that you had plenty of time to organize and get ready."

"I'm awake," she said. "I've just been lying here asking myself why we're going to do this."

"I know," I replied. "I'm wondering the same thing. But we're here today to get this done. We've known it's been coming for over a year. I hate being here, but I also want to live normally."

Mandi didn't say anything. I could tell she was on the verge of tears, and anything more I said would only have hastened their arrival. "I'll get things packed up if you want to get Kenzie up and ready."

It was a cold November morning. There was a biting chill in the air. Mandi put a new full-length fleece sleeper on Kenzie, who was not pleased that she was being awakened and taken out in the dark, frosty morning.

"I'll get the car and warm it up," I said as Mackenzie voiced her disapproval. "I'll take the bags downstairs, and you can bring the baby and meet me at the front door."

Traffic was very light that time of the morning. We quickly navigated the two or three stoplights before pulling into the drop-off zone in front of the hospital.

Pops and Gigi were waiting there to help Mandi with Mackenzie. I parked in the garage across the street and sprinted through the cold morning air toward the hospital's front doors. Meeting back up with everyone in the lobby, we rode the escalators up to the second floor where the inpatient surgery center was located.

I got Mackenzie checked in and filled out her paperwork while she remained asleep on Mandi's shoulder.

"We'll call you back for pre-op vital sign readings shortly," the nurse said. "Mackenzie will be the first patient Doctor Grant sees this morning."

Sitting next to Mandi, I glanced around to review who else was in the waiting area. I watched as multiple families arrived, checked in, and started their paperwork. I wondered what brought their children to the hospital, what their families must be going through. I tried to tell myself others were facing something similar as we were, and we weren't the only parents going through this today, even though it felt like it.

Mandi's parents and my mom were talking to pass the time. I wasn't in much of a chatty mood. I kept a close eye on the clock as it ticked past 6:00 and then on to 6:15. The anxiety of the moment was eating away at me. I played the scene over and over in my mind, giving Kenzie to the nurses and returning to the waiting room with a pager and a prayer.

"Mackenzie Fisher?" A nurse came around the corner holding a large folder. Mandi and I stood up, looking at each other with anxious eyes, and made our way to a small set of cubicles just off the waiting room's main floor.

"The third one on the right, Dad," the nurse said.

Mandi sat down with Kenzie in the chair next to the small desk. They needed to evaluate Kenzie for any illnesses and check her vital signs before being approved for the procedure.

"Oxygen level is ninety-three," the nurse said as she wrote down the number in the chart.

"That's her normal," Mandi said. "She was a micro-preemie and was on a ventilator three times."

"Well, I would say that's good then, Mom," the nurse replied.

She continued checking Kenzie's temperature, blood pressure, and asking us additional questions—many of which another nurse had covered with me two days prior on the phone.

"We're just verifying that you do not want to give her morphine for the pain, correct?" she asked.

"Correct," I replied. "We asked for a suitable substitute because she did not do well with morphine during a previous procedure."

"Got it," the nurse said. "I see the notes here."

We reviewed the remainder of the prior conversation, confirming all the details I had already shared. The time was now approaching 6:45 a.m. We were inside an hour until the start of the surgery. After thirteen months of watching monitors, reading charts, and asking questions, I was confident I knew Kenzie's normal vitals, and I knew we were ready to proceed with the surgery.

"Okay, have a seat out in the waiting area. A nurse will call you back momentarily, and you'll accompany Mackenzie to her prep room. You'll meet with the anesthesiologist, and he'll answer any questions you have. Doctor Grant will then come in and talk to you before the procedure starts. Do you have any questions for me?"

My mind was racing. Mandi was holding Kenzie close, already anticipating having to hand her over to a nurse.

We shook our heads to indicate "no" and returned to our seats. Fifteen minutes had passed when the moment arrived.

"Mackenzie Fisher?"

I looked at Mandi. We had reached the point of no return. The family wished us the best and told us to stay strong. With that, we followed the nurse down a series of hallways until reaching the prep room. No more did we get into the room when there was a knock at the door.

Dr. Bussey was a highly experienced anesthesiologist and came strongly recommended by the nurses. He was sensitive to our prior issues with surgery and knew we were downright frightened at the prospect of putting Kenzie to sleep again.

"I know you're concerned, and I have read over Mackenzie's information thoroughly. You have quite the history already for this young girl," he said. "I see nothing in her chart or this morning's vitals that cause me concern. I would say she's ready."

Dr. Bussey reassured us, answered a few additional questions from Mandi, and then walked out the door.

"Good morning," Dr. Grant said as he knocked and came through the door just a few minutes later.

Mandi had been playing with Mackenzie on the bed, keeping her occupied. I used my phone to snap a couple of pictures of them together. Mandi then took the phone from me and did the same as I posed with my baby girl.

"Good morning," we replied.

He looked different than the last time we saw him; his cartoon tie was replaced by the all-too-familiar blue surgical scrubs we had seen many times.

"Looks like everything is a go. I just wanted to go over the process one final time, and then we'll take the princess back for the procedure," he said.

"Mackenzie is having a repair of a complete bilateral cleft of the hard and soft palate. To guard against the unlikely possibility that her tongue swells and falls back into her airway, we will put a piece of string through her tongue and leave it hanging from her mouth. If her airway were to become obstructed, we would pull that string so that she could breathe. It rarely happens, but it is a possibility, so we do this as a precaution."

We had known about the string from our first visit with Dr. Grant. He had explained it thoroughly and answered our questions during the first visit. Still, it's a bit alarming to hear that your daughter will have a needle put through her tongue and a surgical string run through the hole.

The nurse unlocked Mackenzie's bed from the wall and began rolling it toward the open door. We accompanied Mackenzie down the hallway until we could go no farther. A set of doors that required a code to enter stood between Mackenzie and the operating room. We knew this feeling well. It's a feeling you never want to experience as a parent. You no longer have control when giving your child to medical professionals so they can fix what nature got wrong.

Tears flowed down Mandi's cheeks as she hugged Kenzie. I did my best to hold it together so that both of us weren't outwardly sobbing in the hallway.

"I love you, Kenzie-bug," I said as I kissed the top of her head.

"We'll take great care of her, Dad," the nurse said as the set of double doors opened, exposing the long, cold hallway that led to the operating room.

Mandi said "goodbye" in much the same fashion, then wiped her tears. Glancing behind us one final time, we saw Mackenzie's profile get smaller and smaller until the doors swung shut.

We returned to the waiting room and sat next to our parents. Mandi seemed relatively composed. To that point, I had held it together—primarily to help keep Mandi strong. But inside, I was a mess. With my anxiety building as we approached the start of the procedure, I broke down.

I lowered my face into my hands to hide the overwhelming feeling of hurt and fear enveloping me. I kept seeing my little girl's face as we handed her over. I remembered the scariest moments of the NICU and silently wondered when all this would end so we could just be normal.

"Jase," my mom said. "She's going to be all right. She's in good hands."

I could not stop worrying. I worried about her not waking up. I worried about the pain she would experience. And I worried about the success of the surgery, nervous we would again defy the odds that were supposed to be in our favor and end up needing a second procedure. Overwhelmed with anxiety, I could not reply to my mom. I openly started sobbing.

Other families in the waiting room were watching and undoubtedly wondering what was happening, perhaps fearing the worst. I realized their children might have a scarier procedure ahead of them that day. Perspective does help. But it didn't matter in that particular moment. I was frankly unable to hold it together.

I stayed seated for a few minutes and then decided to excuse myself. I felt guilty that Mandi was comforting me, and I couldn't be more composed for her at that moment. I suppose I had held in the anxiety for so long that it needed to come out. I walked around the hallway for a few minutes, then eventually headed back toward the waiting room.

Mandi met me in the hallway. "The pager went off. There must be an update."

We returned to the waiting room, meeting Dr. Grant as he walked toward us. Still dressed in scrubs, he motioned us over to the side and told us Mackenzie was just fine, but they had a complication. My heart sank.

"We could not intubate Mackenzie," Dr. Grant said. "The smallest tube I was comfortable inserting would not get past the upper trachea. I think it's best to call off the surgery for now until we understand what is obstructing her airway."

I had a strange mixture of emotions. On the one hand, I was glad the surgery didn't happen, and Mackenzie wasn't in pain. On the other hand, like Mandi, I had wanted it over with, and now there was yet another problem that was still undiagnosed. It felt like déjà vu from the NICU. We simply could not catch a break.

"What happens next?" Mandi asked Dr. Grant through her tears.

"You'll need to return for a bronchoscope to see what is causing the obstruction," he said. "It felt like an unnatural narrowing of the upper airway, but we won't know until we can get a scope in and take a look."

Deflated, we listened and took mental notes. We made an appointment to return for the scope, but I was already processing what Dr. Grant had told us and jumping to the worst-case scenario in my mind. Of course, I immediately searched the internet with a description of the symptoms he gave us and came up with several potential problems, none of which were good.

The four-hour ride home to Mobile was long and strange. We felt relieved that Mackenzie was with us, and we were going home. Still, the new issue and potential diagnosis meant even more anxiety was layered on top of our existing emotions.

Three weeks passed by before we returned to Birmingham for the bronchoscope that would help us understand what was occurring.

"Mackenzie has two small nodules on her vocal cords that are consistent with cysts, likely caused by the ventilator rubbing against her voice box while she was in the NICU," the pulmonologist said. "They are almost certainly benign and common in young children that were on ventilators. The nodules were big enough to interrupt the intubation process, but I feel we can safely navigate them for Doctor Grant whenever they can reschedule the procedure. In short, they are nothing to worry about."

A sense of relief came over us. Finally, we had good news! Something had gone our way.

"Mackenzie does have a touch of asthma, though," the doctor said, showing us pictures from the bronchoscope he had just finished. "It's mild, but you can see the red areas here that have more mucous than the other parts of the right lung. It's likely caused by being on the ventilator when she was in the NICU. It shouldn't be a major concern, but it is something to keep an eye on."

Once again, the news was mixed. On the one hand, we could reschedule the cleft palate repair and begin the process of transitioning Kenzie to eat and drink like a typical child. On the other hand, a diagnosis of asthma meant that a simple cold could lead to lower oxygen levels. And if Mackenzie were to get RSV, a respiratory virus in children, it would be even more complicated and concerning.

The first available date for her surgery was Tuesday, March 9, 2011—about eight weeks away. The anxiety for the second attempt was, unfortunately, as palpable as the first. However, I was determined to be calmer and stronger. I made no apologies for being overwhelmed the first time, but I knew I needed to let Mandi focus on Mackenzie instead of having to comfort me.

After checking in and going through the paperwork, Mackenzie's vital signs were once again measured before we took her to the surgical prep area. We were as ready as we could be, tired of the anxiety of waiting and prepared to get this behind us.

"Hello, once again!" Dr. Grant said as he entered the room. "I know you're still worried about putting her to sleep and the pain medication, so nothing has changed for our process since the first time we tried this in November."

With the routine unchanged, Mandi and I nodded, acknowledging that we understood and were ready. Once again, we hugged and kissed Mackenzie and said our goodbyes at the doors to the surgical area. Pushing the knots in our stomachs down, our baby was once again in a surgeon's hands.

I hugged Mandi and kissed her on the forehead. I wanted her to know I would be there if she needed me. Tears welled in her eyes, and we told each other she was going to be okay, we had chosen the best surgeon and medical facility, and we were going to get through this event and the recovery.

Mandi's parents had driven up for the procedure like they had in November; my mom did not, given the distance and time it took to drive to Alabama. Since Mandi was not alone, I decided to head downstairs and look for something caffeinated to drink. I never acquired a taste for coffee and didn't drink colas, so finding a needed boost that wasn't loaded with sugar was sometimes challenging.

The snack shop was just beginning to open its doors when I walked through. I carefully looked through the refrigerated section to find something decent that might wake me up and get me through this two-hour procedure. Spotting a sugar-free energy drink, I paid the small ransom they were charging and headed back to the elevator.

Given that the waiting room had a no food or beverage policy, I walked up and down the hallway to finish my beverage before returning to join the others. I sat down next to Mandi and began participating in the conversation she had going with her parents. I don't recall what we discussed, only that we were in better spirits than the previous surgical attempt, despite still anxiously waiting for the first update.

Finally, the buzzer alerted us that the nurse had an update. We headed up to the front desk. "Mackenzie is asleep. The intubation was successful, and there were no issues. Doctor Grant is ready to begin the procedure."

The first hurdle had been cleared. Mandi and I breathed a sigh of relief but also now knew that this was really going to happen. Mackenzie would be undergoing a painful procedure that would take at least fourteen days to heal.

Sitting in the waiting room, I envisioned what the surgeon was doing at any given moment during the two-hour wait. Since I had watched a video of the procedure, I had a good idea of what Mackenzie was going through. I may not have liked my thoughts, but I didn't regret my decision to watch the video. I took comfort in educating myself, knowing it was far more critical to understand what we were facing than it was to bury my head in the sand and question nothing.

The procedure generally involves slicing through the roof of the mouth near the gumline to the bone, lifting the tissue off, and pulling it together in the middle. Sutures would be used so that the tissue healed together in the middle to form a complete palate. The area next to the gumline where the tissue had been removed would eventually "fill in" while it was healing.

"The procedure is underway, and Mackenzie is doing great," the nurse said as she provided us with a second update. "The next time we come out will be to let you know that the procedure has ended, and Doctor Grant will then come out to answer any questions."

The minutes ticked by slowly as Mandi and I both watched the clock. We had become accustomed to complications with Kenzie, so we half-expected to see a nurse well before the two-hour window was up. However, this time nobody else came to see us until the surgery was done.

"Everything went great! Doctor Grant will be out shortly to talk to you," the nurse said with a smile.

"Oh, thank God!" Mandi said, feeling a sense of relief.

A few minutes later, Dr. Grant appeared in the waiting room. "It went perfectly. No complications. The repair is solid, and I expect a full recovery and a strong new palate. Give her a few weeks to heal, and she can run with scissors!" he said jokingly.

We were elated. We knew Mackenzie would have a period of recovery ahead of her, but she would finally have the chance to eat and drink like a typical child. Still, we were careful not to let our guard down given the complications from the pain medication during her G-tube placement.

Mandi and I steeled ourselves for what we were going to see after the surgery. The nurse guided us back to a small room in the corner off the main hallway. As we pulled the curtain back, we saw our baby still unconscious with a nasal cannula supplying her oxygen. She was puffy and swollen; the aforementioned black string dangled from the edge of her mouth. Braces had been applied to her arms so she could not bend at the elbows and get her hands close to her face.

Mandi and I stood and stared at Mackenzie for a few minutes. We hugged and held each other as we looked at our baby, aching as we anticipated the pain Mackenzie would be experiencing as the sedation wore off.

I took several pictures and texted them to Mandi's parents in the waiting room, letting them know Mackenzie was recovering well. The mere fact that Mackenzie's oxygen levels were good, and she was off the ventilator was great news to us.

Within fifteen or twenty minutes, Mackenzie began to wake up. She was still groggy and not yet recognizing us, but she had come through the surgery and anesthesia without a problem. We could now say the healing had officially started, though we knew there would be many difficult days and nights before we could formally put this behind us.

Mandi was remarkable during the entire experience. She showed her emotions and vulnerability, but it always came with her uncanny ability to compose herself during the most difficult circumstances and find time to comfort others. She needed hugs as well, but there was always a feeling that she was walking right beside me—never ahead and never behind.

After two nights in the hospital recovering, Mackenzie was ready to be discharged and go home. Dr. Grant came by one final time to admire his work. Agreeing that she was ready to go, he cut the string he put through Mackenzie's tongue, pulling it out and leaving a tiny hole that would heal along with the cleft palate repair.

Mackenzie's recovery was largely unremarkable. Dr. Grant had warned us there would likely be one day or night when her pain would seem unmanageable. They didn't understand why this happened, but it usually occurred around seven to ten days after the procedure.

Mandi and I had cleared our schedules for the week of the surgery, but both of us had responsibilities that would take us out of town the following week. I would be gone from Sunday to Tuesday in San Diego and Mandi during the second half of the week, Wednesday through Friday, in Indiana.

Day seven of Mackenzie's recovery was by far the worst. Just as Dr. Grant had warned us, she had an inconsolable day where the pain was more significant than medication or distraction could manage. Unfortunately for Mandi, I was in San Diego getting ready to board a plane to return home on a red-eye flight and arrive in Mobile on Wednesday morning.

"We got no sleep. And when I say no sleep, I mean zero," Mandi said to me as I walked through the door about 9:00 a.m.

"Oh no," I said, feeling terribly guilty. "How bad was it?"

"Horrible," Mandi said. "She screamed and fussed the entire night."

I regretted my trip even more than before I left. Mandi had drawn the short straw—the night Dr. Grant had warned us might occur. Mandi and her mother dealt with the worst of Mackenzie's pain and were both exhausted.

"Way to go, Fish," Miss Sheri said. "Go out of town for night seven, and Kenzie has her worst evening. You couldn't have planned that better if you tried," she said with a hint of sarcasm.

Miss Sheri had dedicated the entire week to helping us out. She stayed each night one of us was gone, assisting with watching Mackenzie and being the extra set of hands we needed while comforting our baby girl.

"I feel horrible," I replied. "I thought for sure it would happen on my watch."

"Well, it didn't," Mandi quipped. "Now, let's hope it's the only bad night she has."

In hindsight, we should have just blocked two weeks off work for this procedure, but we were both somewhat hesitant to ask for too much time off, given how generous our employers had been with us to that point.

The doctors had prescribed a mild painkiller for Kenzie to manage her symptoms. Frankly, the pain medication didn't seem to help much. However, what did help was the Baby Einstein cartoons she loved so much. As long as Baby Einstein was on the video player, Mackenzie seemed happy and tolerated the discomfort without much fussing.

Mackenzie has a strong tolerance to pain. It's been reported through research that many children with Distal 18q-, her syndrome, also have a high pain threshold. Perhaps there's something in her genetic makeup that helps lessen the symptoms of injury or discomfort. All we knew was Mackenzie was proving herself to be one strong little girl.

The surgery was a resounding success. Mackenzie's palate was completely repaired and fully healed within a few weeks of the procedure. However, because of her cognitive impairment and the moderate sensory processing disorder that often accompanies premature babies, learning to eat regular food would be a very slow process. It took months for Kenzie to learn to eat a jar of baby food. For years, she rejected certain textures and foods out of hand. And ultimately, she did not get her G-tube removed until June of 2021.

\* \* \*

Mandi and I were fortunate to have full-time jobs working for good organizations. We both had traveled for work on a fairly regular basis, but we began to think about how we could convert one of our jobs into a non-traveling position. The goal was to have Mandi go part-time or quit working altogether. Ever the planner, I had a strategy for doing just that and a budgeted savings goal in mind for when we could make that decision.

Like any set of plans, circumstances are never static. Adjustments must be made. Ultimately, a few things held us back from making that decision. First, 2010 and 2011 were still tricky years economically. Even though the markets had rebounded some, and the Great Recession had eased a bit, good jobs were still hard to come by. If Mandi were to quit, and we had a financial setback, it might not have been easy for her to get back into the workforce at a place she enjoyed working and that gave her a good level of autonomy.

Second, Mandi liked to talk about a day where she could focus exclusively on Kenzie, but she also enjoyed the social aspect of her job. Mandi was excellent at her work, and she truly enjoyed contributing to her team's success. However, I know she was ready to walk away as soon as we could make it work financially. And she reminded me of it quite often as Mackenzie got older.

Ultimately, what held us back from making that decision was fear. The fear of struggling financially. The fear of going further into debt or perhaps even borrowing against our future. And most of these fears originated with me.

I grew up in a middle-class family, but I struggled to watch my parents get laid off from their jobs when the economy sank. I remember the days of getting free school lunches because my dad lost work, and we fell below the poverty line. And I knew what it was like to shop at second-hand stores because we could not afford anything else.

I started working at the age of fourteen in the hot farm fields of Iowa, detasseling corn and walking rows of soybeans to chop down weeds. I baled hay, worked in a henhouse, and had a newspaper route that got me up before dawn. I was never afraid of working hard. What I was fearful of was not having any work or a paycheck when I needed it. That fear motivated me to go to college, to give myself the best chance of finding a good job that allowed me to weather the inevitable downward economic cycles ahead.

The truth was that Mandi going part-time wasn't just a logical decision for me, it was an emotional one. Even if it wasn't my job directly, I still saw the pitfalls if we had planned wrong. I still felt the anxiety of suddenly falling behind with our bills if we caught a bad break. I truly wanted Mandi to quit or ask to go part-time when the time was right, but I also wanted to ensure we could take care of our family with just one job. My job.

As a family, we hit our maximum out-of-pocket expenses on our health insurance plan every year from 2009 to 2012. I joked that I should just write our insurance company a check up front so we could save the endless amounts of paperwork. I have little doubt this also influenced my decisions. If Mackenzie were healthy and typical, Mandi likely would have stopped working, and we wouldn't have looked back.

The undeniable fact was Mackenzie wasn't typical, and she wasn't likely to be the picture of good health in the immediate future. In her first year home, we saw multiple specialists and sought several second opinions. Plastic surgery. Cardiology. Two pulmonologists. Neurology. Endocrinology. Gastroenterology. Pediatric ophthalmology. Orthopedics. And there were still the routine medical visits, well-baby checkups, and dentistry. We knew there could be more surgeries, endless specialists, procedures, medications, and nonreimbursable medical expenses. These factors weighed heavily on us as a family and probably led to much of my hesitation in shifting to just one full-time job in the household.

In hindsight, this is one of my biggest regrets. I wish Mandi had had more time to spend with Mackenzie in the early days, working with her on those areas she was developmentally behind and just enjoying her daughter instead of worrying about a difficult client somewhere in Nebraska.

***

Many people have experienced the dilemma of a good job offer—one too good not to consider strongly.

In early May 2012, I received a phone call at my home office from the owner and chairman of the board of RuffaloCODY. I had been an employee for the better part of twenty years at that point.

"Jason, I wanted to reach out to you and let you know of some movement at the company and some opportunities coming up. I am stepping down from the day-to-day responsibilities and handing the reins over to Duane," Al said.

Duane was the supervisor who had allowed me to work from home and move to Mobile when I was dating Mandi. A close confidant and friend, Duane had much to do with the paths I traveled in my adult life to that point.

"Duane is interested in talking to you about a position located in Cedar Rapids, where we want our executive leadership to be placed. Are you interested in talking about the opportunity?" Al said.

Based on what Al described, I assumed the job would be one I enjoyed, and I would receive an acceptable offer. I was short on precise details, but when the owner of the company calls you and asks if you're interested ... .

"Yes, absolutely," I replied.

My mind was racing with possibilities. Was this the job that would allow Mandi to quit working or go part-time? What would that mean for Mackenzie's medical treatment? What would we tell Mandi's family? Would Mandi even want to move to Iowa?

"It's not my A choice, but the thought of going part-time and focusing on Kenzie is appealing," she said at dinner that evening.

"Besides the cold weather, what would hold you back from saying yes?" I asked curiously.

"I don't see myself being buried in Iowa," she replied succinctly.

Wow. That was a statement I was not expecting. At that moment, I knew that unless Mandi had a change of heart, I couldn't move our family again from the home we had planned to raise our babies in, even if this job was a potential career changer.

"Okay," I said. "I will call Al back tomorrow and turn him down."

"What's your interest in the job?" she asked. "Is it to move back to Iowa, or is it genuinely a career interest?"

"It's not Iowa. I honestly don't want to move again. I'm perfectly happy here and at home in Alabama. The job sounds like a career-changing possibility. Those don't come around every day."

"Ask Al if there is any room for negotiation on where the job can be located," said Mandi.

I had asked Al on the first call if the position had to be based in Iowa, which he affirmed. There was no reason to think he would change his mind. Still, it was worth asking.

Moving would require changing all Mackenzie's specialists. The quality of the medical care she would receive in Iowa City would be comparable to Children's Hospital in Birmingham. The University of Iowa had a new children's hospital that was very highly rated. The truth was, Mackenzie already had doctors who knew her in Alabama who had performed procedures on her and were familiar with her syndrome. With her rare condition, it was vital we didn't have to refight the learning-curve battle.

"Al, I'm interested in the position, but I'd like to ask you to reconsider the role being located in Cedar Rapids. I feel I'm the right candidate, but I don't feel it's the right time to move my family."

Al was understanding of the circumstances but held firm to his requirement that the position be in Iowa. "Duane needs his team here in Cedar Rapids. I certainly understand your situation, but we'll have to continue with the search if you're not interested in moving."

"I'm sorry, babe," Mandi said when I told her. "Something else will come along that will be interesting and fulfilling."

Mandi knew I was hoping for a new role in the organization to continue my professional growth. Still, she was right in that I currently had a great job. But for whatever reason, something just didn't sit well with me when I told Al "no."

Several days passed, and I was still brooding about the job, contemplating what I might have given up. Through the window, I watched Mandi push Kenzie in her play car down the sidewalk. I thought about what it would be like if she could do that every day, and we weren't both traveling all the time. I walked outside to join them.

"Babe, I'm not sure that turning down the opportunity without hearing more about the details was the best move," I said, staring down at the grass next to the sidewalk.

"I don't understand why you can't let this go," she said with a sigh.

"I feel that I'm passing up a great opportunity. That isn't easy for me. I think about our future, you possibly quitting your job, and wonder if turning this down is the right move."

"Fine," Mandi said, clearly exasperated with me. "Call Al back and tell him you want to interview. This will drive you crazy if you don't at least hear what they have to say."

I felt a strange mixture of satisfaction and guilt. I was happy that I would be learning more about the job, but I was exploring something that was not Mandi's first preference, and I knew it. Our marriage was always first in my decision hierarchy. This decision was going against the grain to an extent, and it felt awkward to be in this position.

I called Al back and told him I wanted to reconsider and work out a date for the interview. I would fly up on the fifth of June, meet with Duane and other members of the team, and fly home the next day. I did not tell my family in Iowa I was coming into town because I did not want to get their hopes up about us moving back.

Mandi was open enough to the possibility that she was looking for houses online. But I knew I would still have a tough sell ahead of me if I liked the terms of the job. I had heard Mandi loud and clear when she spoke of her preference. Yet, my ego now put me in a position where I was interviewing for a job I might not be able to accept unless the offer was overwhelming enough to convince my wife. What that would take, I wasn't completely sure.

I had faced other difficult decisions and listened to a few lucrative job offers before. I was often open to the possibilities, but I had always turned them down because I put family first. However, the tough part about this situation was that, in many ways, I considered RuffaloCODY to be family as well. Many of my closest friends worked there.

I was hoping the offer was either really good or very disappointing, making my decision easier either way. I was fearful it was a great career move but perhaps not lucrative enough.

As fate would have it, the job decision would become the least of my worries. A destiny awaited me that I couldn't have possibly imagined, one that would change the course of my entire life in the blink of an eye.

*\*\**

In early May 2012, I began to experience occasional heart palpitations. They would occur at all times of the day and night in a seemingly random way. Given that it was time for my annual physical, I booked an appointment with my physician and had a complete checkup.

"You need to eat," the doctor said to me. "You're too thin for your height."

"I do eat … all the time," I replied. "I'm on my bike, riding about one hundred miles a week. Mandi can't keep food in the house because I'm constantly hungry."

Over time, Mandi and I had settled into a groove with Kenzie, and I had returned to a regular cycling routine. I had a twelve-and-a-half-mile loop around the adjacent neighborhoods and would usually ride two loops three to four times a week, weather permitting.

"I've been having some weird sensations where it feels like my heart is skipping beats," I said to the doctor. "I've never felt them before."

The doctor finished his exam and had the nurse escort me back to the lab, where they drew blood and took several chest X-rays.

"You're very fit but could stand to gain a few pounds," the doctor said. "Otherwise, all looks good. I don't hear anything with your heart that would give me concern, but we'll check your labs and X-rays and let you know if anything comes back abnormal."

The following day, I flew to St. Louis for a work conference to meet with our sales and operations team. More importantly, I got the chance to see my friends and colleagues again for the first time in many months.

"Those things are bad for you," one of my colleagues said as he saw me sipping on a sugar-free energy drink as I checked in to the hotel.

"So is four hours of sleep at night because of a restless two-year-old," I quickly replied with a laugh. "Don't judge me."

In my room, I noticed I had received a voicemail while I had my phone off during the flight.

"Jason, this is Brittany, a nurse with Family Practice. The doctor would like you to come back in for another chest X-ray. Something showed up on your X-ray, and we want to take a closer look."

I immediately called back. After getting transferred to her line, I nervously asked, "Something's wrong?"

"Not necessarily," Brittany said. "The doctor just wants a better image to rule out any potential issues."

"But you saw something?" I said as I sought clarification.

"The doctor did see something, but, again, the X-ray is inconclusive, which is why we need another image. The doctor will talk to you about that when you come back for the X-ray."

It was only Tuesday, and I wasn't scheduled to depart until Thursday. The earliest I could get back in for the follow-up X-ray was Friday. A mild panic set in. I contemplated what they possibly could have seen on the X-ray. Were the heart palpitations related to some sort of blockage? Did they see something in my lungs that made them suspicious? I was cycling one hundred miles a week, had never smoked, and led a relatively clean lifestyle—absent the occasional shot of caffeine.

I'm not the kind of person who can patiently wait and easily write off such uncertainty. Needing answers, I turned to my computer and looked up the possibilities. Seeing nothing positive online, I needed some reassurance that I was overreacting. I called Mandi.

"Babe, the doctor wants me to come back for a second chest X-ray. It could be a bad image, but they wouldn't tell me why they were concerned. I'm nervous."

"Really? I'm sure it's nothing," she replied. "They are probably just being thorough."

After a few minutes of her comforting me and hearing Kenzie updates, we said "goodbye" and hung up. I tried putting the X-ray out of my mind. But like so many other times in my life, the circumstances being out of my control drove my fear and occupied my thoughts.

Three days was a long time to sit and think about my mortality. I needed to do something, so I called Michael. "Hey, man. I have just a few minutes before I need to go back into meetings, but I wanted to see if you can get me some quotes. I know I'm underinsured, and it's probably time I addressed it."

Michael had entered the insurance and financial business about a year earlier and had set Mandi and me up with small-term life policies when he began his work.

"Let me run some numbers on some different policies, and I'll come over when you get back into town," he replied.

I knew Mandi and I were significantly underprepared when it came to this type of financial planning. All our focus had been on Kenzie's health, not our own. As many young people do, we procrastinated on making out a will and had only taken out short-term life policies in addition to what our employers offered. Discussing the subject was uncomfortable. There was always another day to take care of it.

The reality was, I was ten years older than my wife. I couldn't bear the thought of leaving her and Kenzie struggling because I never ensured their financial security. The inconclusive X-ray made me recognize I had the responsibility of protecting them after I was gone, in addition to taking care of them in life.

\*\*\*

As soon as I got home that Friday morning, I made my way to the doctor's office to retake the chest X-ray.

"The doctor just read your second X-ray, and what we were concerned about did not show up. It was just a bad image," the nurse said.

All my worrying was for naught. I was given a clean bill of health. Utterly relieved, I headed home.

\*\*\*

Memorial Day weekend was upon us. Mandi, Mackenzie, and I went to her parents' house to celebrate the holiday. We ate barbecue and swam, thoroughly enjoying the family time together.

A few days later, Michael came to the house to discuss our insurance and fiscal situation. As he was making his way up the stairs, he peeked inside Mandi's office.

"Hi, Mandi," he said in his usual jovial manner.

"Michael, why are you trying to sell my husband something we don't need?" Mandi replied with equal good humor.

"Just doing my job, Mandi … ."

Michael was chuckling as he walked into my office. We made some small talk before he started going through a quick presentation.

"Do you have a will prepared?" Michael asked.

"No, I need to get on that," I replied sheepishly.

"Yeah, that's step one. You honestly need more than what I'm about to quote you, but this will fit your budget for now, and we can work on the long-term plan later."

"Okay, let's cover me for now, and we'll discuss the bigger plan once I get the will completed." We would revisit the coverage in a few weeks after knowing more about my job situation. The good news was I was covered immediately and only needed to do minimal tests in the coming weeks to verify my health.

Michael said "goodbye" to Mandi and headed back to his office. I set the paperwork on my desk to be filed while we waited for the next steps from the insurance company. I felt relieved.

The next day was Friday, June 1, 2012. At around nine thirty that morning, less than twenty-four hours after purchasing a half-million-dollar life insurance policy for me because I feared my own death, Mandi died from an undiagnosed, sudden blood clot. "It was a massive, deep-vein thrombosis," the medical examiner later told me. "It likely traveled up her leg and got caught in her back."

The cause of the clot was never listed by the medical examiner. There are numerous factors that can increase the risk of blood clots. However, Mandi had just received a clean bill of health in a physical several weeks before her death, so many of those risks could be ruled out. After several weeks of research, it became evident that the new generation birth control Mandi had been placed on after Kenzie was born was the prime suspect. It carried a significantly higher risk factor than other forms of oral contraceptives, and unbeknownst to Mandi, the Food and Drug Administration had taken steps just weeks before to have warning labels added to the medication due to the increased risk of blood clots.

The irony of me adding life insurance to my policy the day before her death was overwhelming. I felt a strange sense of guilt and relief at the same time. The guilt came from even starting the discussion about life insurance and wills, somehow making it relevant in our life when it wasn't before. But I also felt a weird relief understanding the genuine possibility that I would have suddenly had many more problems had I covered Mandi with any of that policy.

I naturally figured I would be the first to die. But the order of the universe was turned upside down. God's timeline was not my timeline—and I had no say in the matter. I had to deal with a new world, a world I could never imagine in my worst nightmare.

The new job was never meant to be. Instead of flying to Iowa for the interview with Duane and Al, they flew to Alabama and comforted me on the day I buried my wife.

My career aspirations were rendered all but meaningless the moment the doctor gave me the news. Instantly, I reflected on Mandi's chilling words a couple of weeks before. "I can't see myself being buried in Iowa," she had said. For many years, I blamed myself for making Mandi's final days more stressful than they should have been. Though my intentions were good, I pushed harder than I should have, given her initial response. I felt as though I let her down—and I carried that guilt with me for a long time.

# CHAPTER 9
# Half My Soul

To say my mind was foggy with grief that first night after Mandi died is an understatement, and to this day, I still don't know why I felt compelled to answer the phone.

"Hello?" I said, my voice raspy from crying.

"Can I please speak with Mister Jason Fisher, husband of Amanda Fisher?" a woman asked in a soft, polite tone.

"This is he," I replied, curiously trying to figure who was calling me from Birmingham.

"Mister Fisher, I'm so sorry for your loss. I'm with an organization in Birmingham that harvests corneas from organ donor patients to help save another person's sight. Our records indicate Amanda wanted to be an organ donor."

I felt my airway constrict, and my response was staggered and uneven. "Yes, she's an organ donor."

"I realize this is an extremely difficult moment for you. However, time is so important in organ donation ... we would like your permission to harvest your wife's corneas."

Mandi definitely wanted to be an organ donor, but memories of conversations with her instantly raced through my mind.

"You have to promise me that if anything were to happen, you won't let them touch my eyes," Mandi had told me. She must have repeated that dozens of times throughout our ten years together.

I had Lasik eye surgery in 2001 and told Mandi about the procedure in one of our conversations when we first began to date. Even the thought of that made her squeamish and uneasy.

Now, in the most unbelievable of circumstances, I was thrust into the role of being her voice the first night she could no longer speak for herself.

Mandi's family was seated around the living room, where I took the call. It took a minute for them to gather what the call concerned. I watched their reactions, curious at first, then a look of horror as their imaginations began to dominate their thoughts.

"Ma'am, I'm sorry. My wife is the most generous person I've ever known, but she made me promise that I would not let anybody touch her eyes."

The room was silent as I hung up. Everyone was looking straight ahead, pretending the call did not happen, pretending that the absurdity of what was taking place was not real, that Mandi was very much alive, and this was all a big misunderstanding.

That was the only phone call I took regarding organ donation. Despite Mandi being an organ donor, no other organization called. Had they done so, I would have followed her wishes. But I never got the chance to say "yes."

It was also not lost upon me that I took that call in front of her parents. They had spent their lives taking care of and protecting their little girl, only to listen helplessly as their son-in-law made decisions for their deceased child.

\*\*\*

I was in no condition to drive the next day—my mind was wandering, sleep-deprived, and in a fog—so Mandi's Uncle Danny took me to visit Father Viscardi, where I spent an hour crying and searching for answers. Uncle Danny waited patiently in the parking lot alone, grieving the loss of his niece. Returning to his truck, I told him I had one more stop I wanted to make before he took me back to my in-laws' house. I had been thinking all morning about staying connected to Mandi. I knew we were spiritually connected, but the physical connection was now gone, and in the blink of an eye.

"There's a jewelry store on Cottage Hill Road, right down from Knollwood," I said. "I'd like to see if they can help me with something."

I walked into the jewelry shop in the heat of the afternoon. The air conditioner kept the inside of the building very cool, a welcome escape from the afternoon heat of a sunny Alabama day.

"Can I help you?" a salesman said, approaching from the back of the store.

My head was down as I scanned the display cases through swollen eyes. I knew what I wanted but couldn't quickly locate it. "I am looking to purchase two identical necklaces."

The young man sidled up next to me and could clearly see I was despondent. He chose his words carefully, not knowing what was wrong but understanding I had a purpose for my visit.

"Is there something specific you had in mind?" he asked.

"I am looking for two silver or white-gold chains, two crosses, and one square about this big." I put up two fingers about an inch and a half apart from each other. "I'll need the chains to match in size, the crosses to match, and I want to cut the square in half and have each part inscribed."

Listening intently, he pulled a pen from his pocket, grabbed a piece of paper, and began writing down my request. After a few scribbles, he asked me to follow him to the adjacent display case. Inside were dozens of cross pendants of all types. Being in the Bible Belt, the jewelry shop didn't have to worry about Christian symbols not selling well.

"I'm looking for something relatively simple," I said.

"How about this one?" he asked as he pulled out a cross and set it under the bright lights above the display case.

"That's too big, and I don't want a diamond in it," I replied. Remembering my purpose for being there, I held back the tears while I reviewed more of the pendants. At this point, I felt I needed to explain the circumstances to help the young man understand what I had imagined before I walked in.

"My wife passed away yesterday ... unexpectedly." Another salesperson helping a customer across the room paused, his voice trailing off as he realized something out of the ordinary was being shared. I felt all the eyes in the store glance toward me as I finished my thought.

"She was a very modest person and didn't like flashy. It doesn't need to be large. Just silver, white-gold ... something that is pure but can't tarnish." The room was quiet, the other staff and customers listening but trying not to be obvious about it.

The young man helping me seemed stunned, looking at me and undoubtedly judging by my relatively youthful appearance that my wife must have been very young. "I'm so sorry for your loss. I will certainly help you however I can."

He showed me several cross pendants and allowed me to inspect each of them up close.

"This one," I said. "Is it silver?"

"It's white-gold, so it won't tarnish."

"Okay, I think this is it. Next, I need a chain. Something to match the cross, yet strong and not able to be broken or kinked very easily."

We walked down the row of display cases until we arrived at one that housed different-sized chains. I reiterated my interest in keeping it simple yet very nice. He pulled a chain from the case and showed it under the light. Handing it to me, he told me it was of high quality; strong, yet brilliant, and it would not tarnish.

"Okay, now I need a piece of silver that is a square," I began. "This is important to get exactly right. I want you to cut it in half. I would like you to inscribe my wife's name and our anniversary date on one of the halves. I want to attach this to the necklace so that it hangs next to the pendant. On the other half of the square, inscribe my name and our anniversary date."

Early in our relationship, Mandi often said I completed her, that I was the "other half of her square." She even drew a picture in a letter to me to explain how she was feeling. I understood exactly how she felt because I thought the same. She just articulated it much better than I ever could.

The salesman began to draw the square. "What was your wife's name?"

"Mandi," I said. "The date of our anniversary is 7-22-06."

"And you want your name on the other half with the date, correct?"

"Correct. Jason. 7-22-06," I stated. "My wife will wear one with my name and anniversary date. And I will wear her name and the date."

The other customer and salesperson continued to eavesdrop on the conversation. I could tell they were paying attention to our discussion by how they reacted to my statement, fidgeting with a piece of jewelry and trying too hard to pay us no mind.

"It's very important that these be attached in such a way that there is no chance they could come off or be lost," I said. "If that means drilling a hole in the pendant and looping the chain through, let's do that." If I was going to be wearing this necklace regularly, I could take no chances that I would lose my half or break the chain.

"That shouldn't be a problem, sir," the young man replied. "Our jeweler is very good, and he will make this hold up."

"I know I'm asking a lot," I said. "But I need it by Monday at noon."

The salesman looked at his watch. It was Saturday afternoon, just a few hours before closing. He disappeared in the back to call the jeweler. I continued to look at the pendant and the chain, imagining the finished product. I realized I hadn't even bothered to ask what the cost would be. But I didn't care. I would move forward with the purchase as long as the jeweler could do the work.

Monday wasn't an arbitrary date. The service was set for Tuesday, but the funeral director needed the necklace by Monday to properly place it on Mandi. Always the other half of my square, she would wear the necklace with my name forever. And I would do the same with hers—a commitment I have kept to this day.

"Okay, we will have it ready by Monday at noon," the young man said.

We reviewed his drawing one more time to ensure names were spelled correctly, and the date was right. We had just one chance at this, so there could be no errors. My eyes welled up once again, and I choked back tears. How in the world had it come to this?

Afterward, Uncle Danny drove me back to Mandi's parents' house, where I essentially got out of his car and into theirs and headed across town to the funeral home. My in-laws had already been in touch with the funeral director and set the date for Tuesday, but we still needed to pick out a casket and iron out some details.

\*\*\*

I breathed my last breath of outside air before opening the door to the funeral home and walking inside. Perhaps it's the result of being forced inside a building where you don't want to be, but funeral homes have a distinct smell to me, and it is highly unpleasant. And there's something about shaking the hand of a funeral director that is unintentionally repugnant. I have respect for the profession—not many people could handle that job—but it requires them to be stoic, which makes them appear desensitized to loss.

The funeral director met us near the door. "Mister Fisher," he said in a soft, hushed tone. "I'm so sorry for your loss."

"Thank you," I said calmly as I shook his hand, glancing away at my first opportunity.

There was a quiet hush before he delicately began the conversation, as if he knew the natural order of the universe had been upended for us. One day after my wife passed, and I'm supposed to make plans that require the ability to think clearly?

I was there, sort of, but my mind was adrift with thoughts of Mandi, the painful moments of the day before, and a sudden hole in my spirit that made it seem as though life was over for me as well.

"What do you think about this, Jason?"

"I'm sorry, ma'am, could you repeat that?" I said.

"On the projector screen. The passage we just wrote. Do you want to add anything to it?" Miss Sheri gently asked me.

I had been sitting at the table for fifteen minutes, doing my best to follow along, but could barely comprehend what they were asking. I hadn't even noticed they had begun to write her obituary. My mind was in a thick fog. Simple words and phrases were not making sense. It was as if I was trying to interpret a language I did not speak.

"I think it's okay," I replied. "I just want to make sure it includes everyone. I'm honestly having a hard time reading and understanding right now. I apologize."

I knew I had to get it together and try harder. I couldn't let Mandi's parents do this alone, but I was clearly struggling, and they knew it.

Miss Sheri sat in the chair next to me. She helped guide me through the process like an interpreter, making certain I was included in the decisions even though I offered very little in the way of constructive input. I wanted to be anywhere but in that seat.

The funeral director was patient. I'm sure I wasn't the first person to be mentally checked out at the planning of their spouse's funeral.

Finally, the group finished writing the obituary. As the final version was read aloud, I was satisfied it contained all it needed to. Still, it was unnatural to write about Mandi in the past tense. It seemed like mere hours ago that Mandi was texting me from the farmer's market, asking if it was raining at our house. Less than forty-eight hours later, I was making decisions I had never dreamed I would have to make.

"What do I owe you?" I asked the funeral director, and then asked him for a pen.

"The total will be eleven thousand dollars even," he replied.

I laid my checkbook flat on the table. The balance in our interest-earning checking account had been steadily climbing as we saved for the day when Mandi could comfortably work part-time and take care of Kenzie. The irony of the prior discussions just days before about our future and the job I was considering now haunted my thoughts. I wrote the check slowly, having to think about each space I needed to enter information. I signed my name, detached the check, and handed it to the funeral director. A good portion of our savings, of which Mandi had contributed to considerably, was now paying to lay her to rest.

*\*\**

Reflecting on somebody's passing, one can always find some prophetic or ironic statement that made little sense when it was said but resonated true just a short time after the person has died. I can attest that this happened to me many times over, the first time being the eve of Mandi's funeral.

In the weeks leading up to her death, Mandi had become more vocal about the elusive balance between home and professional life tipping too far toward the latter. She felt I was too focused on my career, and we needed to reaffirm that family came first as often as possible.

"If you died, they would send flowers, attend the service, ask for your laptop back, and post your job," Mandi said. "Your friendships are strong there, but you're not married to RuffaloCODY."

The night before the funeral, Mandi's parents hosted a small get-together, and several of Mandi's friends from work stopped by to pay their respects. They had driven all day from Arkansas, and it was good to see them; Mandi very much enjoyed working with them.

Near the end of the night, one of Mandi's coworkers approached Mr. Skip. Likely seeing I was in no shape for extended conversation, he bypassed me and went to the person most likely to help answer a few questions.

"I hate to ask, but Mandi was working on some critical projects for several clients," he said. "Would it be possible to get her work laptop while we are in Mobile? I'll burn any personal files or pictures to a CD and mail it to you."

Sitting in close proximity, I heard the conversation fairly clearly. Mandi's statement to me just weeks earlier had come true. It wasn't anybody's fault. It wasn't even a callous request, or one delivered in poor taste. I understood the circumstances, but I couldn't help but think how right Mandi was about never losing sight of the bigger picture, of what is most important.

Her prophecy had come true. Her company sent flowers. Her friends from work attended the service. They asked for her laptop back. And management, though no doubt shocked and thrown for a loop, had an obligation to move forward for the rest of their employees and clients. Like it or not, there are very few situations in the corporate world where an employee is indispensable.

A year or so after her death, Mandi's company planted and dedicated a tree in her memory outside its Arkansas headquarters. I was told her death reverberated throughout their organization for quite some time. Like it did for me, her passing was a wake-up call to many. They were hurting too.

To this day, I still receive an email from her boss on the anniversary of her passing. I still exchange Christmas cards and stay connected on social media with some of her coworkers. I'm thankful for their friendships and how good they were to my wife. Had it not been for them, our experience in Little Rock might have been much more difficult.

\* \* \*

June 5, 2012: the fourth time we rose from our scattered dreams and dried tears to realize Mandi was indeed gone.

Kenzie and I were living out of a duffel bag, sleeping in the recliner at Mandi's parents' house, and getting dressed in the living room. The suit I had asked my sister to grab from my house hung on the back of the door to the entrance of the foyer. My toiletries were thrown in a plastic bag that was draped from the doorknob.

I tried to be quiet as I took a shower, pretending everyone was still asleep despite the echoes of sobbing coming from the bedrooms. I hadn't eaten anything since Mandi passed. My energy was low, but I was not hungry. Food repulsed me. I drank only to clear my throat as my stomach was still in knots, the anxiety controlling both my mind and my physical body at the same time.

I stood in the shower in disbelief. The clock on the bathroom wall ticked by, each second marching me closer to my next nightmare. I did not want to get out of the shower. I did not want to start my day. Not this day. Not the day I had to say "goodbye."

Text messages came in one after another. Friends let me know they were thinking of me. I could tell they chose their words carefully; each sentence was constructed with great thought so as not to inflame my emotions more than they already were.

I felt lost. I didn't know how I was going to handle the day. My lack of nutrition and dehydration led to irrational thoughts, though I could have cared less at the time.

*I don't think I can do this, Lori,* I said in a text message to my friend.

Lori had been a speaker at our wedding and a longtime work colleague. Nobody could do anything to help, but I still thought I had to reach out to somebody and let out what I was feeling.

*You'll make it,* she replied. *Just one step at a time.*

*I can't say goodbye. I can't.*

*You have friends and family there to support you. Lean on them, Jason. You'll get through this.*

Tears flowed down my cheeks. I had a difficult time catching my breath, and my chest felt tight. The air conditioner paused and, with the white noise it delivered on that hot morning suddenly missing, my loud sobs echoed through the hallway.

I had been able to keep Kenzie relatively quiet for most of the morning, but she was now awake and playing in her playpen. I lifted her out of her makeshift crib, laid her on a blanket, and changed her diaper.

Kenzie always looked like her mother to me. She had Mandi's big blue eyes, long eyelashes, and perfectly shaped eyebrows. It was difficult to look at Kenzie that morning, seeing Mandi with every smile that made its way to her face. How was I going to be all she needed me to be?

I put Kenzie back into the playpen to finish getting dressed. She still was not walking or even pulling up onto furniture, though she was much closer to doing so than we knew at the time. On this morning, she moved about her playpen on her hands and knees in a pirouette fashion, hopping to all corners, determined to find a way to see what was happening beyond the mesh nylon walls.

One by one, the rest of the family was begrudgingly starting their day. Mandi's dad started the coffee and did little tasks around the house to keep his mind off the coming event. Her mom came in to check on Kenzie and make sure I had seen where she had hung Kenzie's dress for the service.

It was a busy Tuesday morning on Hillcrest Road, the main road behind my in-laws' house. The hot, steamy air reverberated with the sounds of cars and motorcycles speeding by. The noise level was much higher than I was used to at our house in Semmes. I couldn't get over how loud the world was that morning. *Don't they know I'm burying my wife today? Don't they have any respect?*

I loaded up the car with Kenzie's diaper bag, feeding supplies, and an extra box of tissues. My eyes were swollen and my head congested; my mind was cloudy and adrift with thoughts of the last time I saw Mandi alive.

Slowly, Mandi's parents and sisters emerged from the house. We needed to take two vehicles. Amber, Abby, and Evan—Abby's fiancé—drove in one car, and Kenzie and I rode with Pops and Gigi in Mandi's SUV. I couldn't concentrate and was in no shape to get behind the wheel, so I crawled in the backseat with Kenzie and let Mr. Skip drive.

The drive time to the funeral home was about twenty-five minutes if traffic cooperated. It may have taken longer. I don't remember. My thoughts were consumed with my wife. I knew this would be the last time I would see her, and the anxiety I felt was overwhelming.

There was a private viewing and service for family that started an hour before the public could attend. The early-morning air was already hot and sticky. It would be an unforgiving day in many respects, and the steamy weather would only add to the misery.

Once again, as I had done just days before, I breathed in my last breath of fresh air before entering the funeral home. My hands were shaking, and I struggled to find my composure in front of Mandi's gathering family.

The funeral director shook our hands; I wanted to be anywhere but in that building. He showed us to the room where my wife's body lay lifeless. The casket was open, but I couldn't look. Holding Kenzie, I went over to the bench at the back of the room and somberly sat down. Mr. Skip and Miss Sheri immediately went to the casket and stood beside their oldest daughter. Amber and Abby were patiently waiting behind her parents, but like me, they were having a difficult time comprehending what they were experiencing.

Nobody wanted to be in that room, yet we all wanted to be with Mandi. It was an odd sensation, a push and pull of emotions, knowing this would be our only opportunity to say "goodbye" but not wanting to acknowledge the reality of the circumstances.

I sat on the bench, holding Kenzie close to me. At two and a half years old, Kenzie weighed barely twenty pounds and was still well under her ideal height and weight on the growth chart. I was exhausted from the emotions, but the isolation I felt was made a little easier by being with my daughter.

After a few minutes, Mandi's mom came to the back of the room and talked to me.

"Jason, I know you don't want to go up there, but you have to. Mandi looks beautiful, and you need to see her and talk to her," Miss Sheri said.

She understood the overwhelming feeling I had, a feeling of senseless despair mixed with physical pain. My chest tightened as I silently acknowledged her request, handing Kenzie to her and getting to my feet for the short walk to the front of the room.

As I approached the casket, I broke down. Sobbing uncontrollably the last few steps, my grieving became mixed with incoherent words as I spoke to my wife.

"Why?" I asked out loud, squeezing my eyes with my fingers as tears rolled down my face and off my upper lip. My memory flashed back to her lying on the floor gasping for air. "I'm sorry, baby! I didn't know what was happening. I didn't know how to help you."

An hour is a painfully long time to be in such an environment. Most of the time is spent crying, with weird periods in between of silence and the contemplation of life. I thought not just about the meaning of life and physical death, but a subconscious feeling of uncertainty about being forced to continue while your best friend has gone.

I continued sitting on the bench most of the hour of private visitation. Nearing the end of our time, I once again stood up and went to see Mandi. I knew this was likely the last time I would ever see her with my own eyes on this Earth. The pain I felt while I comprehended the meaning of that thought was indescribable. Sadness, anger, fear—none of these words could perfectly fit what I was thinking.

It was as though ten years of history together, of our spirits and lives intertwined, was being physically cut from my body. My head was pounding from the intense sobbing, and my stomach was hollow. I was just a shell of myself.

I looked in disbelief at my beautiful wife. I reached down and embraced her hand in mine one last time. I don't know what I was expecting, but the shock of grabbing her ice-cold hand made me recoil. The reality was clear; she was really gone. Her body was lifeless, and I would never hear words from her mouth again. I would never see those big, beautiful eyes touch my soul as they had so many times.

Pushing down my shock and fear, I bent over and kissed her on the top of her head one last time.

"I love you, baby. I will always love you, and I will see you again," I said with tears streaming down my face. With that, I closed my eyes and turned away. I walked to the back of the room and sat down on the bench once again.

Several people had been helping with Kenzie while I was saying my goodbyes. I grabbed my daughter, hugged her tight, and sat in relative silence as the doors to the room opened up, and visitors began coming in to pay their respects.

Mandi's parents were greeting people in line as they slowly moved through. After the experience I just had, I needed a few minutes to collect myself and attempt to make it through the rest of the day. We were barely an hour in, and I was already emotionally spent.

"Jason, you need to come up to the front with us and greet Mandi's friends and people that came to pay their respects," Miss Sheri said. "It's one of those things you have to do. I don't know how to tell you to get the energy or summon your strength, but Mandi would want you to do this."

She was right. I needed to be thanking people for coming to pay their respects and share their grief. Selfishly, I wanted to be as deep in the corner of the room as I could be, practically hiding from the experience as though physical distance could somehow make it easier to cope.

"Thank you for coming and being here," I said a few times as Mandi's friends, some of them strangers to me, walked through the line. I did the best I could to be present and in the moment. Still, my mind would occasionally flash back to seeing Mandi on the floor with the paramedics or her arm dangling from the gurney as they pushed it quickly out of the house and lifted her into the ambulance. The horror of those moments would not leave me alone.

Mandi's parents worked the line and met everyone who came through. I was amazed at their composure and their ability to keep their emotions in check. I know they were devastated in ways I couldn't even imagine, yet they were able to rise to the occasion while I stumbled my way through it.

I quietly drifted away from the line and went to the back of the room once again. There, I sat silently, putting off a somber vibe I'm sure was not welcoming to those who thought about approaching me. It wasn't anger but rather an unmistakable energy that I just wanted to be alone in my thoughts.

After some time had passed, and the line was still out the door, the funeral director stepped in and asked folks to start gathering in the chapel for the service. The family was to say "goodbye" one last time and then take their seats.

I could not approach the casket again; I had said my goodbyes, and I couldn't go back to the emotional hell of staring at her lifeless body. I waited for everyone to have their moment and then accompanied them out of the room, down the hall, and into the chapel.

The chapel was filled to capacity by the time I entered the room. Carrying Kenzie, I felt heads turn—all eyes were on me as I walked down the aisle toward Mandi's casket. Soft music filled the somber room, but I couldn't listen to it. In many respects, my mind was absent; the shock of the moment had moved me into an adjacent world. I knew everyone was staring at Kenzie, too, and thinking about the consequences of such a senseless loss. A young, disabled child missing her nurturing mother, forced to navigate the world with just one parent.

Escorted to a seat near the front, I sat down and held Kenzie on my lap. Mandi's parents and sisters sat nearby, though I cannot remember whether they were in front of me or behind. My thoughts were consumed by the surreal moment, a place I never dreamed I would be.

There was a young man playing acoustic guitar and singing. I didn't recognize the music but wasn't paying much attention to the lyrics anyway. I felt a strange sense of comfort that so many friends and family had come from distances near and far to say "goodbye" on a hot Tuesday morning in June.

My recollection of the service is fuzzy. As Mandi would sometimes tell me when I was deep in thought, I must have been a thousand miles away. Before the service began, I asked Mandi's cousin Lamar—who would be delivering the eulogy—if I could say a few words once he was finished.

"Are you sure you can do it, buddy?" he asked me.

"Yes," I responded. "I have to."

Lamar spoke proudly of Mandi, the beautiful person she always was and the mother she had become. Poised, he delivered a wonderful tribute in what must have been a painful experience for him. He gazed at me questioningly, and I nodded, handed Kenzie to a family member, and walked to the front of the room.

I had not prepared any remarks. I did not even think much about what I was going to say. I just wanted to be sure everyone in that room who knew Mandi understood what she meant to me, to remind them of how she loved me, and I loved her.

"I want to thank you all for coming here today, for remembering Mandi and loving her," I began. "Please bear with me as I try to find the words ... ."

I started at the beginning, sharing with everyone how we met and connected. I cracked a joke about Mandi bringing me a bag of peanuts from her flight to Cedar Rapids when she interviewed for the job, getting some smiles and laughs as they affirmed that it sounded like something she would do.

I kept talking and reaffirming how much she meant to me, seeking a way to end my speech. In reality, I didn't want that moment to be over. I didn't want to leave the podium because it meant we would then have to bury my wife. And in my mind, so long as I kept talking about her, she would still be alive. "I love you, Mandi. I will forever," I finally said.

The ride to the cemetery was long and silent. The drive took nearly thirty minutes in midday traffic, winding through the interstate, main highways, and finally to the side roads that led to her final resting place. The cemetery is located off Snow Road, on the outskirts of West Mobile. Mandi and I had taken this same road home just a few days before, after the Memorial Day cookout with her family. Now, I was taking the long and winding road to say my final "goodbye."

Many of the guests had arrived to the cemetery ahead of us and were standing out in the hot sun, waiting. The ladies were fanning themselves to keep cool while the men dabbed their foreheads with handkerchiefs.

Father Viscardi, the Jesuit priest who had married us, had agreed to officiate the final gathering. He greeted the family under the tent and gave us each his condolences, working down the row until he reached the end of the line.

The final tribute was very quick. Prayers, words of comfort, and blessings were said by the priest as we asked God to accept Mandi into His kingdom. As the service ended, I found myself standing at her casket. Once again, I did not want to leave. I felt the overwhelming urge to stay right there. I had nowhere to go if it wasn't with her.

I bent over and gently kissed her casket. I rested my forehead on the metal case and began sobbing. I was frozen in place with raw emotions and pain. The tears flowed heavily, and no amount of crying seemed to relieve the agony. It felt endless.

After a few seconds, somebody came and gently put their hand on my back to guide me to the car. I never turned around to find out who it was. My eyes were so painfully sore from crying and so filled with tears that I could barely recognize people I knew.

On the short walk away, I passed by several of my coworkers. Duane grabbed me and gave me a giant hug. I could see his eyes glisten, the emotion of the moment threatening to overwhelm all of us.

"Jason, we're here for you," Duane said.

I thanked him and hugged Al, Maureen, and Cutler. Nate, my friend who worked at my college alma mater in Iowa, made the long trip down as well. I gave him a big hug and thanked him for coming. All those hugs were more than appreciated. They were needed and gave me a glimmer of hope that I would make it through this nightmare. I was feeling distraught and completely alone, missing my best friend.

"Are you all coming over to Mandi's parents' house?" I asked.

"Our flights are early this afternoon, so we'll have to go to the airport soon," Duane replied. "But we're with you in spirit. Anything you need, you call us."

I gave my thanks to each of them for making the trip down. They were more than my coworkers; they were my mentors and friends who all wanted to be there for me. Unfortunately, schedules and overseas travel didn't allow others to attend, but I felt the spirit of the entire company with me.

This show of support was an example of the RuffaloCODY I will always remember. Yes, they were a bottom-line business, but the leaders always recognized that people made the company what it was. As Duane would often say, "We aren't in the widget business … we are in the people business."

I saw a few more people I knew from Iowa and Arkansas who had made the long journey and thanked them for attending. I know I missed many people who were there for me, either because I didn't see them through the crowd or just don't remember moments of interaction during that painful time.

I was so relieved when the service was over, but the reality of a life without my wife unrelentingly pounded away at my conscious thoughts. I now had to find a way to move forward when half my soul had died.

# CHAPTER 10
# The Fog of Grief

A crack of thunder reverberated through the air as dawn was breaking, an eerie combination of a summer sunrise and thickening storm clouds. The sun painted the puffy clouds varying shades of orange and gray as the day was making up its mind whether it would start bright or whether it would rain. Shortly after sunrise, the heavens opened up and gave us the answer.

In the days after the funeral service, I had barely peeked my head outside to review the weather conditions. It had been hot and sunny for the funeral, but just as life was changing for me, so was the atmospheric pattern. Just a few days prior, a beautiful Friday morning turned tragic. The days grew warmer and unrelenting in the aftermath of that awful day, staying hot through the service that following Tuesday and subsequently building to a point where the air was so saturated and full of moisture that it just had to rain.

For days after the service, the skies were cloudy and stormy. There was hardly a break in the rain. All that could be done was to stay inside and grieve. It was as if God knew how bad we were hurting and cried along with us. Wicked, forked lightning would light up the sky day or night as the flooding rains pounded onto the soil. I kept thinking about how the rain must be eroding Mandi's freshly dug grave, washing away the precious soil that now covered the last place I had stood next to her just days before.

I continued to stay with Mandi's parents after the funeral. Under normal conditions, I didn't need the help with Kenzie. But this wasn't a typical situation, and my mind was in many ways not functioning well enough to take care of her on my own. Plus, I couldn't go home and stay in the last place Mandi was conscious. I was having panic attacks from the trauma, though I didn't know that was what they were at the time. I just knew I couldn't step foot in that house without memories from just a few days prior rushing back to me and exacerbating my grief.

Being close to Mandi's family also gave me a measure of comfort to know I wasn't in this new world alone, our togetherness could help get us through our combined grief. The reality was that I was in shock and scared. The heavy feeling of death followed me wherever I went, as if there were no escaping it. I was like a young child who sought my parents' reassurance that the monsters weren't real. Except, in this case, my nightmare was vivid, and I was living it nearly every waking moment of the day.

\*\*\*

The day before Mandi's funeral, I left a message for a psychiatrist I had seen to help reconcile some leftover stress and anxiety from Kenzie's NICU experience. I had mentioned it to Mandi at the time and let her know it had nothing to do with our marriage; I just wanted to rid myself of the general feeling of malaise and the mental exhaustion that comes along with it.

About ten minutes after talking with the receptionist, I received a call from the doctor.

"Jason, this is Doctor Brown. First, are you okay?" she asked.

"I'm in shock and am overwhelmed right now," I said as my voice quivered.

"Can you be at my office this afternoon?"

"Yes, I can be there," I replied.

Arriving at the doctor's office, I stepped into the restroom quickly before checking in. Looking at my appearance in the mirror was quite a sight. My eyes were swollen, and my face was red from crying nonstop. My reflection truly told the story of a horrible situation.

I pulled myself together as best I could and went to check in with the receptionist. Soon, the doctor appeared.

I stood up and walked slowly through the doorway. Once again, I felt the eyes of the room upon me, following me until the door closed, and I entered the doctor's office.

"What happened?" Dr. Brown asked after I had sat down.

"I honestly don't know yet," I replied through my sobs. "Her back hurt. It grew worse very quickly, so I called an ambulance at her request. The next thing I knew, they were telling me she was gone." I explained the details of the previous Friday that were burned and etched into my memory, and we discussed the circumstances. "I'm just ... shattered ... trying to take care of Kenzie ... my wife's funeral ... I have no idea what I'm going to do now."

"You don't have to know right now," she replied calmly. "That's for another day. Right now, we have to get you through tomorrow and make sure you have plenty of support. Okay?"

"Yes," I said quietly. I didn't have the first clue how I was going to make it through this crisis. My future was gone. I couldn't go home. My grief devastated me and left me unable to properly tend to Kenzie's needs. And the thought of having to raise her without Mandi scared the hell out of me.

Had I not already been in contact with this doctor just weeks before Mandi's death and established a patient record, I have no idea who I would have called. The truth was, I needed immediate help. I wasn't eating or drinking. My sleep cycle was thrown completely off, and I was mentally exhausted. There was no way I could have managed that without an impartial voice of comfort.

\*\*\*

Our intent had always been to have one of Mandi's sisters be Kenzie's legal guardian if anything had happened to us. It made the most sense given their familiarity with Kenzie and Mandi's close familial bond with both of her siblings. Still, we did not have a will designating Kenzie's guardian if the unthinkable would have happened. Michael reminded me of this the day before Mandi passed.

The irony of that discussion the day before her death was not lost on me. Instead of this scenario being improbable, I was now one accident or illness away from Kenzie being an orphan. No matter my foggy state of mind, I needed to make a few calls and make them fast.

I asked a few people for recommendations on local attorneys to call who specialized in wills and trusts. Nobody had any names they could offer. I decided to do what I do best in these situations— conduct an internet search. Using my phone, I searched for attorneys handling wills in the Mobile area. I reviewed the list and randomly chose what seemed like a reputable option on the first page.

"Hello, this is Henry," the voice said on the other end.

I introduced myself, then told him why I was calling. "I'm in a tough spot right now, Henry. I'm forty years old, my wife just passed unexpectedly, and I have a special needs daughter. I do not have a will, and I need to make sure I have a plan if something happens to me."

"Jason, I don't know how to say this, but I feel we were meant to talk," Henry said. "My best friend is your wife's sister's boss. He told me about your situation over the weekend. I just have this strange feeling that I was meant to help you."

Mobile is a big city but also a small town in many ways. Connections run deep, and family histories and friendships are intertwined, going back many years. Still, it was a little unexpected that he already knew my story. Henry handled that call in such a way that made me very comfortable moving forward, so I agreed to meet him at his office and begin discussing what I would need.

A week had gone by since Mandi had passed, and my emotions were raw. I had lost about fifteen pounds in six days. In my mind, I didn't want to eat because I would somehow erase my last meal together with Mandi. Of course, that wasn't true, but a traumatic situation like this can put your mind in strange places.

When I met Henry in his office, I had difficulty comprehending everything I would be facing and precisely what I needed. We discussed how quickly the will could be finished to ensure that the courts wouldn't be the people deciding where Kenzie would go should something happen to me. As I was telling Henry about the emotional events of the previous week, I noticed he was tearing up.

"I'm sorry for getting emotional," he said. "I got into practicing law to help people. I suppose I'm not your typical attorney ... ."

Henry's reaction was just fine with me. I needed somebody who listened and understood what I was going through and could help me think about the next steps logically. While I was outwardly grieving as I spoke, I felt slightly better about taking some sort of action to protect Kenzie. I suppose it was a way for my mind to think it had a level of control over the situation, even though, in reality, nothing could change the painful fact that I had to do this without Mandi.

Planning for my life as a single parent would prove to be the easy part. What I ultimately needed was a document that protected Kenzie's assets if something happened to *me*.

"I need a special needs trust, Henry," I said. "My daughter is disabled, and I need to have an instrument to protect her inherited assets in the event of my death. Can you help with that?"

"I've never created a special needs trust before, but I know somebody who has, and I'm confident I can write it up," he replied.

"I know it is a rare instrument, but it's necessary to make sure Kenzie doesn't lose any federal disability benefits she might have because I suddenly die, and she inherits all my assets."

Henry scribbled some notes on the paper and agreed to work on it over the next few weeks. He promised a quick resolution to the completion of the will, and we decided to touch base thereafter about generating the special needs trust.

I believe most of the ironies in life are largely coincidental. But fate and destiny sometimes intervene. It could have been a simple random chance that I connected with Henry. However, the fact that I called somebody who had a connection to Mandi's sister, and who already knew my story, gave me the extra reassurance I needed to feel a measure of peace in such a tumultuous period. The thought that Mandi was intervening and guiding me most definitely crossed my mind.

*\*\*\**

Life was far from normal in the weeks after Mandi's passing. I had taken Gracie over to Mandi's parents' place, given that I was still unable to go inside my home. Every few days, I would drive by the house quickly to check the mail and make sure everything was secure. The neighbors were helping to keep an eye on the property as well, knowing I was spending a lot of time away. On the drive back to Mandi's parents' house, I would take the long way back, avoiding the hospital or the cemetery at all costs.

I was also seeing a grief counselor in addition to the psychiatrist to help with coping. I honestly question if I could have made the transition to life without Mandi on my own if I did not have the help of these qualified professionals.

Two to three times per week, I would go in for an hour session and talk through my grief. My sadness was crushing me and making it difficult to function for Kenzie. After using up an entire box of tissues, the grief counselor would give me a book recommendation and reschedule me for another appointment.

Making a significant life transition is never easy, particularly if what you have experienced was traumatic. I felt a wide range of emotions that would cause the sudden onset of grief, panic, anxiety, and "ultimately" profound guilt for not being able to help Mandi in those final minutes. I could not see a reason to forgive myself. It was my job to protect her—and I had failed.

I had significant problems with post-traumatic stress disorder symptoms. Though I didn't understand the reason at the time, I would feel my chest tighten and experience a sudden flashback to the ambulance being parked in our driveway every time I heard a siren. I would relive my decision not to ride in the ambulance with her that morning, questioning whether I made the right choice staying with Kenzie instead of going with my wife.

To this day, I still associate any siren I hear with visions of Mandi's arm dangling from the side of the gurney, her head lay back on the pillow with the oxygen mask on, and the EMT shutting the door. It was the last time I ever saw her alive, and the memory of that moment remains extraordinarily painful.

I had taken a leave of absence from work. I needed time to get through the initial shock and grief, get my legal and financial affairs in order, and continue my therapy. Honestly, I was no good to my clients or coworkers at the time. I could not concentrate for more than a few seconds before my thoughts would drift to Mandi.

Maureen, my direct supervisor, would call to check on me from time to time. Under the circumstances, I don't believe I could have had a better boss for that moment in my life. She had my best interests in mind, checking in with me to see how I was progressing and talking about anything I may have needed.

One afternoon in late June, Maureen and I talked for a few minutes about when I could potentially start back at work again in my current role. The team needed me, and I wanted a distraction. I *needed* a distraction. But I was still drowning in my new reality. We agreed to talk again later in the week about when the right time would be and what the circumstances of easing back into my role would entail.

"Okay, Maureen. I'm going to try coming back to work," I said during our follow-up discussion. "Next week might be good because it's a short week due to the Fourth of July holiday. That will help me ease into things, I think."

"Thank you, Jason. I appreciate your willingness to give this a shot," Maureen said. "I know this is not easy. I'm hopeful this will be a much-needed reprieve for you."

My return date was set for Monday, July 2. We would get Wednesday off for the holiday, which would allow me to work two days, take a day off, and work another two days before the weekend.

When Monday arrived, I set my laptop on the dining room table at Mandi's parents' house and got the things I needed out of my work bag. Feeling as though it would be similar to working from a hotel room, I thought I could handle any moderate distractions that would come my way. After all, I was used to working while traveling.

Miss Sheri watched Kenzie and kept her occupied while Mr. Skip worked from his home office in the back of the house. I fired up my laptop, opened my email, and began scanning. Maureen had done an excellent job of keeping up with my email while I was out, but there were so many messages I hadn't seen. I knew it would take me several days to respond to everyone.

Almost immediately, I could feel my mind drifting off to Mandi. I fought back the tears and continued to try focusing on the task at hand. Frustrated, I stopped working for a minute to collect my thoughts.

*There's not a shred of importance in any of these messages*, I said to myself. *My life is turned upside down, and I'm reading emails from a month ago, trying to catch up on things that have already been solved.*

In truth, everything in my inbox that needed attention seemed trivial compared to the challenges I was facing and the omnipresent grief. Work, it turned out, was not the welcomed distraction I had hoped for.

I did my best to keep up that first day or two. I found my phone not ringing as often as it did before. My coworkers were apprehensive about reaching out to me, not knowing what to say and how to bring up the uncomfortable subject that was the elephant in the workplace.

In reality, nothing was going to usurp what was happening in my personal life. While I enjoyed my job and had a great boss, just about anything I did to keep my focus essentially bore little fruit. I would find myself daydreaming and reimagining horrific details on conference calls or discussions with clients. I was often a silent participant on calls, either because I was distracted with thoughts of Mandi or unable to keep the pace of the conversation and remember the details. My brain was just not working right.

"Maureen, I think I came back too soon," I said one afternoon a week or so later. "I can't concentrate on anything right now, and I'm not helping anybody on the team."

Maureen understood where I was coming from, but she preached patience.

"I'm happy to give you as much time off as you need," she said. "I can only imagine how difficult it is for you. All I ask is that you come back when you're confident you're ready so that we don't throw the rest of the team off with you being in and out of the office."

"Sounds fair," I replied.

I spent a good portion of July 2012 in intense grief therapy several days per week. The next time I came back to work, I vowed it would be with a new plan to see the bigger picture and maintain my focus. Still, the wounds were raw and the therapy difficult. It would not be an easy transition, and I would have to dig deep to reclaim some semblance of a typical workday.

Duane would occasionally call to check in and see how I was doing. We'd talk for a few minutes, I would give him any updates on my end, and we'd agree to check in again soon. The team was behind me 100 percent—I could feel it. I just needed to make sure I could return something close to my full effort and not try to take advantage of the generosity and patience already being extended.

***

July proved to be as rough as June. With my birthday on the tenth, Mandi's birthday on the twentieth, and our wedding anniversary on the twenty-second, it was a trifecta of pain that caused a great deal of stress and anxiety. My birthday was hard, but Mandi's birthday and our anniversary were highly emotional experiences. I nicknamed them "Park Place" and "Boardwalk." These are two of the costliest days in terms of hurt and anxiety—and every year, I'm guaranteed to land on both of them. There's a sense of relief when I reach July 23—as if I've passed GO and collected my two hundred dollars.

Mandi's birthday in 2012 was just fifty days after her death. She would have been thirty-one years old. The anticipation of her birthday and our anniversary was breathtaking for all of us close to her. For her parents, her birthday is especially difficult, as one might expect it to be. In our world of perceived chronological order, you're not supposed to outlive your kids. July 20 is an incalculable source of pain for them, an annual reminder that they are still here while their firstborn child is gone.

It was difficult to acknowledge Mandi's birthday, but we each did our best to make the day as good as it could be. Thinking about what she would want me to do, I purchased household supplies and wish-list items for the Ronald McDonald house, her favorite charity. I dropped them off that afternoon, talking to their executive director to explain that the donation was in honor of my wife who had passed away six weeks prior.

The executive director and the staff were greatly appreciative. They asked if they could take a picture of Kenzie and me along with the donated items so they could share it in an upcoming newsletter with friends and donors. I sat on the couch surrounded by grocery bags and placed Kenzie on my knee. As I looked at the camera, I mustered the biggest smile I could, which wasn't much. With my eyes swollen and puffy from fifty days of tears, I thought about Mandi and the wonderful person she was to the world. I hoped I had made her proud.

That evening, we returned to Pops and Gigi's to have a birthday dinner in Mandi's honor. We made macaroni and cheese and hot dogs, her favorite meal as a child, and did our best to numb ourselves by watching television.

Just as we were about to get Kenzie ready for bed, something remarkable occurred. Kenzie had been showing signs of trying to stand up on her own, but she had difficulty with the strength and coordination it took to make it to a standing position.

With her tablet sitting on the ottoman, Kenzie was playing her favorite cartoon. She reached up with both hands, got herself to her knees, and put one foot down on the ground. This was usually as far as she got before backing off. However, this time, she shifted her weight and pushed off with both hands to a standing position! At two years and nine months old, Kenzie stood up on her own for the first time.

I looked over at Gigi in awe.

"Did you see that?" I asked excitedly. "She stood up on her own!"

Tears formed in Gigi's eyes. "On Mandi's birthday," she said as the emotions overtook her.

What had been a day of acknowledging our loss suddenly got just a smidge brighter. Mandi had worked with Kenzie so much on her physical therapy—rolling over, sitting up, crawling, and standing. After all the time and energy invested in that goal, Kenzie finally did it.

The fact that Kenzie had hit this milestone on Mandi's birthday was bittersweet. I know she made her mama proud, but Mandi was not there to celebrate the moment. Nobody said anything, but I'm confident we were all feeling that Mandi had sent us a message, that she was still helping and looking out for Kenzie.

Watching Kenzie stand up on her own and cruise the furniture was as bright a moment as I had experienced in months. I felt like a small weight had been lifted off my shoulders. Yet, I also felt the extreme guilt that comes along with being the surviving parent, knowing Mandi had worked so hard for that moment and didn't live to see it.

\*\*\*

Our sixth wedding anniversary came just two days later. Other than the annual date of her death on June 1, it continues to be, by far, the most challenging day every year for me. And in 2012, the wounds of her passing were still fresh when July 22 arrived.

In truth, all the important dates were incredibly difficult that first year without Mandi. Father's Day without her was hard because it was just days after her passing. My birthday was difficult because I felt little reason to be festive. And Mandi's birthday was bittersweet; a day to remember my wife and feel good about Kenzie's progress. But our first wedding anniversary after her death was simply torture, knowing I would remember my best day on Earth without my wife with me to celebrate.

Never a late sleeper, I was up early at the crack of dawn. The late July sun shone brightly through the windows, heating the front room quickly and making it difficult for the air conditioner to keep up. I did whatever I could do for those first few hours to keep my mind occupied, but nothing seemed to work. All I could think of was my late wife, wishing I was anywhere but in this position.

Late in the morning, my anxiety reached its maximum threshold, and I needed to get out of the house. I got in Mandi's SUV, turned up the air-conditioning to full blast, and headed toward the cemetery. On the way, I stopped at a grocery store to buy Mandi some fresh flowers, a dozen yellow roses—the color of the flowers in our wedding, and what I got Mandi every anniversary for the previous five years.

I went to the refrigerated floral section and picked out the best roses I could find. I found the first checkout lane that was open and put my purchase on the belt. A young man, likely a high school student, began to ring up my item.

"I saw you here a couple of days ago, buying flowers," he said with a slight grin. "You either really like this girl, or these are make-up flowers."

It was clear he was just trying to be friendly. I wasn't angry at him but didn't have the capability of filtering my response.

"These are for my wife," I told him matter-of-factly. "Today is our sixth wedding anniversary. She died last month. I'm taking them to the cemetery to put them on her grave. So, to your question, the answer is neither."

The young man's eyes quickly shifted down as he apologized.

"It's okay," I said quietly as he put the flowers in the bag and handed me the receipt.

There are some places in conversations that you just don't go with strangers. This was one of them. We've all had uncomfortable moments in life where we've said something we didn't mean or intend to be hurtful. Those moments serve as learning opportunities. I wasn't out to set that example for him, but I also didn't feel like ignoring his blunder either.

I got back in the car, put the flowers on the front seat, and headed west on Cottage Hill Road toward the cemetery. Since Mandi's passing, I had spent several days each week alone at her grave, talking to her and crying. With our anniversary falling on a Sunday, the churches were in the process of letting out after their morning services. Families were herding their children into their cars.

"How in the world can I be doing this today?" I said out loud with a touch of self-pity. "I should be with my wife and daughter at home, enjoying family time."

As I rounded the large curve on Snow Road and approached the cemetery, my heart began beating loudly in anticipation of the emotional moment. Like usual, tears had already started flowing. I was living my worst nightmare. Every day was horrible, but our wedding anniversary was especially painful.

I parked underneath the large shade tree on the side of the path and walked the fifteen yards to where Mandi's still barren gravesite was baking in the hot sun. There, I knelt and touched the ground, speaking softly amid the tears flowing down my cheeks.

"I'm sorry, baby. I'm so sorry I couldn't help you. I don't understand why you were taken. I miss you so much. I just wish you could come home."

I cried for several minutes until the tears ran out. Sitting silent, I stared at the dirt covering the ground above where she lay at rest, contemplating what this day now meant. It was still our anniversary, but she was no longer able to celebrate it with me. What did this all mean? What was my life worth now that she was gone?

The emotional pain I was experiencing had begun to take its toll in recent weeks. My anxiety was still omnipresent, and I had yet to go back to work. I was hopelessly lost, and the world had little meaning without my wife.

In the extreme grief leading up to our anniversary, I had searched the internet for how to make a hangman's noose. I figured that if worse came to worst, I could find a rope and a tree in the cemetery tall enough to get the job done. In the back of my mind, I knew this wasn't going to happen. I never seriously considered it. But intense grief does funny things to an idle mind. I just wanted the pain to lessen and kept thinking about being close to Mandi.

In my daily thoughts, I could not see an obvious way out of the cycle of emotional turmoil. There seemed to be little in life to inspire me to keep going. My parents were distant, both physically and emotionally. I was living with my in-laws because I was afraid to step foot in my own home. Most critically, the person I leaned on the most in crisis was Mandi. I had never opened up to anybody else as I did with her, and now she was gone. With the exception of my daughter, I felt alone in so many ways. And even though I had Kenzie to keep me company, she was still nonverbal, which added more silence to an already muted new life. I began to turn inward and self-isolate.

I spent as much time as I could talking out loud with my wife, who could not answer me. With sweat dripping from my forehead, the oppressive heat eventually chased me out of the cemetery. I said "goodbye" to Mandi for the day and sat in her car for a minute to collect my thoughts. My eyes were on fire and raw from the constant tears, and my head was pounding from the same. I wasn't ready to go back to Pops and Gigi's house. I wasn't prepared to drive back to my house, either. On that horrible Sunday afternoon, I had nowhere to be and no place to go.

I decided to drive to St. Joseph Chapel, the church we were married in just six years earlier. The images of our wedding were still fresh in my mind, and I just wanted to visit and remember.

The campus of Spring Hill College was quiet that Sunday afternoon. Summer classes may have been happening, but everyone was gone for the weekend. Seeing nobody around, I decided to get out and walk closer to the chapel. I hadn't planned on going inside, but something told me to enter. It was the first time I had stepped foot in the church since the day we were married, and memories came flooding back to me. I closed my eyes and pictured Mandi walking down the aisle toward the altar, arm-in-arm with her father. I remembered his words as he gave her away to me. "Take care of her."

Guilt washed over me. I failed my wife. I failed my in-laws. I couldn't help but blame myself. Was there something I could have done differently? Did I miss the signs in the days before June 1 that something might be happening?

I walked slowly down the aisle and stood in front of the altar. There, I kneeled and prayed aloud. "God, I'm sorry. I'm not strong enough to make it through this life on my own. Why did you take the one person I couldn't live without?"

My words echoed through the empty church. The silence was deafening as I contemplated what the answer could be. An hour passed as I cried and talked to God. Why was He this cruel? Why did He choose Mandi? Why was He punishing me, and why did He take Kenzie's mother? I asked every question aloud. I didn't expect to get any answers but would have welcomed any divine intervention that came my way—physically, spiritually, or emotionally.

Looking back, going to the chapel was somewhat cathartic and precisely where I should have been that day. I needed the time alone to let out the pain that had been excoriating my body.

\*\*\*

In the weeks that followed, I made some strides in my grief. I was growing keenly aware that I was essentially running from my emotional pain by not going home. One day, in early August, I decided the time had come to confront my demons.

"I'm planning on taking Kenzie and spending the night at our house," I told Pops and Gigi. "I need to do this, or it will own me."

"Are you sure you're ready?" Gigi asked.

"No, but I have to at least try."

Both Pops and Gigi supported the decision and helped me mentally prepare for the experience, knowing I could very easily get there and decide I wasn't ready. But on a Saturday afternoon, I put Kenzie's feeding items and my toiletries in a duffle bag and drove the twenty minutes to our home in Semmes. Pulling into the driveway, I pushed the garage door opener like I had hundreds of times before. The open door revealed the reality that I was coming home to nobody, a feeling that would be amplified once I was inside the house.

As I entered, I immediately turned on the television for background noise, opened the blinds for light, and made sure the door to the master bedroom was shut. Dozens of times every day, my memory would fixate upon Mandi lying on the bedroom floor, pale and pleading for help. I couldn't be in that room for any considerable length of time without anxiety rushing through my body.

Prior to arriving, I had made the decision to stay in the guest room. I could not sleep in the master bedroom, especially in the bed I had shared with Mandi. The memories were too painful, and I had no intention of making them worse by pushing beyond the limits of my comfort.

I placed my things in the guest bedroom, put Kenzie's feeding supplies in the kitchen, and pulled out toys to put in her playroom. We spent the rest of the afternoon playing, my mind, at times, drifting back to an extreme state of sadness and anxiety. I was glad to be back home, but home felt much different than it once did.

After feeding Kenzie dinner, I dressed her in pajamas and rocked her to sleep while watching television in our living room. It was a routine I had done a hundred times before but always with the comfortable feeling of a true parenting partnership with Mandi. Now, I was a solo act. The pressure of Kenzie's health and happiness fell squarely upon my shoulders. There was no backup.

Once Kenzie was asleep, I walked her down the hallway and lay her in her crib. I situated the baby monitor so I could see her and walked to the adjacent bedroom where I would be sleeping.

Our home in Semmes was in a newer subdivision on the outskirts of the city. Behind our house was a landscape nursery. The green space out back made for peaceful nights. Typically, that's a great thing. But the extreme silence only seemed to feed my heightened anxiety. I missed Mandi, and being in the house without her was emotionally difficult.

In the days before she passed, Mandi had picked out new furniture for the guest room. Once I finished painting the room, we brought the bedroom suite home and arranged it like we had imagined when we bought the house. Slowly, over time, we had transformed our beige residence with standard construction details into something much more personal to our tastes.

The guest bedroom furniture was refurbished by a local woman who specialized in the "distressed" look, which was becoming very popular. Mandi loved the dresser and headboard, and we were excited to start inviting more guests to our home now that Kenzie was growing up and not as medically fragile.

I sat on the guest bed for a minute to collect my thoughts. My heart was racing. I felt extremely uncomfortable—as if I didn't belong in that room either. Mandi's presence was everywhere in the house. I knew I couldn't sleep in the master bedroom. And going upstairs was out of the question given the distance I would be from Kenzie. So, I grabbed the blankets off the guest bed, walked into Kenzie's room, and made a makeshift bed on the floor.

At the time, I had no idea I was having panic attacks. I just believed I was extremely uncomfortable and in a very emotional state. I was still relatively new to the grieving process and genuinely bewildered when my hands would shake, and I could not relax.

I did my best to take my mind off my uncomfortable circumstances. I surfed the internet on my phone for a while to try to get comfortable enough to relax and drift off to sleep. But my mind was never far from Mandi. I wondered if she might visit me in my dreams now that I was home, a way to comfort me because she knew how bad I was hurting. While I was anxious about being in the house, I also hoped and prayed I would get a sign that she was with us.

Kenzie was sound asleep in her crib, the first time she had been in her bedroom in over two months. I finally drifted off to sleep, only to wake up again a short while later. This sleep-wake cycle went on for most of the night until the early dawn hours. As soon as I awoke, I would immediately think about Mandi, and it would take me some time to relax enough to fall back asleep.

As the night was coming to a close and morning was near, the lavender shade of Kenzie's walls slowly began to show their vibrant color. Kenzie remained asleep, but I was now wide awake, listening to the ticking of the clock hanging on the wall in the living room outside Kenzie's bedroom door. The rhythmic clicking of the moving hands is seldom heard in a normal setting. But in the early-morning hours of that Sunday, I listened to every second loudly pass by.

Our home had a split floor plan downstairs. Kenzie's room and the guest bedroom were on the west side of the house. The master bedroom was on the east side of the house. The dining room, kitchen, and living room—where the clock was located—were in the middle. This had been a main selling point in the floor plan

Mandi and I liked as we envisioned the need for occasional peace and quiet from our intended large family.

I lay on the floor, hiding from the day as long as I could. Finally, I gave in to my restlessness and decided to get up. I rose quietly and made my way across Kenzie's bedroom. Taking a deep breath, I mustered up the courage to open the door and slowly creep into the living room. I intended to open the blinds and let the light in so the house didn't feel so claustrophobic.

The sun had risen to the point where the east side of the house was illuminated while the west side was still relatively dark. As I moved through the living room, my eyes were immediately drawn to the door of the master bedroom. The room, emotionally off-limits, seemed to be calling my name. As my heart began racing, I could barely believe what I was seeing.

The door to the bedroom was shut tight, but the light of that bright Sunday morning would not be denied. The small spacing around and under the door was just wide enough to let through the sunlight. The rectangular outline of the doorframe was illuminated in a radiant yellow and orange color, almost as if another world lay just beyond that boundary.

I stood frozen, looking across the room, hearing only two sounds—the ticking of the clock and my heart beating in my ears. My initial reaction was fear, but something about the sight of that doorframe outlined in bright light was also comforting. I wondered if it was Mandi telling me she was okay, that she was at peace and in heaven. Or perhaps it was a symbol of my recovery, that the sun was rising again, and I was strong enough to face down my fears.

I had made it through the night. Overcoming such a simple but emotionally challenging objective was the first step out of the suffocating fog I had been immersed in all summer. Many more obstacles were ahead, but for this moment in the healing process, I conquered what was unthinkable in the days following the loss of my wife.

# CHAPTER 11
# Baby Steps

Following Mandi's passing, I had received a significant number of phone calls from people asking what they could do to help. One of those calls was from Goodwill Easter Seals, where Kenzie was in early intervention therapy for physical, occupational, and speech services.

I did not recognize the gentleman on the phone. And with all that was happening, I failed to write down his name. He introduced himself as the executive director of Goodwill Easter Seals in the Mobile area and explained the purpose of his phone call.

"Jason, I just wanted to let you know how sorry I am to hear the news about your wife," he said. "Whatever I can do for you in this time of need, you just say the word."

"Thank you," I said politely. "I can't think of anything specific off-hand with the potential exception of your preschool program at the Spring Hill Child Development Center. I know there's a waiting list, but now that I'm a single parent and have to work during the day, it would be great if Kenzie could attend."

"I can certainly check into that for you and see what I can do," he said.

With that, we hung up, and I went back to focusing on reading the information my attorney had sent regarding the special needs trust he was constructing for Kenzie. Given all I had on my plate, I didn't think about that call again until the phone rang a few days later.

"Jason, I have some good news," the Goodwill Easter Seals executive director said. "We can accommodate Mackenzie on a limited schedule three days per week."

"That really helps me out!" I said. "And it's greatly appreciated. Thank you so much!"

"I'll have the school's director get in contact with you to set up a start time and share any necessary details," he replied.

I was thrilled. This particular child development center accommodated preschool children with special needs and was highly recommended by Kenzie's therapist. In the back of my mind, I couldn't help but think of the irony of the moment. Mandi had dreamed about taking Kenzie to her first day of school since we started talking about having a family. It was not lost on me that the only reason Kenzie was admitted was because Mandi had passed away. I would have never received that phone call under normal circumstances.

Kenzie's first day of school arrived quickly, just a week or two after the call. I had purchased all the required supplies and prepared her school bag and snack. Gigi picked out her outfit for the day, which made her feel as though she was helping her daughter and being a good grandmother. However, she also felt guilty. She stepped in and helped me prepare but wanted so badly for Mandi to be the one who would have the experience of taking her daughter to the first day of school.

Predictably, we arrived fifteen minutes early out of nervousness. I could tell Kenzie was extremely anxious in this new environment. She had only spent considerable time in two places, our home and Pops and Gigi's house. This new adventure would test the limits of her adaptability.

Dressed in a purple shirt that said, "I love my Mommy," Kenzie tensely observed the unfamiliar surroundings as I pushed her in a stroller across the parking lot. Her golden-blonde hair radiated in the morning sun, and her big blue eyes were open wide as she absorbed the new landscape.

As we entered the classroom, we were greeted by her two assigned classroom teachers, Miss Molly and Miss Jodi. Molly had attended high school with Mandi's sisters and was already familiar with our circumstances, which was comforting. Both Molly and Jodi were very patient teachers, but each had high expectations for Kenzie.

Since Kenzie is an only child with special needs, I'm confident she is a bit spoiled in many ways. Reflecting, I arguably haven't pushed her as hard as I could have to make developmental progress, given everything we had experienced with the NICU and with her syndrome, surgeries, and more. Molly and Jodi, as educators, saw Kenzie's potential and worked hard to bring it out of her.

When it was time to leave Kenzie with them for the first time, I felt the tugging of my heartstrings so many parents talk about when dropping their child off on the first day of school. There's joy and happiness, as well as worry and anxiety, all mixed together.

"Daddy loves you, Kenzie-bug," I said as I kissed her on the forehead.

I stood up, took one last look to make sure she was okay, and proceeded with Gigi to head out the door. My baby was in preschool. I had to admit that not only was she growing up, but my life was changing very rapidly. Over the course of a few weeks, I had gone from a two-parent household with a part-time sitter watching Kenzie at home to being a widowed, single father of a special needs preschooler. In my wildest dreams, I could never imagine such a scenario happening.

\* \* \*

My second attempt to return to work in August had been more successful, though I continued to struggle at times with my focus. I made contributions to projects and began to find my way through the most intense grief of the summer. Most importantly, I was working some of that time from my office at home. While it was difficult knowing Mandi wasn't in her office across the hall, I took solace in the fact that Kenzie was often there to keep me company and help me get through the day.

Early in the fall of 2012, an internal job posting came across my email. It wasn't unusual to see announcements once or twice a week for various positions. Our company was relatively large and still growing. This particular position was for a vice president and consultant, essentially, the position I was supporting in my role as assistant vice president of marketing and business development.

I enjoyed the marketing and consulting work I was doing and felt I added something valuable to the organization with my data analysis and creative approach to writing. I had also carved out a niche for myself in the company that allowed me to contribute directly to the bottom line with my consulting work while helping to convert leads into sizable business for the sales staff.

Having turned down the opportunity to move to Iowa back in June, I doubted I had much work capital to apply for the VP position that was now open. After all, I had to take two separate leaves of absence to deal with my grief and get my life in order. Ultimately, I decided it wouldn't hurt to show interest and called Maureen to ask her for more information.

"We're hiring another one or two more vice presidents to focus on managing existing accounts," she told me.

Maureen's "existing accounts" comment caught my attention for two reasons. One, I had a good reputation for creating tools and making recommendations that took my clients' existing results to the next level. And working with the same clients would mean I would have familiar travel routes. When you're selling new business, you often need to drop what you're doing and make a visit at a moment's notice. The "account manager" part of this position would allow me to plan travel well in advance, which would be imperative now that I was a single dad. Best of all, the position continued to report to Maureen, for whom I had tremendous respect.

"I know you likely already have folks in mind for the job, but I wanted to at least call and express my interest," I told her. "This could be a great way to challenge myself while also benefiting the company. I would just need to make sure that childcare could be covered with Mandi's parents, but outside of that, I can see only positive things for me in this role."

"We don't have anybody in mind right now," Maureen said. "I would certainly consider you for the role given your background and history. Why don't you talk it over with the family and make sure you have a solid plan for Kenzie before you formally apply."

I hung up the phone and began thinking about how I could make it work. It would take considerable help from Pops and Gigi to meet the travel demands of the position, but the upside was significant, both professionally and personally. And frankly, I needed a new challenge.

For the first time in a while, I felt a flicker of intellectual curiosity and competitive spirit return as I thought about this job possibility. Plus, I felt that a change in responsibilities and learning a new role might help me climb further out of my grief. But Kenzie's well-being was my top priority, and any interest I had in this position would be secondary to making certain she was taken care of while I was on the road traveling.

"Are you sure you can handle the travel and still have time for Kenzie?" Gigi asked me.

"I'll have a consistent set of clients, most of which are close to home. But I would need you and Pops to help for the one or two nights during a trip that I would be away."

Gigi had long been concerned that I had lost interest in most things after Mandi passed. She was equally concerned with Kenzie's welfare, and no doubt felt compelled to make sure her daughter's baby girl was properly taken care of when I was away. I approached the opportunity with a level head, knowing Kenzie's needs came first. But after four months of intense grief and depression, I was finally starting to show some interest in reshaping my future.

"I ask that you continue to provide us with some nanny help during the day with Kenzie, but if your schedule is manageable, and this is what you want to do, we will watch Kenzie while you're away," Gigi told me the next day. "I have to make sure Kenzie gets what she needs because that is what Mandi would want."

I felt good enough about that answer to formally apply for the position. Several weeks later, I had my interview with Maureen and accepted an offer from her a few days thereafter.

I took two things away from the decision to apply for this new opportunity and subsequently getting the new job. First, Maureen and the company's management team had faith in me and wanted me to succeed. There aren't many organizations, particularly corporations, that would have given me a chance, knowing the difficult road I had just traveled and the uncertainty of what was ahead. I was very fortunate to work with some truly exceptional human beings.

Second, there are times in the grief journey when you have to roll the dice and take a chance on yourself. The easy thing to do would have been to stay with the familiar role and not pursue the promotion. It certainly would have been less risky for a suddenly single parent. But I knew I had reached a fork in the road of life. I had to start moving the needle in a positive direction or risk falling further into depression. At that particular moment in time, the vice president position was what I needed to propel my healing process.

* * *

The holiday season can be especially difficult for people battling grief. So many of the memories we carry of our loved ones are tied to special occasions and family celebrations.

I felt very disconnected the first holiday season without Mandi. I more or less went through the motions. As usual, Pops and Gigi went out of their way to make the days special for Kenzie. But whether it was her third birthday party, Halloween, Thanksgiving, or Christmas, I was subdued and aloof.

Some people will tell you that the first year is the most difficult when grieving the loss of a loved one. To a large extent, that was my experience as well. However, I still felt somewhat numb and in shock during these times. It had only been four to six months since Mandi passed. My passive and apathetic approach was indicative of how I felt overall. It was only after most of the shock and numbness wore off that I started feeling the acute pain others describe. In some ways, the second year and beyond were more difficult for me. I suppose reality had fully set in at those later times that Mandi was never coming back home—a fact I was stubborn to accept.

The holidays eventually became a time when I grieved personally in isolation rather than spending long periods of quality time with family and friends. Because my work at RuffaloCODY largely followed an academic calendar, our clients often took much of December off. Given this annual break, the company had a slow period for the weeks around Christmas.

I used the time around the holidays to reflect. I might pull out photo albums to digitally scan pictures of Mandi, go through her notes and letters to me, or spend time creating tribute videos that reflected on our life together.

Digging through Mandi's belongings almost always led to a depressive episode, though I often couldn't see it happening at the time. My desire was to save everything I could find associated with her. I would spend hours backing up digital photos, videos, or computer files to different locations in the cloud and on flash drives. I would organize and then reorganize her personal effects to make sure they were properly preserved. And I would read the journals Mandi wrote Kenzie while she was in the NICU. It was the perfect breeding ground for my PTSD to resurface, and I would often give in to temptation and walk right into that trap.

I eventually saw the pattern I had created for myself. It was my only method of control over the circumstances that had turned my life upside down. I needed to preserve as much of the past as possible to ensure Kenzie and others could someday truly understand who

Mandi was and who we were as a couple. And I was determined to make sure Mandi was never forgotten.

* * *

By the spring of 2013, Kenzie was threatening to walk solo at any moment. Many children follow standing by taking their first solo steps quickly thereafter, but Kenzie has always been a very cautious, risk-averse child in many ways. While she had the strength and coordination to walk sooner than she did, she was careful not to get adventurous too quickly.

One afternoon in April of 2013, I received a text message from Kenzie's teacher. Miss Molly excitedly wrote me that Kenzie had taken her first steps and began walking during recess! I admit I was skeptical at first. Did she just mean a few steps and then sitting down? Or was this a genuine attempt on Kenzie's part to throw caution to the wind and roam free?

Molly sent me a short video showing Kenzie walking on her own across the playground, one foot in front of the other, and relatively steady.

"Wow!" I said aloud to myself in my office.

I grabbed my keys, cellphone, and let my coworkers know I would be away from my desk for an hour. Driving the twenty minutes across town to the preschool, all I could think about was how Mandi would have reacted to this news. When Kenzie had begun to crawl for the first time after months and months of physical therapy, Mandi cried tears of joy. Some of the pain and guilt she carried as the mother of a special needs child was lifted when she watched Kenzie bunny hop across the floor and proudly display her newfound independence.

Arriving at the school, I headed inside to Kenzie's classroom and attempted to see her actions for myself. I was not disappointed. Peeking around the corner, I watched my daughter confidently walk to where I was standing, squeeze past other people gathered near the open door, and proceed to walk the length of the hallway.

Fortunately, I had the presence of mind to get the moment on video to share with others.

The video serves as a reminder that Kenzie is one of the most perseverant human beings I know. She doesn't know how to give up. After three and a half years, she walked for the first time and ushered in a whole new world of opportunity.

Mandi and I had never been assured by doctors or therapists that she would walk, though most felt she would. To see the happiness on Kenzie's face as she confidently moved around the school on her own two feet was bittersweet. Nearly a year after Mandi's passing, Kenzie had fulfilled what her mother dedicated a portion of each day to help her accomplish.

Kenzie walking was also symbolic of my own baby steps I had taken since Mandi's death. While I was still facing daily anxiety and challenges finding happiness, I had changed jobs and was doing relatively well in the adjustment. I managed to return home permanently in early 2013, though I was still sleeping in the guest bedroom with the master bedroom door always closed. And I had gone back to the gym to start working out again, finding a bit of my old athletic interest that completely fell by the wayside in the months after Mandi passed.

\*\*\*

As the spring months continued along, the date of June 1 began to creep closer and closer. I had dreaded the upcoming first anniversary of Mandi's death. My thoughts became more consumed by the day; my anxiety heightened as I began to think about how I would react. I looked for things I might be able to do that would provide a necessary distraction if needed, but I also wanted to remember Mandi properly and not run from my feelings.

Around mid-April, I began to think about removing my wedding ring. It was a very upsetting thought process, but I felt that the longer I kept the ring on, the more difficult it would be to remove it down the road. I knew the first anniversary of Mandi's death was approaching, and I didn't want to let the calendar dictate my decision. Having been subject to so many things out of my control the prior year, I wanted to be the one who determined the circumstances so I would be at peace with my choice.

For close to seven years, I faithfully wore my ring every day, even when playing golf and other sports. I was proud to be Mandi's husband, and displaying my dedication to the woman I loved so much was very important to me. During the entirety of our marriage, I never even thought about taking off the ring. Now, I had to make the conscious decision to remove it and acknowledge I was no longer married, even if my heart and soul still believed I was.

I made a plan to place my ring alongside Mandi's engagement ring in the safe deposit box at the bank. I felt better knowing our rings would be together. On a Friday morning in April, I pulled my wedding ring off my finger and placed it next to the ring I had given Mandi seven years prior. Carefully, I put the small white ring box back in the safe deposit box next to copies of my will, Kenzie's special needs trust, our wedding CDs, and other personal effects from our marriage that were irreplaceable.

"Is that all you need, Mister Fisher?" the assistant manager at the bank asked as I was leaving. She could tell I was emotional as I wiped away my tears, heading for the door.

"Yes, thank you," I said simply as I walked outside. I sat in my car and cried. My finger felt bare, and my heart felt hollow. My dreams had been crushed, but acknowledging it in such a visible way was more difficult than I had imagined.

Looking back, the act of removing my ring was another way I was trying to gain some level of control over my still-chaotic life. I had switched jobs, moved back into my home—though living in the guest room—and I took off my wedding ring as time crept closer to the first anniversary of her death. Nothing felt within my power to control, but I was doing my best to find a way forward.

\*\*\*

The approach of June 1, 2013, was an exercise in anxiety management. I had dreaded this day for months, and it was now almost upon me. In many ways, the anticipation of the day was just as difficult as the day itself. Fortunately, it was a Saturday. I didn't have to take a day off work because I couldn't function. I just wanted to be with Mandi in my heart and soul that day, not having to think about work deadlines or trying to artificially distract myself with my job.

As I often did on days when my heart was hurting, and I needed to get the pain out, I jotted down my thoughts. At times, I put them out there for friends or family to see, but I would often keep them to myself. The anxiety had built to a point where I needed to pour out my feelings. So, on May 31, the morning before the first anniversary of her death, I decided to post my thoughts to her social media page.

*52 Fridays ago, I lost my best friend. A beautiful spring morning turned out to be a nightmare. It was beyond comprehension. In a split second, without warning, you were gone. The randomness of that moment left me asking questions for which there are no answers. It shook my faith and my very being to the core. It left Kenzie without a mother and left me wondering how I would make it to the next 52 seconds, let alone the next 52 weeks.*

*We are promised nothing in this life. Nothing. Yet, we expect so much. We're conditioned to think that tomorrow will come, that it will be better than today. Except, sometimes tomorrow doesn't come, and the order of the universe is thrown completely upside down for those that remain. Nothing makes sense, and everything is chaos. I've spent the better part of 52 weeks scratching and clawing to return some sort of order to our lives. Yet, there are still moments that I feel as out of control as I did at 9:30 that Friday morning.*

*I've made peace with what happened. I cannot change it despite my best efforts to bend reality, to live in a world where you're still here. There is part of my soul that will always be scarred, devoid of life because you're not physically here with me. I miss your laugh. I miss your smile. I miss your hugs, your kisses, and your thoughtfulness. I miss everything that was, and is, Mandi Cowart Fisher. I'm a better human being because of you. Still flawed in many ways, but better. Perhaps the best compliment that can be paid to another person is your impact on positive change in somebody else's life. If that is the case, there are a tremendous number of people paying compliments to you.*

*If I knew the outcome and could see the future, I would still have married you. You were my soulmate, my best friend. I would have endured all this pain because I was loved unconditionally. And I loved you the same. That's what you search for in life, to be accepted, cherished, and loved—to give it back the same way, as best you can. We're not promised to find somebody like that. I had it, if only for a short time. I have come to view that as a gift.*

*I miss and love you, babe. Now and forever.*

It was just seven o'clock in the morning, but it took every ounce of energy I had to put that on paper and share it publicly. The rest of that day was unproductive. My anxiety was essentially paralyzing me, and I wasn't getting much accomplished at work. All I could think about was Mandi.

I arranged for a babysitter to watch Kenzie on Saturday. I needed to go to the cemetery and spend some time talking to Mandi. Once again, I stopped on the way and picked up a dozen yellow roses to leave on her grave.

The early-morning dew was just evaporating off the grass when I arrived. The day wasn't too warm yet, so I felt I had plenty of time to be with her. I brought a blanket, laid the flowers on her grave, and kissed her headstone.

*Babe, I don't know how it's been a year since you've been gone. I'm doing the best I can moving forward, but it's hard. I miss you every second of the day. My life feels so void without you in it.*

I talk to Mandi every day whether I'm at the cemetery or not. I've never heard a response, but it always makes me feel better knowing I'm sharing my feelings with her. It's helpful in many respects to feel as though she's still listening.

*I don't know how to keep doing this without you. Nothing is easy. I can't make decisions like I used to because you're not with me to listen and help me through it.*

Many people will tell a grieving spouse not to make decisions for six to twelve months, largely to avoid emotional choices that will lead to further difficulty down the road. I tend to agree with that general advice, but I have come to believe the timeline is different for everyone. In my situation, I *had* to make decisions immediately given Kenzie's special needs and my work schedule. Getting her into preschool was a blessing. The promotion helped with the lost income from Mandi's passing, and childcare was more expensive than before. I had no need for two cars, so I sold my car back to the dealership and kept Mandi's SUV for vehicle safety and practicality. I had no problems making logical or financial choices. It was emotional decisions that were paralyzing me.

*** 

I was not forced to move from the house I shared with Mandi. Financially, I could make the payments and take care of the property. However, emotionally, I needed to leave. I had given it several months, and while things were better, I still couldn't go into the master bedroom or Mandi's office without shutting my eyes and moving quickly.

The decision to sell the house was a difficult one to make. The real estate market was not in great shape at the time. We had a 3,025-square-foot home with four bedrooms and a bonus room for Mandi's office. It was going to be the home we raised three kids in, or so we naïvely thought.

Big homes in our location were not selling well in 2013, and I would likely take a significant financial hit. Still, I knew I couldn't stay there much longer. Psychologically, I needed the change. Unfortunately, the house sat on the market for about seven months. I knew the process would require patience, but I began to get the feeling the real estate agent I had picked wasn't using the latest marketing techniques to get my property seen by potential buyers. I decided to switch agents, using a friend of Michael's who had a good reputation for finding buyers quickly.

I introduced myself to Sam and told him Michael had referred him. "I've had my house on the market for nearly seven months now but have not had any viewings. I know the market is slow, but the property is in immaculate condition, and it's priced aggressively."

"Let me pull it up and take a look," Sam replied.

I could hear him typing on the keyboard as he reviewed the details that were currently online. "You need some better photos that show the property in a way that is consistent with the verbiage on the listing," Sam said, pointing out areas where he would make changes.

"Sam, my situation is a bit unique," I mentioned. "My wife passed away last year. While I could stay, I simply want to get out from underneath the house, downsize a bit, and start over."

"I completely understand," he replied. "I think your price is okay, but I would recommend lowering it again to get the foot traffic out to take a look at it. The problem isn't the property. You're in a tough market, but you have to get potential buyers to see it in person, or you'll never get an offer."

Sam and I agreed on a lower sale price, and we set up a time the next day for an early afternoon photo shoot to give the house the maximum amount of natural sunlight.

As I pulled into the driveway the next day, Sam was already outside taking pictures.

"I love the property," he told me as we shook hands. "I think we're going to be able to move this house quickly if I can generate some traffic."

"Are you thinking about having an open house?" I asked.

"Honestly, most of my sales don't happen at open houses. I work the internet hard, push social media, and maintain many past client contacts. I have a lot of repeat buyers," Sam said.

Sam was a younger man, perhaps in his late twenties at the time. His style was very friendly, but I could quickly tell his biggest asset was knowing this industry well.

"How soon until we can list it again?" I asked.

"I'll go home and pick out the best photos. We should be able to have it up and on the market tomorrow," Sam said.

"Wow, that's fast. I appreciate it!"

Once the house was listed online, it was apparent that Sam's tactics were working. Like changing bait while fishing, it took just a day or two before we started getting "bites"—in this case, calls and requests for walk-throughs. The desired result came quickly.

"We have an offer," Sam said with a matter-of-fact tone. "The offer is low compared to your listing price. But the owner will guarantee the sale goes through because he'll pay in cash."

I quickly ran the numbers in my head. I would be taking a significant loss, particularly after paying the real estate fees. I thought about counteroffering but didn't want to lose the opportunity for a guaranteed sale and quick move. I knew I may not get another offer any time soon.

My instincts told me it was time to go, I had met the challenge of going home again, and I had nothing else to prove. I no longer felt comfortable in the house, and there was little sense in torturing myself daily over a few thousand dollars. "Accept it," I told Sam. "I'm willing to take the loss at this point to start over."

I found a small apartment in West Mobile closer to Kenzie's school and just down the street from Pops and Gigi's house. It was a significant downsize, but I was looking forward to having less responsibility with my home and focusing more on Kenzie. I had re-homed our dog, Gracie, to Samantha, a good friend whose family could give her the love and attention I was struggling to provide. All that was left to do was pack up the house and move.

As moving day quickly approached, I took a few days off work and made arrangements for Kenzie to be watched by Mandi's parents. I purchased the boxes, packing materials, and totes I needed to make the move. Many of Mandi's items had remained untouched to that point. I knew packing would be much more difficult emotionally than it would be physically.

I started with Mandi's office. I'm not sure why, other than perhaps I felt the need to jump into the deep end of the pool and immediately begin the tough task of methodically going through her things to carefully preserve those items I needed to keep. It was all but impossible to pack her desk quickly. Every note she had made to herself on a scratch pad had meaning. Every work journal she had used was priceless. Even her favorite pens had value. I couldn't bring myself to give away any of it. There were too many memories to preserve.

I boxed up her remaining office equipment, all the supplies she had used, and set aside items I thought I could incorporate into my own office as a way of keeping her with me. I spent several hours going through her desk, stopping every few minutes to read something she had written and have a good cry. I felt her presence with me, and I did my best to pack up her items with the utmost care.

As I went room by room, the accumulating memories began to feel suffocating. I had to take frequent rests to stop from completely breaking down emotionally. I was making good progress in boxing up the entire house by myself. Yet, I had left the most challenging room until the end—the last place Mandi was alive. The master bedroom would take all my energy and focus.

Mandi's clothes still hung neatly in the closest. Her favorite pair of earrings still sat on top of the wooden jewelry box on her dresser.

I hadn't slept in our bed for over a year. It was as if time had stood still in our bedroom, the horrible events of June 1, 2012, still only a split-second away in my memory at any given point. The entire year that had passed could not adequately prepare me to pack up Mandi's things.

I had made a conscious decision not to give any of her belongings away until I was ready. Everything would be put into storage until I located a more permanent place to live and could take my time sorting through the items, deciding what to keep and what to donate.

I took each item of Mandi's clothing, enclosed it in a plastic garment wrapper, and taped the opening shut to give it maximum protection. All her shoes and her purses were placed inside giant zipper bags and sealed. Occasionally, I would find articles of clothing that would bring back a memory, causing me to stop and have a hard cry before eventually moving on to the next item.

I carefully went through her jewelry box, matched each pair of earrings, and placed them in small bags to keep them from being separated. If I found a particularly special item, like a necklace I had purchased for her, I was careful to set that aside and keep it in the safe deposit box. I even packed up her haircare items and toiletries, unable to simply discard them and move on.

Working late into the night, I finally finished boxing up the master bedroom. I sat on the floor near where the paramedics had attended to Mandi, lying my head down on the spot where I thought she might have had her last conscious thoughts. I closed my eyes and prayed for a sign that she was with me, that she could hear me, and that everything was going to be okay. I wanted so badly to see her again, to tell her I loved her and was sorry. But I heard or saw nothing. Exhausted, with visions in my mind of my beautiful wife lying next to me, I drifted off to sleep.

The movers came early the next morning. They backed the long moving van into the driveway, leaving just enough room for the ramp into the back of the truck to comfortably extend toward the front door.

I had already sold the living room furniture, knowing I could never use it again, so some of the heavy items had already been taken away. Piece by piece, the three guys they assigned loaded up the carefully packed belongings. It wasn't long before the house looked eerily empty, similar to before we had bought it. It was a bittersweet moment. I could not stay there and expect to thrive again. It was our home, but it was also the last place Mandi was alive and conscious. I needed to change the scenery to avoid reliving that day again and again.

After my furnishings were delivered to the apartment and the storage unit, I went back to the house one last time to clean and lock up. Before leaving, I sat on the floor and talked to Mandi.

"Babe, I don't know if I'm doing the right thing, but I'm not sure how else to move my life forward. I miss you. I want to come home to you here, but I can't," I said out loud, as if she could hear me. "I love you so much. I'm sorry if you're still here, and I'm leaving you. Please come with Kenzie and me."

For the prior thirteen months, I had sought signs that Mandi was still in our lives. I had heard or seen nothing remarkable during that time, which was both comforting and disappointing—comforting in the sense that I didn't need the additional trauma of having an unexplainable experience. But I missed her terribly and secretly hoped for a magical moment of interaction that would give me some measure of peace.

Before I locked the door behind me, I gave the inside one last look. All the dreams and hopes were gone. I had nothing left now but memories. It was up to me to find the strength to keep those memories alive. I pulled out of the driveway and did not look back, making up my mind that my only direction now was forward. Driving out of the neighborhood in July 2013 would be the last time I physically laid eyes on our home of so many promises.

I never returned, choosing to remember the house in my mind and through our pictures rather than feeling the pain of days I could not get back.

# CHAPTER 12

# The Escape Artist

Going from 3,025 square feet of living space with a big backyard to a cramped 1,300-square-foot apartment with no yard was quite a shock to our lifestyle. But it was a relief not to be visually reminded daily of the tragedy that had unfolded in our house, and I was looking forward to a fresh start with Kenzie. The size of our home was unimportant compared to the opportunity to move forward.

The apartment was in a newer complex. It was a three-bedroom, two-bath with an attached garage. Nothing too fancy, but it had what Kenzie and I needed at the time: a ground-floor layout with no stairs and closer proximity to Pops and Gigi for assistance with childcare when I traveled.

At the onset, the apartment felt like a new beginning. Sure, it was small. But Kenzie and I did not need a lot of space, and the change of scenery helped my comfort. I had sold most of our furniture to downsize considerably. I kept the futon that was in my home office and used it for a couch. And I kept the guest bedroom furniture Mandi had purchased and used it as my bedroom furniture for the time being. I maintained my office furniture and kept Kenzie's room intact, sending everything else to a storage unit to accommodate the reduction in space.

I knew the apartment would be a temporary stop; I signed a year lease, intending to find a more permanent location within that timeframe. My main focus was to continue my therapy and healing, establish myself in my new role at work, and be the best dad I could be to Kenzie. I started exercising regularly at the gym just down the street and concentrated on the meteorology classes I had just started taking as a way to jumpstart interest in living life again.

Compared to the prior summer, I was in a better place mentally, still grieving but functioning. I had grown so isolated in the year since Mandi passed and lost many of the connections I once had to outside activities, so I had been thinking about ways to keep my mind off the negative feelings of losing my wife and rechannel that energy into something positive.

Prior to Mandi's passing, I had shared with her some information about a certificate program in broadcast meteorology at Mississippi State University. Almost entirely online, the program was meant for working professionals who were already in broadcast journalism but perhaps lacked an official certification to deliver a weather forecast. The certificate would allow you to sit for the National Weather Service's Seal of Approval and further advance your career.

There were also non-broadcasting professionals who were interested in the weather, potentially as a career, but lacked the formal training needed to switch professions. Some students wanted to help their careers in emergency management, and other students, like myself, just had an intense passion for meteorology.

I had been fascinated with the weather since I learned to walk and talk. Growing up in eastern Iowa, we saw our share of severe storms. On the eastern edge of tornado alley, we were trained by teachers and our parents to be weather-wise. By age five, I could tell you the difference between a watch and a warning, knew which directions tornadoes typically tracked—to the northeast in the northern hemisphere—and understood the basic requirements to classify a severe storm. I had a favorite meteorologist on our local television news and always made sure I was tuned in about twelve minutes after the hour for the start of the weather segment.

"Babe," I said to Mandi one afternoon in March of 2012. "I've been looking at this online meteorology certificate program at Mississippi State. It's seventeen classes total. You go part-time, completely at home, except for a few days during the last semester where you have to be on campus for the final comprehensive exam."

"You should do it!" Mandi replied quickly.

She knew I loved the weather and likely felt that I needed a positive goal to focus on after our experience in the NICU. Mandi had also been looking at going back to school for an MBA, which I encouraged her to pursue.

"I'm not sure about the program," I said. "I'm worried that a certificate won't be enough to potentially switch careers if that is what I want to do at a later time."

"Who cares?" Mandi said in a sarcastically funny way. "You're doing something you love, and you get to do it completely remote. What other meteorology options are there for that?"

She had a point. The options for online coursework in meteorology were limited at the time. Still, I had the mentality that I wanted something more than a certificate if I spent time completing seventeen classes.

"I'll think about it," I said. "I have some time to apply."

I never filled out that application. June 1 happened, and my goal at that point was survival and stability, to readjust to life without my best friend. But gradually, over time, my outlook began to change. I needed to learn how to live again and began to think about *how* I would live now that Mandi was no longer with me. She had been my motivation and my inspiration for so many years; with her death, a part of my spirit for living a fun, adventurous life left me. But I remembered the discussion we'd had about going back to school part-time—meteorology for me and an MBA for her.

Sitting at my desk one Saturday afternoon early in 2013, I pulled up the website for Mississippi State's online meteorology certificate and once again looked at the criteria. Unlike a year prior, I viewed the program from a different perspective. Instead of looking at it from a career-only standpoint, I remembered Mandi's words to me.

"Who cares?" she had said.

Mandi wanted me to enjoy myself, to live life happily and to the fullest. To her, it was about the journey—not the destination. She lived life in the present, not the future, and certainly not the past.

"I need to do this," I said to myself. "I need to start living again."

I printed out the information on the website, requested transcripts from the colleges I had attended, and started putting together the basics for the application. The classes would begin in August, which was a long way off at that point. I could have easily changed my mind and backed out. I may or may not end up being a practicing meteorologist, but I was okay with the uncertainty. The most important factor was that I would had something positive to look forward to and enjoy, which I desperately needed at that point in life. I decided to go for it.

After formally applying and being accepted, I purchased my first textbooks and started classes in August of 2013. Almost instantly, I became hooked on the material in my Intro to Meteorology class. Many of the weather concepts I already understood were explained in greater detail. I found myself loving the learning process again. Already having an undergraduate degree in both political science and business administration from Coe College, and my master's degree in public service from the Clinton School at the University of Arkansas, I had a solid foundation in liberal arts and social science. Now I was challenging myself in physical sciences and math, which required a different type of thinking—a more robust focus to relearn the basics and overcome my relative fear of algebra and calculus.

Learning is a lifelong process. I firmly believe this to be true. We should never stop challenging ourselves to be better, whether formally in school or informally in other ways. When I applied for the meteorology program, I learned I was only an additional five classes from a full bachelor's degree because of my prior coursework. So, I changed my schedule and pursued the full program curriculum. In all, it took me six years to finish the program, taking one or two classes per semester as my schedule would allow.

In addition to learning a new skill, the meteorology program served as the perfect distraction for me when I needed it most. I wasn't running from something but rather toward something when I decided to pursue the certificate and, eventually, the degree. Taking classes in a subject matter I enjoyed allowed me to begin a vital transformation after Mandi's passing. I was taking a lesson she taught me and making it happen: don't get caught up in chasing goals for the wrong reason. Enjoy the journey. It matters far more for your happiness than the destination.

\*\*\*

Mobile and the surrounding community was the only place I had ever lived in Alabama. I thought about leaving to go someplace close, yet far enough away where everything felt like a fresh start. I still felt unsettled and did not want to deeply put down roots when I wasn't sure exactly where I wanted to live.

My mind flashed back to the summer of 2010. On a Sunday afternoon, while reading the paper, I had casually thrown out an idea to Mandi. "Hey, babe. What would you say if we bought a condo at the beach for a weekend rental?"

"Don't tease!" Mandi exclaimed.

Property prices then were distressed, given the state of the economy and the collapse of the real estate market. The beach area of Alabama was hit particularly hard. "There are a ton of condo and beachfront properties that are in foreclosure right now. Prices are very affordable. If there were ever a time to buy something at the beach, now would be the time to do it."

"Can we afford it?" Mandi asked.

"That depends on how nice of a place we would want," I said. "But I can check things out online. Maybe if rates are good, we take the plunge. You know the market will come back sooner or later."

"I would love to live at the beach, even if it were just a weekend place," she said. "Yes, let's look."

After a few weeks of looking and reviewing the budget, we decided it would probably be more intelligent to focus on paying down the mortgage on our home in Semmes rather than investing in another property and getting too financially extended. However, we kept the conversation alive by continuing to talk about it.

As the August 2014 deadline to extend my apartment lease grew closer, I found myself remembering my condo conversations with Mandi and reviving the discussion—if only in my own head. Making decisions on living arrangements was much easier than choosing where Kenzie would go to school. That decision loomed as well.

Mobile County and Baldwin County are the only two counties in Alabama that touch the coastal waters. Many families live in Baldwin but work in Mobile, connecting the two counties economically as well as by proximity. On an average day, it took only about an hour to drive to Gulf Shores or Orange Beach from Mobile.

My work at RuffaloCODY—by then called "Ruffalo Noel Levitz" after a merger—could be done remotely from my home office. As long as I could continue to travel to client sites and conferences as I had before, I could live anywhere technology allowed me to.

Kenzie had started her third year of preschool at Goodwill Easter Seals Child Development Center, and I wanted to find a permanent home for us before she began her elementary school years. Unfortunately, there are very few specialized options for children with disabilities in Alabama, particularly in the southern part of the state. And with a recent diagnosis of autism in addition to her rare syndrome, it was especially important I find the right multi-disability classroom environment for her.

In the spring of 2014, I had taken her to San Antonio to be seen by one of the experts at the Chromosome 18 Registry & Research Society and evaluate whether her poor social skills, nonverbal status, and lack of eye contact was typical for a child with Distal 18q- or whether she also had autism along with her genetic deletion.

Following a series of evaluations, it was determined that Mackenzie was indeed also on the autism spectrum, further muddying the waters as to which delays could be attributed to her syndrome, and which might be due to her autistic features. In any event, it would not alter the treatment program and the many therapies she would need. Autism would likely just make it more difficult for Kenzie to hit her milestone developmental goals.

Similar to many other autistic children, Kenzie did have some level of speech early in life. She had only said one word, "Mama," for about two to three months when she was fourteen months old before she lost the word. She never regained the ability to talk after Christmas of 2010. Looking back, I'm thankful that the one word Kenzie said, and that Mandi got to hear, was "Mama."

It is both heartbreaking and frustrating to raise a nonverbal child. The frustration mounts for them in numerous ways, particularly when they cannot tell you what hurts, or why they don't feel well. As a parent, you're left solely to your instincts and the medical history of the child to render a guess as to what may be wrong, and whether it warrants a trip to the doctor. The heartbreak for me as a parent comes from seeing Kenzie try so hard to communicate but not be able to connect. And as a single parent, the pain for me is especially amplified when I cannot have a simple two-way conversation with the only other person in my home.

Until 2018, Alabama did not require insurance companies to cover applied behavioral analysis therapy, which is a proven method of interacting with autistic and cognitively challenged individuals to positively modify learning and behavior. It's expensive, but it works. To that point in time, only a handful of schools in the state, public or private, worked exclusively with children with disabilities or autism. The private school in Mobile that served autistic children had a significant wait list. And based on where I was living at the time, I wasn't impressed with the local public school she would attend in the multiple disability classroom.

It became apparent to me that Kenzie's best chance in south Alabama for a quality education would be in Baldwin County, where the public schools had a better reputation for quality academics and good facilities. In the summer of 2014, I decided to research what the best options in Baldwin County might be, should I choose to relocate. I narrowed my list to several schools and locations, ultimately deciding to meet with the principal of Gulf Shores Elementary. I had heard positive things about the environment at the school and felt it was as good a place as any to begin my search.

Before the meeting, I had written up an executive summary of Kenzie's cognitive needs and health challenges, complete with research articles on her syndrome and characteristics that were unique to Kenzie's diagnosis. I wanted the administrators at the school to have a thorough background on Kenzie so they could give me their honest opinion as to whether or not they felt they could help her.

During our meeting in late July, the principal took an hour away from her busy day to meet with me. We covered the summary I had written, which included all the major points of Kenzie's diagnosis. I came away from the meeting thoroughly impressed with the school's compassion toward their special needs children. It would have been easy for the principal to give us fifteen minutes of her valuable time and then go back to her administrative workload. But the fact that she took the time to ask probative questions made me feel we were in the right place.

There was a particular set of condominium-style apartments that I felt would be perfect for Kenzie and me. They were located off a main road in Orange Beach, a city adjacent to Gulf Shores and only a few miles away from Gulf Shores Elementary School.

The condominiums were built in the months leading up to the housing crisis in 2008. The developer had financial issues and ended up selling to a company that managed apartment properties. Unlike many apartment homes, these condominiums were extremely well-built, with thick walls, high ceilings, and nice amenities.

They felt much more like a home or townhome than they did an apartment complex.

Because Orange Beach Elementary School did not have a multi-disability program at the time, children who met the criteria were sent to Gulf Shores Elementary on a waiver. We could live in Orange Beach and not affect Kenzie's ability to attend Gulf Shores Elementary.

Orange Beach was close enough to the University of South Alabama's Children's & Women's hospital for Kenzie's appointments, which was another primary consideration. While Kenzie was no longer as medically fragile as she had been when she was younger, she still had a G-tube for feeding, thyroid medical maintenance, and the uncertainty that generally came with her syndrome.

"I have some news," I said to Gigi in a low-toned voice.

"You found somebody, and you're getting married," Gigi said with a semi-serious reply.

"No!" I said shaking my head. "I've decided to move to Orange Beach and put Kenzie into Gulf Shores Elementary."

"You're moving?" she replied. "That's so far away."

"It's only an hour away," I said, trying to downplay the distance. "I'm still within driving distance of Mobile for hospital or doctor visits, family outings, and other appointments."

"Oh, Jason. Are you sure about this?" she asked.

"I signed the paperwork on the condo rental yesterday and enrolled Kenzie into Gulf Shores Elementary. We will move in mid-September."

I explained my reasoning to Gigi as best I could. I talked about interviewing the principal at the school, researching other options in Mobile and Baldwin counties, and finding a comfortable place to live. I had done my homework on this potential move. I had not made a quick decision without studying the pros and cons.

The move to Orange Beach was exciting in many respects but intimidating in others. I was looking forward to starting anew and not being faced with the familiar scenery of Mobile that brought about so many memories of Mandi—both good and bad. But I also knew I was now on my own more than ever before.

I would be moving to a more isolated location where I knew nobody. I had to find childcare—someone who could work overnight when I was out of town for my job—and establish new pharmacies for Kenzie's medications. However, my primary support system was an hour away. If I needed anything, they would be there as fast as possible. But I was giving up the comfort of having help just a few blocks down the road.

* * *

We moved to Orange Beach in September of 2014. Kenzie started her final year of preschool almost immediately, attending Gulf Shores Elementary three days per week. She was in a small classroom environment with several periods of one-on-one assistance with her multi-disability teacher during the day. I was back at work quickly, taking off only a day or two after the weekend move.

During the two years since Mandi had died, my schedule had adjusted to one where I was early to bed and early to rise. I learned in the beginning that if you didn't sleep when Kenzie slept, she would make sure you didn't sleep much at all once she was awake.

One morning, I woke from a stirring dream of Mandi. I rarely remember the details of my dreams, but this one was so vivid that it was almost impossible for me to forget. We were at a social gathering of some sort—a few of my friends, a few of her friends, and some of our family. There was the idle chit-chat one would expect in a big gathering. And there was Mandi's gregarious laugh that filled the room. But there was also music playing, which wasn't unusual if Mandi was around. I still have vivid memories of her in the kitchen, listening to whatever her favorite band was at the time, singing into the wooden spoon she was using to cook with, as if it were a microphone.

As I approached Mandi in my dream to talk with her, I suddenly woke up. I sat up in the bed for a split second, thinking she was still with me. Recognizing it was just a dream, I immediately felt a sense of disappointment that I didn't get the chance to say "hello" or that I loved her.

My dreams of Mandi were infrequent and often occurred this way: Mandi was in the room, I knew her as my wife, but we would never get the chance to talk. I might try speaking to her in my dream, but it was as if she paid me little attention—as if I was not worthy of her talking to me. Of course, this was foolish thinking. The real Mandi never ignored anybody. She was friends with everyone she knew. And she certainly would talk to me. But the dreams bothered me enough that they started interrupting my sleep patterns.

Crawling out of bed and getting ready for the day, it occurred to me I was humming a song that had been playing in my dream from just moments before. The distinct melody was stuck in my head. I couldn't remember the title or the artist.

It's no surprise that music was in my dream with Mandi. She loved listening to a wide variety of genres. Bon Jovi was her all-time favorite, but she always tried to find new artists to accompany her traditional interests like Elvis Presley, Elton John, or Sister Hazel. Our credit card would constantly show charges for $1.99 or $10.99 on it as she would download her latest favorite song or album.

Like many things that spark my curiosity, I typed a few keywords into the internet search engine, trying to find out more about the song. It didn't take long to discover that Five for Fighting's hit song "100 Years" was the melody I had heard in my dream. At 4:30 a.m. that morning, shortly after waking up, I watched the music video of the track.

I sat dumbfounded as I pondered how my life seemed to fit into the narrative and lyrics of the song. Music often reflects life, and the best songs almost always make you think deeper about the important things in your world. "100 Years" was no exception. In fact, it seemed to be the rule for me.

I downloaded the song on my phone, put in my earbuds, and got Kenzie ready for school. I listened to the music repeatedly, each replay of the lyrics further reinforcing what seemed to be a song I had known all my life. Sure, I had heard it before but not recently. Yet, that morning, it was as if the music had been inside me the entire time, just waiting to be rediscovered.

Everything about the song seemed to resonate. The melody was comfortable, and the lyrics made it easy to see my life as it had unfolded. Each season brings challenges, along with new joys and pain. There are but a finite number of years we have, often marked by the milestones of life. As the years move on, and we reflect on our time here, our memories find us circling back to those we love, and who have come to define our existence for the short time we are alive.

Images of Mandi came into my mind: the first time I saw her in the airport, the first time we kissed in Florida, sharing the altar at our wedding, and bringing Kenzie home from the NICU for the first time.

I must have played the song a hundred times in the days that followed. My eyes would fill with tears as I recalled my life with Mandi. The images and words seemed to mesh so perfectly—as if they were meant to be together.

I felt compelled to create what I was thinking, to make the images truly blend with the music. I got out my laptop and started learning how to put a video together using pictures and music. I added the song first, then the images, timing them to the lyrics to match what was in my mind, blending them together. I refined the video again and again until the quality was good. Then I refined it some more.

Tears would stream down my face as I saw the final product coming together.

*Of course!* I said to myself. *Mandi is speaking to me through music.*

For so long, I had been waiting to hear her voice or perhaps have something happen that would let me know she was there with me. But music was her world. Through the dream and this song, she was communicating with me and whispering in my ear.

Of course, this is a very personalized experience. I could not prove this was actually her communicating with me, nor would I feel the need to try. I used the music as a creative outlet, allowing me to channel my innermost feelings and thoughts into something I could mold and shape until it turned out precisely how I felt it should be. I seemed to have gained a sense of control when I had no control over the circumstances involving Mandi's death. The video creation was part therapy and part art, and it was exactly what I needed to let out a lot of emotional pain.

I'm not a videographer, nor am I an artist, but the sheer power of the video for me was not in recalling the images themselves but rather in the story it told. I discovered that the video mirrored what I had been feeling and thinking for so many months but could not express. The emotions it displayed were in my heart and soul. It was as if the universe opened up briefly and let me connect with what I so desperately needed to see and feel.

There would be other videos I would create as the years went on, each using a different song that would come to me at some point when I was thinking about Mandi. I got better at sharing the story I was feeling and creating the videos, eventually even weaving in actual footage from our wedding and reflecting on our life lived together through cherished photos. But it was the first song—"100 Years"—that opened up a portal into my soul when I needed it the most.

*⁂*

Many young widows and widowers end up throwing themselves into their work as a way to stay focused on something other than their grief. I fell into that category as well, though it did take some time and a position change within the company before I was back up to speed.

From 2013 through 2016, I handled a considerable workload for a single dad with a special needs toddler. Working remotely, I balanced home- and work-life as best I could, using a network of babysitters and family members to piece together my schedule and make things work.

At one point in my job as vice president and senior consultant, I had more than twenty-five accounts across the country that were my responsibility. It was nearly impossible to visit each one regularly, though I did my best to maintain contact via the telephone and email. My time was spread thin, and I was focused on a group of challenging clients, either from a programmatic or results standpoint.

For the first year or two, the new VP job was exhilarating. I worked for Maureen, enjoying new colleagues and friends and feeling as though I was making a substantial contribution to my clients and the company. Given my background and experience, I was often asked to solve problems or give opinions on how we handled larger, big-picture challenges within the industry.

It was also not unusual for me to spend two to three weeks of every month traveling for my job. While it was challenging to find reliable babysitting and overnight care at times, staying busy was good for my psychological health. Work was providing the positive distraction I needed to continue healing. It allowed me to escape from the difficult memories and focus on building something positive instead of tearing myself down.

In 2014, Ruffalo Noel Levitz was sold to an investment company interested in our history of success within the industry. The investors assured us they liked our business model and wanted to enhance our products. They had connections and experiences to make it happen and take our company to another level.

As is the case with many companies that undergo a sale, a portion of the senior management stayed on to help lead the new organization while others decided to go their separate ways. Some retired. Some found new projects outside the company. For me, it was a time of great transition after more than twenty total years of professional stability.

From my standpoint, the sale of the company was a mixed bag. There was a level of enthusiasm for the future and also a measure of sadness with the departure of so many colleagues. Over time, several of my closest coworkers and friends left to try their hand at other things they were interested in doing, including both Duane and Maureen. Another close mentor, Stan, retired, as did Al.

I decided to stay on. And while I was excited to see what the future held for the organization, I didn't know anyone on the executive leadership team. These new managers seemed nice and spoke about a family atmosphere, but they were still learning about our business and history of the company.

Personal relationships had built RuffaloCODY over many years. In the corporate world, the ultimate responsibility of the executive team is to make money for the shareholders, whether they be public or private. The genius of our leadership at RuffaloCODY was they were able to balance rapid company growth while creating a positive, team-oriented atmosphere. Lasting friendships were formed, and a sense of community permeated the environment. That is not easy to do, given the pressure and high expectations of the C-suite jobs.

After the merger and sale, our culture began to change. Part of that change was inevitable. Our product line that had supplied most of our clients and revenue for years was starting to be phased out or de-emphasized on the campuses we worked. We did our best to stay ahead of the curve, but the technology was changing faster than we could adapt and fine-tune our new products to the marketplace, and our clients began to scrutinize their return on investment more intensely.

The importance of sales goals and client reverence had been stressed since the early days the company was formed. But with the changing product line and the growing expectations, the atmosphere became more punitive when goals were missed or errors happened. We knew we had to adapt and be innovative, but there were growing pains with new products and the necessary speed of our changes made it challenging to effectively adjust to the new business climate.

The summer of 2016 became particularly tumultuous for me. Work was as demanding as ever; goals were being missed because of the changing market, and investors seemed to be concerned. Personally, Kenzie was changing and growing rapidly. While her medical needs began to lessen, her cognitive challenges continued to be significant. She was falling farther and farther behind her peers.

When my workload was reasonable, and I had a supportive supervisor, I flourished. However, the stability the company enjoyed for so many years had changed. A new culture of high-pressure sales had replaced many of the personal relationships that, at one time, had nourished our employees' creative minds and gave confidence to our clients in times of turbulence.

By the fall of 2016, I was beginning to feel it was time for a change. With little room for error, and leadership demanding more productivity from fewer people, the stress of the job outweighed the benefit of distraction I had been receiving since Mandi's death. Many of my close friends and colleagues were gone. Work had not been fun in quite some time, and I eventually realized this was not a blip on the radar but rather the new normal.

Following an extensive period of late-summer and early-fall travel, I needed a break. I longed for the days when I could talk to Mandi, and we could balance the workload at home. Instead, being the sole provider both financially and parentally had worn me down.

I pleaded with my boss to cut back my travel or help me find a non-traveling position within the company. I was encouraged to be patient and was told something would come along soon that would limit my travel. But the goalposts kept moving. Ultimately, it never happened. I didn't blame him. He was a friend and under the same pressure I was. The circumstances were such that I could request more family time all I wanted, but beyond my immediate supervisor, the pleas seemed to fall on deaf ears.

I sank into a depression, mild at first, then more significant as the fall continued. My anxiety about job performance, Kenzie's progress, and the continuing pain from Mandi's death ate me up from the inside. I told nobody about what I was going through, fearing for my job as coworkers departed left and right. And I also felt powerless to stop it.

I parted ways with Ruffalo Noel Levitz soon thereafter, allowing two months for the transition of my responsibilities. It had been a long journey, and a fruitful one in so many ways. I had earned eight promotions total, traveled the world, had leadership and management opportunities, learned from the best in the business, and was given significant creative control over my employment destiny.

Change can be difficult for many people, including me. I understand it to be a part of life and something that should be taken in stride. It's necessary at times for the revitalization of the human spirit. But when you're the single parent of a child with a rare syndrome, unforeseen change can have significant consequences.

I had escaped many times after Mandi's passing. I found new places to live, new jobs to perform, new degrees to seek, and new friends to make. I was always attempting to reinvent myself, partly to keep my marketability high and partly because I needed the challenge. Escaping also helped keep my mind off my wife's death. Now, following an eye-opening internal struggle for happiness and self-worth, it was time to move forward with confidence in the skills I had acquired and the accomplishments I had achieved over my many years in business, education, and public service. There were new mountains to climb.

# CHAPTER 13

# An Awakening Spirit

In many ways, finding the path home began with my journey to rediscover who I was in my inner core. What precisely was my self-worth, and what did I want to do with the rest of my life?

Looking back, my life with Mandi had been precisely what I had envisioned it would be when I asked her to marry me. Marriage was the celebration of our life we had already started building together many years before. My identity as a person had evolved. I had become less self-absorbed in my own interests over our ten years together, moving from a person focused mainly on his individual goals to one who learned how to better appreciate the absolute value in putting others first.

June 1, 2012, had been my worst nightmare come true. In the days and weeks that followed, I became lost in so many ways. My best friend was gone. I went from a partnership that was clicking on all cylinders to being a lonely, grief-stricken widowed father of a disabled child in the blink of an eye. I constantly felt the weight of my circumstances. It seemed every day was June 1.

The roadmap I created for our lives had been scrambled. Nothing looked familiar, and everything felt uncomfortable. Each decision I made in those weeks and months that followed became much more complex, carrying the burden of asking myself what Mandi would do and considering the ramifications of my choices. Kenzie always came first; that was the easy part. But I was forced to ask myself what the value of my life was outside of marriage.

As the calendar flipped to 2017, I needed to find the passion I once had to be able to move forward. I pushed myself to relearn how to be okay with prioritizing my happiness and not apologizing for it. Guilt still prevented that from being an easy transition. My identity had become so closely wrapped in my marriage that it was difficult to see how I could function as an individual after Mandi passed.

\*\*\*

Taking the online meteorology courses at Mississippi State was one of the first steps toward improving my self-esteem and seeing my individual worth again. I studied day and night to make sure I got the best grades possible, refusing to go through the motions just to get the piece of paper. I wanted to enjoy the experience and use it as a springboard for a better state of happiness.

Slowly adjusting to life without Mandi, I became interested in other activities I hadn't been involved with before. I joined the board of directors at the Chromosome 18 Registry & Research Society, which served Mackenzie and other children with genetic disorders affecting the eighteenth chromosome. It was satisfying and exciting to advocate and lobby for additional research dollars, raise money through events, and lend a hand in other ways where I could.

Politics and public service had also remained a passion. I enjoyed researching and understanding policy, particularly how it impacted the lives of those less fortunate. Political campaigns captured my interest growing up in Iowa, where we were guaranteed a front-row seat every four years to watch the inner workings of presidential candidates and campaigns—from both sides of the aisle. You couldn't ask for a better setting to learn the political ropes.

From 1988 to 2008, I managed to meet every Democratic nominee for president in person—and a few Republicans too. While living in Iowa, I canvassed houses and helped with errands for some Democratic campaigns, even before I could vote. At twenty-one years old, in my first election I was eligible to vote for president, I was selected as a delegate to the Linn County Democratic Convention for Bill Clinton. In 2000, I was chosen as an alternate delegate for Al Gore.

With so many interests on the list of possibilities for my next professional foray, I began to take steps to identify what I wished to pursue. I networked and looked for new jobs. I researched online and read many different publications to get a feel for my next goal. One afternoon in the spring of 2017, I was watching the local news while cleaning our condo in Orange Beach.

"Governor Ivey issued an order today calling for a special election to fill the seat of former US Senator Jeff Sessions, a seat now occupied by Luther Strange," the newscaster said. "The governor set August 15 as the date for a primary election, with the general election to be held on December 12 later this year."

The previous governor, Robert Bentley, had appointed Luther Strange to the seat after Sessions resigned to take the job as US Attorney General. However, Bentley resigned in scandal shortly after the appointment, leaving the new governor, Kay Ivey, with the opportunity to distance herself from that decision.

To that point, I had not given much thought to politics as a potential career. Sure, I had always appreciated the art of politics and thought I might run for office one day, but I was never close to seriously considering it. Yet, something inside me made me stop and watch the newscast with more intensity than usual.

After I finished cleaning, I went upstairs and got on my computer. I searched the internet for the election results from 2016. Following politics, I knew about what I would find in terms of winners and losers but was curious about the specific numbers and election details. I looked at the victory margins for Trump and Senator Richard Shelby, who had won reelection to Alabama's other US Senate seat. I reviewed each county and each area of the state to better understand the political landscape.

It didn't take a political scholar to know that Alabama was very conservative. But, the tone and tenor of the discourse across the state and nation was rapidly changing, and good people whose opinions I trusted were disappointed in a way I hadn't seen in quite some time.

*\*\**

Just a few weeks prior to the political upheaval in Alabama, I had decided to take time away from the normal routine and head to north Georgia to do some trout fishing with Michael. It would be good to catch up and, no doubt, have another funny story or two to share later.

During the five-hour drive to get my vacation started, I listened on satellite radio to President Trump's first press conference with reporters. When Trump was elected, I prepared myself for an unorthodox presidency. I anticipated great changes in the norms of our institutions, believing that Trump's campaign promises to reshape the White House were for real. However, what I heard was more than unorthodox, it was a blunt departure from anything that resembled normal political discourse. Through my car's speakers, I listened to a narration of incoherent thoughts and incomplete sentences, and seemingly not an ounce of policy details or respect for the role of an independent press that came standard in our democracy.

I respect the two-party system of our government. I believe each political party, Democrats and Republicans, play a necessary role in properly shaping public policy. Being a Democrat for me was a decision born from a deep-seated empathy for those who are less fortunate, particularly those who feel marginalized in society or rely heavily on elected representatives to make decisions in their best interest. From a young age, I was drawn to the optimism most Democrats expressed—the desire to help others and stand up for the working man and the middle class.

Listening to President Trump's news conference was a bit surreal. Here was the president of the United States, duly elected through our system of democracy, being stunningly rude to reporters and calling the media "fake news." Furthermore, he had just entered the office and was already this brazen. I thought about what the next four years may look like if his approach did not change.

I respected the office he held and genuinely hoped for his success despite my philosophical differences with his approach. But this was no act. It was apparent he was incapable of reciting policy or understanding how to nuance language in such a way that got his point across without demonizing those who dared to disagree with him.

After arriving at our cabin, I texted with some friends and a few family members who voted for him to hear and see what they were thinking.

*What about Trump made you vote for him?* I asked. *Did you just see that news conference?*

I continually got a similar answer from most people.

*He tells it like it is,* they said. *I'm tired of politicians always smooth-talking their way through the job but never helping me. He's looking out for the little guy.*

I thought to myself that we couldn't possibly be talking about the same person. Stunned by the responses, I sat and thought about everything I was taught and knew about contemporary politics. I considered myself well-read and always informed of ideology and strategy across the political spectrum. But this was different than anything we had seen in our modern political era. I even dug back into lessons from my political theory classes in college, trying to digest what I was hearing and seeing. *What is the allure with him? Why is he such a cult of personality?*

For the next several weeks following that first news conference in February, I spent a great deal of time reading articles and attempting to understand what the political climate was showing us. It became apparent that few in his own party were willing to stand up to him when he was wrong. And even more were ready to go along with the narrative if it meant some personal political gain for themselves.

In 2017, no Democrat had been elected in a statewide race in Alabama in over a decade. The Democratic Party in Alabama was fractured and disorganized following significant losses in successive statewide elections. The pundits had all but given the US Senate seat to Republicans—it was just a matter of which one made it through the Republican primary to the general election.

However, I saw the political climate a bit differently than the national pollsters or opinion journalists. This contest would be a special election. Turnout would almost certainly be low—particularly in December. And low-turnout elections usually offer the best chance for a surprise. Moreover, my conversations with family and friends led me to believe that many citizens were not happy with the political discourse. The question was, would anybody be running on the Democratic ticket who would offer voters a credible alternative?

Being in fundraising and nonprofit management, my skill set matched up nicely for a political campaign. I figured I could raise some money, write my own policies, and run a short grassroots campaign that focused on showing the state's voters that Democrats could lead and could debate the issues with skill and precision.

After making a couple of calls to trusted friends connected to the political process, I arrived at a decision.

*I'm going to run. I can absolutely do this. I have the skills that match up well, the education needed to understand policy, and the people deserve a choice beyond the rhetoric that we're hearing.*

Regardless of whether I won or lost, my goal was the same: to change the debate. Represent the Democratic Party with integrity, common-sense values, and hard work. Educate the voters with where I stood on the issues. Debate vigorously and hold your ground, but be respectful and do it with a level of dignity and professionalism that shows the voters you can disagree without being disagreeable.

I called my friend and former coworker, Ryan, who was in marketing and internet technology.

"Ryan, I'm tired of the political rhetoric I'm hearing. I'm declaring for the US Senate race in the next couple of weeks, and I could use your help. Can you build me a website?"

"Absolutely! I love the idea!" Ryan exclaimed. "I'll help however I can."

With that call to Ryan, I began to put together the pieces of the puzzle for my run at the Democratic nomination to the United States Senate. I arranged for a temporary, full-time nanny for Kenzie, using a caregiver already familiar with her needs. And I contacted friends and family for my first political donations.

On May 16, 2017, I sent a press release declaring my candidacy in the special election. It was picked up by numerous statewide political news organizations. I handed in my qualifying paperwork to the Alabama Democratic Party and set my campaign in motion. Over the next thirteen weeks, I would travel to every corner of the state—in big cities and small towns—participating in every forum or debate held and meeting with Alabamians who were thirsty for change.

"Do you really think a Democrat can win?" I was asked during a debate hosted by the NAACP in Montgomery.

"I believe that Alabama will go blue in this election, or I wouldn't be in this race," I said confidently. I wasn't playing politics with that answer. I believed it.

There were a few Republicans participating in the debate that night. And while they were respectful, I could sense they thought I was unrealistic. Almost everyone with an opinion in the mainstream press believed there was no chance a Democrat would win the seat. But I said in public and in private that I thought it was possible with the right candidate and the right set of policies. And I worked my heart out to be that person.

What I was attempting was almost unthinkable. There I was, an unknown Democrat with no formal political experience as a candidate from the state's southernmost tip, trying to win election to the United States Senate in one of the most conservative places in the country. I knew the odds were long, and I was very aware that losing would be far more likely than winning. But I trusted my political instincts that told me it was possible, and I believed in my work ethic and skills that told me I belonged in the race.

I put 13,500 miles on my car in the summer of 2017, traveling the state and meeting voters where they lived and worked. I assembled a group of volunteers from events where I met supporters who liked my message and wanted to be part of my campaign. While I received some early guidance from political experts, I acted as my own campaign strategist and frequently talked on the phone with my trusted friends who gave me their thoughts based on what they saw and read about the race.

On the campaign trail, I told my story to the voters. I was a widowed, single father to a seven-year-old daughter with special needs. I understood the struggles Alabamians faced with healthcare and education because I faced those same struggles every day. I talked about my policies—about improving the Affordable Care Act and the many benefits of expanding Medicaid so lower-income folks didn't fall through the cracks and go without health insurance.

I spoke about leadership and taking pride in our elected officials again. I emphasized that public service was a noble profession, and we needed to get back to politicians who thought about the people they represented before they thought of their own political interests.

I introduced the state to Kenzie and talked about Mandi, attempting to demonstrate to those struggling that perseverance and perspective were invaluable tools we can all access in our everyday lives.

I listened intensely to the voters stories as well. Everywhere I went, people wanted to tell me about their personal challenges and circumstances, asking me to advocate and fight on their behalf when I got to Washington.

"I'm a single mom to three girls," one woman in Huntsville said to me after a debate. "I'm doing the best I can to get by, but I make too much money to qualify for any meaningful medical insurance subsidies, and I can't afford the premiums they charge."

A gentleman in Birmingham was concerned that he couldn't afford all his prescription medication that treated his diabetes and other conditions. He often had to choose between paying his rent or buying his medicine.

The young couple I spoke to in Tuscaloosa were concerned about the rising cost of a college education. They were forced to continue to rent when they wanted to buy a home, unable to save enough for the down payment because of the large monthly student loan installments they both had after graduation.

I made many new friends on the campaign trail, including my fellow candidates. Seven other Democrats from all parts of the state had declared for the race. I enjoyed their company and camaraderie—and had many good laughs with them throughout the summer. I wanted to win the nomination, but I came to respect them as knowledgeable candidates with great hearts and a passion for people.

Ultimately, my fellow Democratic candidates displayed many of the characteristics I wanted to showcase in our politics. Every day I was around them, I felt better and better about our chances to win. The crowds grew, and people got involved in a way the state hadn't seen in years. Republicans dismissed the Democrats and gave us no chance to win, but I truly thought otherwise. I saw the grassroots begin to fire up and believed it was possible.

After thirteen weeks of campaigning, the primary election was held on August 15, 2017. The Democratic race for the US Senate was declared for Doug Jones. Doug had won by a convincing margin and avoided a runoff election, which helped him organize and save cash against the Republicans. I immediately endorsed Doug in the media and pledged my complete support for his candidacy. Throughout the campaign, I came to greatly respect Doug as a person and a politician. We were always very friendly, and our political platforms were very similar.

As a former US Attorney, Doug had successfully prosecuted former members of the Ku Klux Klan in 2002 for the bombing of a church in Birmingham that killed four little girls in 1963. The case was unsolved, and neither the families nor the community had ever attained a strong measure of closure. By winning that case and bringing the murderers to justice, Doug had helped the healing process of an entire city and nation that mourned the lives lost.

After the votes were counted, I came in fifth place out of the eight Democratic candidates on the ballot. While initially disappointed, I was proud of my effort and kept my head held high. As promised, I worked hard to help get Doug Jones elected to the United States Senate on December 12, 2017—the first time a Democrat had won statewide in over a decade.

During a portion of his term, I had the honor and privilege of working for Senator Doug Jones as his field representative in the Southern District of Alabama. I enjoyed the job immensely, attempting to better the community I lived in and connecting people with their elected representative. I was proud of that job in a way I hadn't felt in a long time. I had also fulfilled my original objective when I ran for office: to put people first with integrity. Senator Jones is the embodiment of that philosophy, and I am proud to have played a small role in helping him represent the people of Alabama.

\*\*\*

For the first time in many years, I felt a passion return to my spirit. I came to the decision to run for the US Senate organically, trusting my instincts that the time was right to challenge myself in a new way and believing in my skills and abilities—many of them learned from my previous job in nonprofit and business management. In the process of campaigning, I also found my voice that had been silent for several years since Mandi's passing.

At one time earlier in my life, the world seemed to all be going my way. I met a beautiful woman who I grew to love immensely. I had a terrific job with a great company. I ran a half-Ironman triathlon and got married. I graduated from the Clinton School and started a family. All that happened within a short half-dozen years. Then, without warning, the world came crashing down. Kenzie was born premature and diagnosed with a rare syndrome. Within months of each other, my grandfather and my cousin's boy tragically died in separate incidents. Just as I was accepting the circumstances of a family life we did not envision, the horrific events of June 1, 2012, occurred. I had gone from the highest peak to the lowest valley inside three years. As a result, I became more isolated and cautious—my confidence in myself intact but severely bruised.

Sometimes, bad things happen to you that you have no control over. Often, you have no time to prepare mentally or emotionally but are instead left to pick up the pieces of your soul that were tattered and torn by the randomness of life.

I've come to view my political run in 2017 as a time of personal and spiritual awakening. The special election for the US Senate was a gift. It was an opportunity to share my skills, reinvent myself, and approach life with a vigor I hadn't felt in years. I gave back to others and listened to stories that gave me an even greater perspective of the challenges people face every day. I didn't force this moment to happen, but I did take advantage of it when it occurred and reveled in the chance to once again smile and live life to the fullest—just like I had done so many times with Mandi by my side.

# CHAPTER 14
# Finding the Path Home

*I'm entering the final third of my life. I know that sounds
grim, and I am hoping to get more time than that, but I
often do these mental calculations because the clock of life
inspires me to make the most of the years that remain.
That constant tick-tock reminds me to fill the final decades
with invigorating experiences to bank in my inner black box—
a delightful cache of memories to replay over and over
in my mind like a favorite movie.*

—DR. SANJAY GUPTA

The path home following tragedy will be different for everyone.
Just as there is no universal way or timeframe to grieve, there
is no singular way to move forward with your life following
a loss.

The meaning of home is also different for everyone. For some, it
might be a physical location, such as a house or a city. For others,
home could mean family and close friends.

After Mandi passed, I was essentially homeless. I had a physical
location that put a roof over our heads, but the spirit of the house
had changed. Mandi's departure from this Earth took away the
only meaning of a happy home I had ever really known. Therefore,

to move forward, I had to accept what had happened and redefine what home now meant to me.

The truth of the matter is that Mandi's death had fundamentally changed me. I once dealt with adversity by using it as a motivating factor to overcome the obstacle and push through what had set me back. If I experienced a bad day at work, I would counter it by throwing myself into the problem and solving what had been the trouble. If I gained weight and wasn't happy with my physical appearance, I would sign up for a long road race and push to get in great shape. Or, if I did poorly in a particular class, I would calculate precisely what I needed for the remaining points to achieve the "A."

When Kenzie was diagnosed with Distal 18q-, I researched and read every paper I could find on the subject. We enrolled in the research group, donated our blood, and answered every survey they sent. We knew it would be some time before breakthroughs occurred, but that didn't stop us from focusing on overcoming the challenge. I had my wife by my side, and together, we would remain a family that persevered and loved with all we had to give.

But I had no answers for Mandi's death. Nothing made sense about it at the time, medically or spiritually. It was as if the universe screamed out, "Checkmate!" rendering any moves I could make meaningless and leaving me with the intense feeling that the game was over.

*\*\**

For many years after Mandi's passing, well-intentioned people would attempt to encourage me by suggesting it was time to "move on" and reclaim my life. I always carefully corrected them on that choice of phrase. I don't believe one ever "moves on" from significant trauma or grief. Instead, they learn to live with a new normal, find the happiest things in life, and rebuild as best they can.

"Moving forward" is the description I prefer to use. The difference in verbiage is subtle but important to understand for those battling through grief. Moving on could signify that the grief or trauma you faced is somewhat insignificant, that the past is not worth thinking about or doesn't deserve a proper place in your life for memorialization. That phrase, "moving on," can make your grief feel almost disposable or trivial. And frankly, that's simply the wrong type of thinking.

Moving forward is a more appropriate description for somebody who has faced their most difficult challenge, acknowledged it as a significant and potentially life-changing event, but yet continued to work on getting the most out of life. Moving forward means you are not asked to forget your past. Instead, you unapologetically embrace it as a part of who you are. The act of remembering is an essential component when you're ready to step in a new direction with your life.

Guilt is also a powerful obstacle to overcome. You do not have to feel guilty for moving forward with your life when and where you are ready to do so. Guilt can paralyze even the most determined people dealing with grief or trauma and trying to heal. It lurks unnoticed in your daily thoughts but thrives in a mindset where the person grieving cannot bear the thought of how their life has changed. However, having an attitude of moving forward means you can acknowledge the past, remember the circumstances, and honor your loved ones, but you don't have to let guilt or grief dictate your future happiness.

I think of Mandi multiple times every single day. At the time of this writing, over nine years have passed since her death. For many years, I struggled mightily with grief and guilt. At times, I felt as though I was dishonoring her memory by continuing to live and occasionally smile. It was not until I discovered the mindset of *moving forward* that I was able to reclaim the future as my own.

Mandi is an integral part of the life I choose to live, and she will always play a role in my happiness. And while I'm careful never to speak for my wife as though I would know what she thought in every circumstance, I'm very confident she would want me to be happy and live out my years to the fullest.

To honor Mandi, I keep a complete picture and video library saved in multiple places—never to be lost or erased. This visual vault of memories highlights our happiest moments together and reminds me of who she was at her core. She is, in many ways, my continuous North Star. I dedicated myself to our marriage. But because she was the type of person I looked up to and enjoyed being around, she was more than my wife, she was also my best friend. When I make important decisions involving Kenzie, she's always in my thoughts.

In the immediate aftermath of trauma or loss, we may not know precisely how to deal with the circumstances. As I mentioned earlier in the book, it took me several days to eat and drink following Mandi's death. It took several months until I was back working and productive the way I knew I could be. And it took several years before I learned how to help the post-traumatic stress disorder and depression that had come along with watching my wife die a difficult death. It took dedication to my grief therapy sessions and a commitment to heal, look at things differently, and want to improve my mental outlook on life.

I often questioned my self-worth in the moments where I could not muster a sufficient defense against the emotional circumstances I faced. At times, I would lose my way temporarily, believing I was ill-equipped to overcome the guilt and grief, and my best days were irretrievably behind me. I often saw my value as a person tied to the negative circumstances that happened to me, that my identity was forever connected to a tragedy I could never forget.

To effectively move forward, I first had to accept what had happened and how my life had changed. That was not an easy thing for me to do. I had to rid myself of a victim's mentality, feeling cursed or believing the event as it happened would define the remainder of my life. I often failed to stay in the moment and enjoy the little things in my journey that were gifts.

The truth is, it's not disrespectful to the person you lost in your life if you continue to live and enjoy yourself. Of course, there's a period of grief and mourning that everyone faces. The length of that time is different for everyone. But eventually, you learn how to let the happy moments back into your life, just as though you're relearning how to walk. By acknowledging your grief and maintaining your self-worth, you can honor them every time you achieve a positive moment or celebrate a win.

I know Mandi would have been proud that I achieved my second bachelor's degree in operational meteorology. She would have likely questioned whether I was a little too ambitious in my thinking when I ran for the US Senate, but I'm confident she would have been cheering me on as my biggest supporter. And while she was a modest person who may not have wanted the attention this book might bring to her, she would have been thrilled at the determination and courage it took for me to write it, given how much I hurt and miss her every day.

The phrase "time heals all wounds" can give some people the impression that all wounds can be made whole, almost as if there never was an injury at all. I think of it a little differently. Instead, I believe we develop some emotional scar tissue that stops our bleeding and allows us to resume our lives. The scar tissue represents reminders of our grief and trauma. We function, and we can even laugh and smile again, just like before. But the wounds of the past can still be visible; personal clues of a difficult period in life can give those who suffered from intense grief or trauma the perspective they carry forward.

*  *  *

This book is the culmination of many setbacks and failures. For several years, I had the idea of writing down my thoughts and someday turning them into a book that could tell my story and potentially help others with their challenges from grief. But I could never have imagined how difficult of a process it would be to write what I could only visualize—to put to words all the pain and suffering I had experienced.

I started with a passage here and there. Random thoughts about how I felt would come to mind, and I would write them down, sometimes in the notes app of my phone or in an email I would send myself. I began that process a full six years before understanding how best to string together the paragraphs and pages that this book represents.

*Where do I start?* I would ask myself. *There's so much to say.*

After much thought and discussion with therapists and counselors over many months and years, I had an epiphany. I needed to start with the hardest part of the story—the day she passed. I needed to share the details about the most difficult moments of my life. If I couldn't share those transparently, then I couldn't share what I had learned along the way. And I couldn't share the happy moments without acknowledging the sad ones.

For me, home is not a destination. It's a state of mind, a journey toward peace. It's a constant focus and refocus on what is important in life—the ideals I loved so much in Mandi. To live life in the moment. To never take for granted what you love and cherish. To share whatever gifts you have with those around you in the most generous of spirits. To always try giving back more than you take. And to honor those whose lives were so profound and impactful upon your own that you can't even remember a time they weren't in your world.

Remember the past. Plan for the future. But live in the moment. Ultimately, that is how Mandi lived. Through these words I write and the memories I share, I will never lose her. She is always with me every step of the way.

# Epilogue

Kenzie has made considerable physical progress over the past several years. Currently age twelve as of this writing, she's not as coordinated as other typical children due to the neurological challenges of her syndrome. However, she does relatively well with her mobility and has become much more capable in activities that require strength and determination.

Kenzie first crawled at fifteen months, began standing at thirty-three months, and finally walked on her own at three and a half years. And once she got moving, she has not stopped. From 2016 to 2021, Kenzie won her assisted walk/run event in the Baldwin County Special Olympics five times in a row. She is currently undefeated in all five races. While the spirit of the race and the goodness of the cause is rightfully celebrated as the true mission of the Special Olympics games, I must admit that I'm one proud father seeing her standing on the podium with the blue ribbon. It's a testament to the determination she has always shown, whether she was fighting for her life in the NICU or enduring yet another surgery thereafter. Kenzie never gives up.

Cognitively, Kenzie remains significantly challenged. Autism, combined with sensory processing disorder and her rare genetic syndrome, has inhibited her ability to learn and grow. Kenzie is a gentle soul, much like her mother. But her inability to focus for more than a few seconds at a time or make consistent eye contact means it is extremely difficult for her to make progress socially as well as learning intellectually.

As with most autistic children, Kenzie does best in a routine. From early morning baths to snacks and meals, we maintain a regular pattern in life as much as possible to keep her in a good state of mind. As she's grown older, she has become much more tolerant of breaking that routine. But, for purposes of maintaining a dose of sanity, I do my best to keep her in good spirits.

Frankly, I have spread myself too thin at times—working long hours and not focusing enough on Kenzie's long-term functional challenges. Or I might focus on Kenzie so much that my own needs suffer. Finding the proper balance has proven elusive. A friend who also has a special needs child older than Kenzie gave me some advice that helped relieve me of at least some of the pressure.

"I learned a long time ago that you can't be both a therapist and a parent full-time. Love your child. Give them a safe place at home. Push them gently," she said.

I know that too little focus will result in Kenzie not moving forward and gaining skills at the pace she could, all other things being perfect. But, of course, things are rarely perfect.

I've been called "Superdad" many times by well-meaning people. I'm sure the compliment is part encouragement and part wondering how I manage to piece things together. Of course, I'm just a mere mortal like every other parent. I make plenty of mistakes. I miss developmental signs she is giving me that show me she's ready for the next step. And I can be a bit impatient when it comes to her making the necessary strides that move her closer to a more independent life rather than one in which she's a perpetual child.

Regardless of me being a relative novice in child-rearing, Kenzie has a way of watching and learning when nobody is looking. She's very perceptive without being obvious about it and probably understands my weaknesses far more than I understand hers. I haven't given up hope that she will one day learn more effectively or even talk. I constantly make sounds and encourage her frequent vocalization, focusing on trying to get her to say the only word she uttered for just a few short months early in her life, "Mama."

That said, I'm a realist by nature. I see her challenges for what they are and do my best not to put my own personal bias into the equation. When that happens, I tend to expect too little from her, often remembering the baby girl Mandi and I were raising together instead of the beautiful young lady Kenzie is quickly becoming.

Aside from grief, childcare has always been the single biggest challenge to a more "normal" life for me. Mandi's parents and aunts were very helpful in the first months and years after Mandi passed, watching Kenzie so I could travel for my job and providing me with some occasional, much-needed downtime. But since I moved to the adjacent county in 2014, I've had to rely almost exclusively on paid childcare.

I've interviewed and hired many caregivers in that time, always searching for that elusive blend of experience with special needs children, an affectionate and trusting approach, and enough availability and flexibility to match my needs. Thankfully, Kenzie has always been loved and taken care of by those whom I have entrusted with her needs.

*＊*

I try to remember that the future is wide open—a time yet to be shaped or experienced. I have spent a considerable amount of time the past nine-plus years reflecting on my life. My past, like most people, is one filled with both happiness and sadness. Perhaps what is different from many others is the very short period when I went from one extreme to the other, with traumatic events in succession that compounded my grief. But my dreams are still intact. I refuse to give up, despite some days admittedly getting the best of me.

I still enjoy exercising when I can, though irregular or expensive childcare sometimes means I don't get my workouts in as frequently or as consistently as I would like. I don't take as many individual vacations as I should, largely for the same reason. To the extent possible, I know I need to change both of those things going forward. I have come to understand I need a healthy amount of respite from the daily grind to stay fresh and sharp.

Two weeks before Mandi passed away, she had told me that if anything were to ever happen to her that she would want me to find somebody who is good to me and Kenzie, somebody special I could rebuild a life with. I dismissed the statement at the time as just a playful conversation. Given our ages and health, that would never happen. We had the whole world in front of us as a happily married couple. I couldn't see anything else in my mind's eye.

It has been somewhat difficult to discuss my private life after Mandi. I've dated, but I have rarely opened myself up publicly. I've not yet introduced another woman to my family or Mandi's family. But when I find somebody who is right for me (and Kenzie), they will be among the first to know. And I know they will be happy for me—because Mandi would be happy for me. She was as selfless a person as I have ever known. And my love for her is absolute and unending.

CPSIA information can be obtained
at www.ICGtesting.com
Printed in the USA
FSHW021831160222
88254FS